… a Glance

岸野めぐみ

EDITORIAL CONVENTION

Romanization

Japanese words are spelled in this book according to the Hepburn system of romanization.

- Long vowels are indicated by macrons on all words, including place names (Tōkyō, Ōsaka).
- This book follows the Hepburn practice of using "m" instead of "n" before "p," "b," or "m" (e.g., tempura, not tenpura; *shimbun*, not *shinbun*; Gumma, not Gunma).
- An apostrophe is used to distinguish final-syllable "n" from "n" at the beginning of a syllable (e.g., *Manyōshū* versus *Man'yōshū*).

Historical periods used in this book are based on *Japan: An Illustrated Encyclopedia* published by Kodansha.

凡例

ローマ字

この本では、ローマ字のつづり方は、ヘボン式に従う。

- 長母音は地名も含めて、母音字の上にマクロンをつけてあらわす。
（例：Tōkyō、Ōsaka）
- はねる音「ン」は「m」「b」「p」の前では「m」を使う。
（例：tempura、shimbun、Gumma）
- はねる音「ン」はナ行と区別するために「'」を使って表す。
（例：Man'yōshū）

歴史年号

講談社発行の「英文日本大事典」による。

Published by Kodansha International Ltd.,
17-14, Otowa 1-chome, Bunkyo-ku, Tokyo 112-8652.

First Edition 1997

ISBN4-7700-2080-5
98 99 10 9 8 7 6 5 4

イラスト日本まるごと事典
Japan at a Glance

インターナショナル・インターンシップ・プログラムス
International Internship Programs

Bilingual Books

PREFACE

The number of Japanese people travelling abroad seems to increase every year, and so have the chances of meeting foreigners, both officially and privately. However, the bias toward and misinterpretation in foreign countries of the so-called "Faceless Japanese" still remains. We are publishing this book for people who want to understand Japan better, and for those who want to explain Japan and its culture as simply as possible to interested non-Japanese. Although many publications seek to explain Japanese culture in English, foreigners nonetheless require tremendous time understanding literal translations of Japan's unique culture.

This book is based on the real experiences of more than 6,000 Japanese interns sent by International Internship Programs to various countries as "Cultural Ambassador," for the past 18 years. Fully illustrated and discussing not only the Japanese culture but also its geography, living habits, politics and economy, both in Japanese and easy English, this book is truly a concise "Entire Japan." We will also be very happy if this book could be used for two purposes: one is for Japanese to use as a handbook for their own re-discovery as well as for introducing Japan, and the other is for foreigners as a guidebook about Japan.

Finally, we would like to extend our sincerest thanks to Ms. Kumiko Inui, a participant of International Internship Programs, who has contributed an enormous amount of information and documents, and to Kodansha International, which made the publication of this book possible.

May, 1997
International Internship Programs
Yoshikazu Ikeda, Director

まえがき

日本人の海外渡航者も年々増加し、公私ともに外国人と接する機会が増えてきました。「顔の見えない日本」と言われるなど日本に対する偏見や誤解は、まだまだ海外では根強く残っているようです。日本のことをもっと理解したい、また日本に興味を持っている外国の人に日本文化を分かりやすく説明してあげたいと思っている人のために本書を企画しました。英語で説明する日本文化紹介の本も数多く出てきていますが、直訳的な文語体の難しい言い回しでは異文化の国の人々に、独特の日本文化を理解してもらうには時間がかかります。

本書は、過去18年間6,000人以上の日本人を『日本を紹介する文化大使』として世界中に派遣してきたインターンシップ・プログラムスの参加者の実体験にもとづいて作ったものです。日本文化はもちろんのこと、地理、生活習慣、政治経済まで、初めて日本に接する外国の人にも理解しやすいようにイラストを中心に、できるだけ平易な英語の対訳付きで、「まるごと日本」をコンパクトにまとめました。日本人には日本紹介の手引き書としてだけではなく日本再発見の書として、そして外国の人には素顔の「日本」に触れる入門書として、活用していただければ幸いです。

最後にこの場をお借りして、膨大な資料を根気よく整理しまとめてくれたインターンシップ参加者の乾久美子さんと、出版の機会を与えて下さった講談社インターナショナルに感謝の意を表します。

1997年5月

インターナショナル・インターンシップ・プログラムス
所長　池田吉和

CONTENTS • 目次

PART 1

This Is Japan
これが日本だ

PREFECTURAL MAP
分県地図

Japan is an island extending in a curve along the eastern coast of the Asian continent. It consists of four big islands (Hokkaidō, Honshū, Shikoku, Kyūshū) and almost 7,000 islands altogether. Its land area is about the same as that of Germany (357,000km²).

アジア大陸の東海岸に沿って弓なりにのびている島が日本である。4つの大きな島（北海道・本州・四国・九州）と大小7,000近い島々から成り立っている。その面積はドイツ（357,000km²）とほぼ同じである。

Total Area: 377,829km² (1995)

(Including 5,036km² of the Northern Territories)

（北方領土5,036km²を含む）

JAPAN'S TOPOGRAPHY
日本の地形

Japan is surrounded by the sea. A large portion of its land consists of mountains, most of which are steep and covered with forest. 67% of the land is mountains and only 13% is plains. There are seven volcanic zones, including Mt. Fuji, Mt. Mihara, Mt. Unzen, Mt. Aso, among others. Rivers are usually narrow and rapid, and flat plains surround the areas where rivers run into the sea.

周りを海に囲まれた日本は山地が多く、その大部分は傾斜が急で森林に覆われている。国土の67%が山地で、平野は13%しかない。富士山をはじめ三原山や雲仙岳、阿蘇山などを含む7つの火山帯がある。川幅は狭く流れが急で、海に流れ込むあたりには平野が広がっている。

Top 5

	Mountains (Height)	Rivers (Length)
1st	Fujisan (3,776m)	Shinanogawa (367km)
2nd	Shiranesan (3,192m)	Tonegawa (322km)
3rd	Hotakadake (3,190m)	Ishikarigawa (268km)
4th	Yarigatake (3,180m)	Teshiogawa (256km)
5th	Akaishidake (3,120m)	Kitakamigawa (249km)

THE FOUR SEASONS

四季

There are four seasons in Japan: spring (March–May); summer (June–August); autumn (September–November); winter (December–February). The Japanese take pleasure in the transition of the seasons, and enjoy their duration.

春(3～5月)、夏(6～8月)、秋(9～11月)、冬(12～2月)の四季があり、日本人はその移り変わりを楽しみながら四季折々の生活をしている。

Spring • 春

After the first storm of spring, the temperature rises and beautiful flowers bloom. April 1 is the beginning of the academic and business year.

春一番の風とともに暖かくなり始め、美しい花が咲きだす。学校や会社の一年の始まりも4月1日からである。

Summer • 夏

The rainy season comes to a close, the hot weather arrives, and people flock to the mountains or the beaches. Summer in Japan is very humid and hot.

梅雨が明け、本格的な夏になると人々は山や海へと出かける。湿度が高く蒸し暑いのが特徴である。

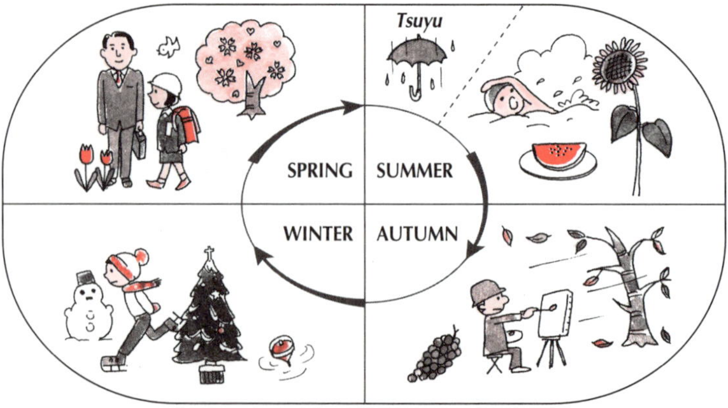

Winter • 冬

It is cold in winter, and snows in many regions in Japan. In areas without snow, a piercing cold wind blows.

日本の冬は寒く、雪の降る地域も多い。冬晴れが続く地域では木枯らしが吹く。

Autumn • 秋

Typhoons come periodically, but fall is a beautiful season with autumnal-colored leaves. People enjoy local autumn festivals and embark on excursions.

時折、台風がやってくるが、木々の紅葉が美しく、各地で祭りが行われ、行楽地に出かける人も多い。

CLIMATE
気候

Stretching from north to south, Japan has different climates from region to region. Also, due to seasonal winds, the Japan Sea coastal area and its Pacific Ocean side have different climates, respectively.

日本は南北にのびているため、地域によって気候がちがう。また、季節風の影響で日本海側と太平洋側とでは、異なった気候になる。

The climate in Hokkaidō 北海道の気候

- Severely cold in winter, cool in summer. 冬は寒さが厳しく、夏は涼しい。

The climate on the Japan Sea coastal area 日本海側の気候

- Heavy snow in winter. 冬は雪が多い。

The climate on the Pacific Ocean side 太平洋側の気候

- Cold in winter but not much snow. 冬は寒いが、雪が少ない。
- Many clear days and not too cold in winter. 冬は晴天が多く、寒さが厳しくない。
- Warm in winter and a much rain in summer. 冬は暖かく、夏に雨が多い。
- Cold in winter and cool in summer (central highland climate).
  冬は寒いが、夏は涼しい。（中央高地気候）
- Mild through the year without much rain (Inland Sea climate).
  一年を通し、雨が少なくおだやか。（瀬戸内気候）
- Not so cold in winter but cloudy.
  冬は寒くはないが、曇りが多い。

The climate in the Southwest Islands 南西諸島の気候

- Warm winter, hot summer and much rain.
  冬は暖かく、夏は暑い。雨が多い。

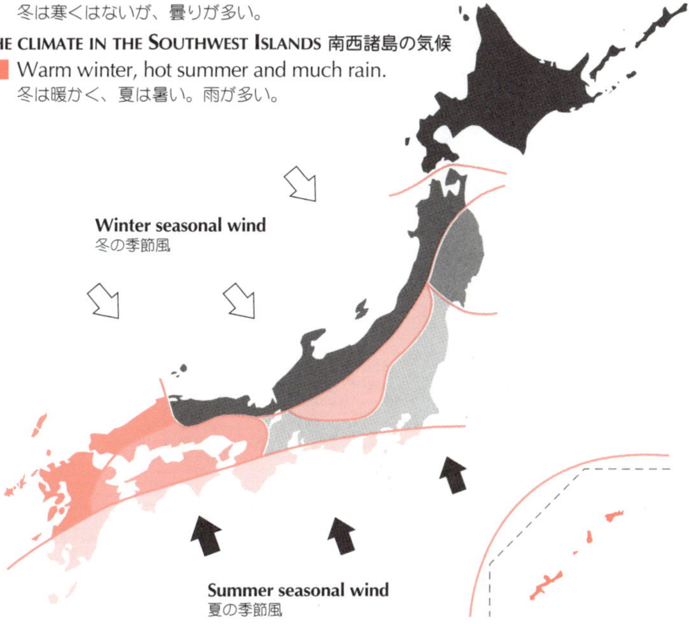

NATIONAL SYMBOLS
日本の象徴

HINOMARU (THE RISING SUN FLAG)
日の丸

The rising sun flag was first used by merchant ships to identify themselves as being of Japanese nationality during the Edo period (1600–1868). The flag then evolved into the national symbol of Japan as "The Land of the Rising Sun." The ratio of length to width is 2 to 3; the circle in the center has a diameter which is 3/5 of the width of the flag.

江戸時代の商船に日本国籍を示すために使われていたものが、「日出づる国、日本」の象徴として、国旗となった。縦・横の比率は2：3で、円が中心に置かれ、その直径は縦の長さの5分の3である。

KIMIGAYO
君が代

This song was arranged from a classical Japanese poem composed in the Heian era (794–1185). It is now the official national anthem of Japan.

平安時代の和歌から生まれた歌である。国内外で国歌として演奏されている。

KIMIGAYO

Thousands of years of
happy reign be thine;
Rule on, my lord, till
what are pebbles now
By age united to mighty rocks shall grow
Whose venerable sides
the moss doth live

(Translated by Basil Hall Chamberlain)

Kimigayo

Words: Anonymous
Music: Hayashi Hiromori

CHERRY BLOSSOMS
桜

Japanese have had an affection for cherry blossoms, the national flower, from ancient times. Cherry trees sent to Washington, D.C. in 1909 as a token of U.S.-Japan friendship still bloom beautifully every year.

日本の国花として古くから人々に親しまれている。1909年に日米友好のためワシントンD.C.に贈られた桜は、今なお美しく咲き続けている。

CHRYSANTHEMUMS
菊

Another flower symbol of Japan, the chrysanthemum is used as the Imperial family crest.

日本を代表するもう一つの花は菊。皇室の紋章にも使われている。

PHEASANTS
雉子（きじ）

This wild bird is native to Japan. It has been designated the national bird.

日本特産の野鳥で、国鳥に指定されている。

JAPAN'S WORLD HERITAGE
日本の世界遺産

Japan has cultural and natural treasures that should be preserved for future generations. These are assets that have gained recognition among other countries around the world.

将来に向けて継承されるべき伝統的な文化や自然。世界的にも認められている価値あるわが国の財産である。

Cultural Heritage • 文化遺産

The Buddhist architecture in and around the Hōryūji Temple (Nara); Himeji Castle (Hyōgo); cultural assets of the ancient city of Kyōto (Kyōto and Shiga); traditional thatched-roof residences in Shirakawa (Gifu) and Gokayama (Toyama); Hiroshima Peace Memorial Gembaku Dome (Hiroshima); Itsukushima Shinto Shrine (Hiroshima).

法隆寺地域の仏教建造物（奈良）、姫路城（兵庫）、古都京都の文化財（京都、滋賀）、白川郷（岐阜）、五箇山（富山）の合掌造り集落、原爆ドーム（広島）、厳島神社（広島）

Natural Heritage • 自然遺産

Shirakami mountains district (Aomori, Akita); Yakushima Island (Kagoshima).

白神山地（青森、秋田）、屋久島（鹿児島）

NATIONAL HOLIDAYS

国民の祝日

There are 14 national holidays during the year. Specific events or festivals take place in each local area on these days, and government offices, banks, and schools are closed. When a holiday falls on Sunday, the following Monday serves as the alternative holiday. May 4 is treated as a holiday.

年間、14日の祝日があり、各地域で祝日のための催しや祭りが行われる。官公庁・銀行・学校関係は休業。祝日が日曜日にあたる場合は、その翌日が休日となる。5月4日は休日として扱われる。

JANUARY 1

GANJITSU **(New Year's Day)**
元日

Celebrates the beginning of the new year.

年の初めを祝う。

→P.20

JANUARY 15

SEIJIN NO HI **(Coming-of-Age Day)**
成人の日

Celebrates those becoming 20 years old, and encourages them to become aware of their responsibility as adults and make a resolution to survive.

大人(20歳)になったことを自覚し、自ら生き抜こうとする青年を祝い励ます。

FEBRUARY 11

KENKOKU KINEN NO HI **(National Foundation Day)**
建国記念の日

This is the day the first Emperor, Jimmu, is said to have ascended the throne. It was thus designated as Japan's Foundation Day.

初代天皇である神武天皇が即位した日として、日本国の始まりと定めた。

MARCH 20 or 21

SHUMBUN NO HI **(Vernal Equinox Day)**
春分の日

→P.25

APRIL 29

MIDORI NO HI **(Greenery Day/Birthday of Emperor Shōwa)**
みどりの日(昭和天皇誕生日)

A day to commune with Nature, to express thanks for its blessings, and to appreciate nature's abundance.

自然に親しみ、その恩恵に感謝し、豊かな心をはぐくむ。

MAY 3

KEMPŌ KINEMBI **(Constitution Memorial Day)**
憲法記念日

A day to commemorate the institution of the Constitution of Japan, and to express hope for the future development of the country.

日本国憲法の施行を記念し、国の成長を期する。

MAY 5

KODOMO NO HI (Children's Day)

こどもの日

→P.26

JULY 20

UMI NO HI (Marine Day)

海の日

A day to be thankful for the blessings of the sea, and to express wishes for the prosperity of Japan as a country surrounded by the sea. This holiday was instituted in 1996.

海の恩恵に感謝し、海洋国日本の繁栄を願おうと1996年より施行。

SEPTEMBER 15

KEIRŌ NO HI (Respect-for-the-Aged Day)

敬老の日

A day to express respect for aged people, to thank them for their contributions to society over many years, and to celebrate their longevity.

多年にわたり社会に尽くしてきた老人を敬愛し、長寿を祝う。

SEPTEMBER 23

SHŪBUN NO HI (Autumnal Equinox Day)

秋分の日

→P.25

OCTOBER 10

TAIIKU NO HI (Sports Day)

体育の日

A day to enjoy sports and to promote a healthy mind and body. The day was established to commemorate the opening of the Tōkyō Olympics in 1964.

スポーツに親しみ、健康な心身をつちかう。1964年東京オリンピック開催を記念して制定された。

NOVEMBER 3

BUNKA NO HI (Culture Day)

文化の日

A day to express love for liberty and peace, and to celebrate cultural developments.

自由と平和を愛し、文化の発展を祝う。

NOVEMBER 23

KINRŌ KANSHA NO HI (Labor Thanksgiving Day)

勤労感謝の日

A day for respecting labor, celebrating production, and extending gratitude for others' efforts.

勤労を尊び、生産を祝い、国民が互いに感謝しあう。

DECEMBER 23

TENNŌ TANJŌBI (Emperor's Birthday)

天皇誕生日

A day to celebrate the birthday of Japan's present emperor, Akihito.

天皇の誕生日を祝う。

ANNUAL EVENTS
年中行事

There are some special traditional events which take place in local areas during the year. Celebrations and rituals differ from area to area, and in some areas they take place in accordance with the lunar calendar.

一年を通じて各地で行われる日本独特の行事がある。地方により祝い方が異なったり、旧暦で祝う場合もある。

THE NEW YEAR
正月

The New Year is one of the most important occasions for all Japanese. Relatives living far away gather together to celebrate the New Year, wishing for the future health of every family member.

日本人にとっては、最も大切な行事の一つで、遠くに住む家族も集まり、皆で新しい年を祝い、一年間の家族の健康を願う。

New Year's Day • 元旦

People pay the first visit of the year to shrines and temples with their families, or visit their relatives to deliver New Year's greetings. Quite a few people wear kimono on this special day. (January 1)

家族で神社や寺に初詣に出かけたり、親類の家に年始の挨拶に行く。着物を着て出かける人も多く見かけられる。（1月1日）

New Year's Decorations • お正月飾り

New Year's decorations are made to welcome in the gods at the beginning of the year. They consist of propitious decorations.

お正月の飾りは神様を迎えるためのもので、あしらうものは縁起のよいものである。

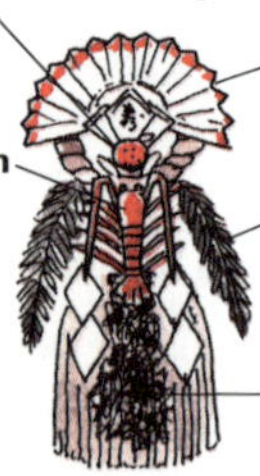

Shimekazari
(to be put at the sides of entranceways)

Kadomatsu
(to be put at both sides of gates)

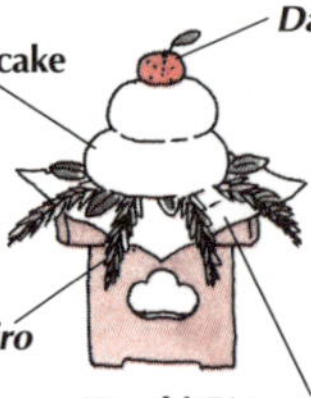

Kagamimochi
(to be displayed at the alcove or in the kitchen, etc.)

Osechi ryōri • お節料理

Specially prepared New Year's food, beautifully arranged in lacquer boxes. Many of the delicacies inside are named in hopes for the family's health and prosperity.

漆塗りの重箱に盛りつけられたお正月用の保存料理。家族の健康や繁栄を願った名前の料理が多い。

Zōni • 雑煮

A special New Year's soup with rice cakes, vegetables, etc. In the Kantō (Eastern) district, people prefer clear soup; in the Kansai (Western) district, people prefer white miso soup.

汁にもちや野菜などを入れたお正月料理。関東地方ではすまし仕立て、関西地方では白みそ仕立てが多い。

Iwaibashi
(Chopsticks for New Year)

Toso • 屠蘇

Sake steeped in *toso* herbs. Drinking *toso* on New Year's Day was traditionally thought to prevent illness.

屠蘇散（とそさん）をひたした酒。元旦にこれを飲んで一年の邪気を払うといわれる。

Hatsumōde • 初詣

People visit shrines and temples to pray for health and happiness for the comming year.

新しい年が健康で幸せに満ちた一年になるよう、寺や神社へ参拝する。

●THE WAY TO WORSHIP AT A SHRINE

① Throw coins into the wooden box.
さい銭を投げ入れる

② Ring the bell.
鈴を鳴らす

③ Bow twice.
2礼

④ Clap hands twice.
2拍手

⑤ Bow again.
1拝

New Year's Cards • 年賀状

People send New Year's postcards to their friends, relatives and colleagues to express their New Year's resolutions as well as to give updates on their lives. Usually special New Year's lottery postal cards are issued for this purpose.

新しい年の決意や近況を、友達や親戚、仕事仲間に伝えるもので、お年玉付き年賀葉書が一般的に使われる。

Otoshidama (New Year's Gift) • お年玉

Originally *otoshidama* referred to the giving and receiving of gifts among adults on New Year's Day, but the custom has changed to that of parents, grandparents or relatives giving money to children.

お正月の贈答品のやり取りが次第に子供達へのお年玉と変わってきた。親や祖父母、親戚の人などが子供達に現金をあたえる習慣。

Kakizome (The First Calligraphy of the Year) • 書き初め

The first calligraphy of the year is conducted on January 2. People write their resolutions for the coming year, facing a lucky direction.

1月2日に、その年の吉の方向に向かって毛筆で1年間の目標を書く。

Nanakusagayu (Rice Porridge with Seven Grasses) • 七草がゆ

Rice porridge prepared with the seven grasses of spring is eaten for breakfast on January 7 as a way of wishing for good health throughout the year.

1月7日の朝に食べる春の七草の入ったかゆで、一年の無病息災を願う。

Kagamibiraki (Division of New Year's Rice Cakes) • 鏡開き

On January 11 the round "mirror-shaped" rice cakes used in New Year's displays are taken down, divided up, and then cooked in a traditional dish of sweet adzuki bean soup.

お正月に飾っていた鏡もちをおろして、割って汁粉などに入れて食べる。1月11日に行われる。

Traditional New Year's Day Games • 伝統的正月遊び

Hanetsuki • 羽根つき

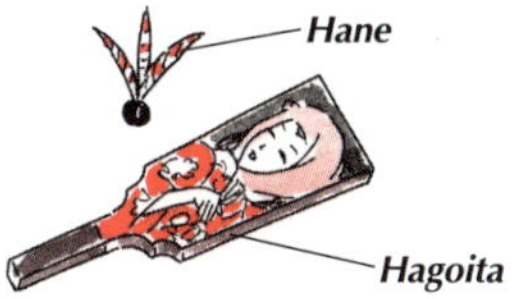

A game like badminton for two people, where the shuttlecock is hit with the wooden racket. The person who loses has an "X" mark drawn on their face with India ink.

羽子板で羽根を打つゲーム。負けると顔に墨で印をつけられる。

Takoage (Kite-flying) • たこあげ

A traditional children's pastime of flying kites.

子供の伝統的な遊びとして受け継がれている。

Koma (Top) • こま

Wind a long string around the top and pull it. The top will start rolling.

長いひもをこまに巻きつけ、そのひもを引くと同時にこまが回る。

Karuta • かるた

A traditional game in which people compete to pick up picture cards that match opening lines read out aloud by a referee from proverbs and ancient Japanese poems.

ことわざの「いろはカルタ」などで、読み手の読んだカードの絵札を探すゲーム。

Fukuwarai • 福笑い

Players are blindfolded, and place ears, eyes, nose, mouth, eyebrows on the outline of the face of Otafuku (a chubby-cheeked woman), and enjoy comparing the results.

目隠しをして、お多福の顔に耳、目、鼻、口、眉を置いて、出来ばえを楽しむ。

Sugoroku (Parcheesi) • すごろく

A player moves forward according to the number he/she throws on the dice. The first one who completes the steps wins.

さいころの出た目の数だけ進めるゲーム。先に上がると勝ち。

SETSUBUN
節分

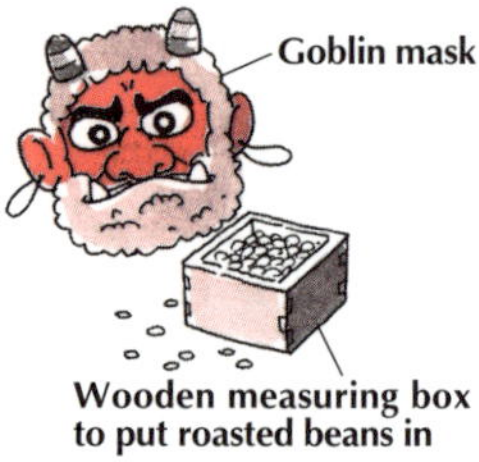

A ceremony held on February 3, the day before spring, in which people scatter roasted soy beans in order to drive away goblins and draw in happiness. People collect up and eat an amount of beans that corresponds to their age, expressing the wish for good health.

立春の前日の2月3日をさし、この日に豆をまくことによって、鬼を追い払い福を招く儀式をする。また、自分の年齢の数だけ拾って食べて、無病息災を祈る。

VALENTINE'S DAY
バレンタイン・デー

This has become an important day, particularly for young people. In Japan, women give chocolate to men to express their affection. (February 14)

女性から男性に愛を伝え、チョコレートを贈る日として、近年、特に若者の間では大切な日である。(2月14日)

DOLL FESTIVAL
ひな祭り

Families with daughters celebrate March 3 by displaying *hina* dolls on a stepped shelf to express the wish for their daughters' good health and growth. The dolls are dressed in gorgeous kimono modeled after those worn by women in the ancient Heian court. *Hina* (Empress) and *dairi* (Emperor) sit on the top shelf, followed by *sannin-kanjo* (three ladies of the court), *gonin-bayashi* (five court musicians), *zuishin* (escorts) and *eji* (guards). Diamond-shaped rice cakes, sweets and white sake are also displayed.

Hina ningyō

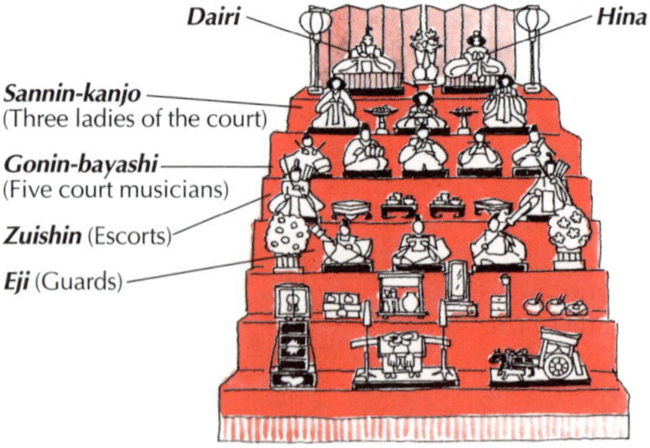

女の子のいる家庭では3月3日にその子の健康と成長を願いひな人形を飾って祝う。ひな人形は平安時代の宮廷の豪華な衣装を着ている。お内裏様とおひな様を最上段に、三人官女、五人ばやし、随身、衛士などがそれぞれの段に飾られる。また、あられやひしもち、白酒などを供える。

HIGAN (EQUINOX WEEK)
彼岸

Buddhist services performed during the week of the spring and autumn equinoxes (around March 21 and September 23, respectively). People visit their ancestors' graves, burn incense, and pray for the souls of the departed.

春分の日（3月21日頃）、秋分の日（9月23日頃）をはさんだそれぞれ1週間に行う仏教の行事。墓参りにいき、線香をたいたりして先祖を供養する。

Water is sprinkled over gravestones to purify them.
墓に水をかけて清める。

HANAMI (CHERRY BLOSSOM-VIEWING)
花見

People enjoy outdoor parties under the cherry blossoms in early April. They sit on mats under the cherry trees, eating, drinking, singing cheerfully and viewing the blossoms.

4月上旬の桜の美しい季節になると、公園や広場の桜の木の下にござを敷き、飲んで歌って陽気に野外での宴会を楽しむ。

GOLDEN WEEK
ゴールデン・ウィーク

A vacation that begins at the end of April and lasts until the beginning of May. Many national holidays are concentrated together during this week. Tourist resorts are crowded during this week, and recently foreign travel has increased.

4月下旬から5月上旬にかけて祝日が集中しているのでこのように呼ばれている。観光地はどこも満員になり、海外へ旅行する人も急増している。

CHILDREN'S DAY
こどもの日

May 5, also called "Boys' Festival," is a day to celebrate the healthy growth of children. Families with boys display a helmet replica or samurai dolls inside the house, and fly *koinobori* (carp streamers) outside. The carp is thought to be a lucky fish symbolizing success in life.

5月5日は端午の節句ともよばれ、子供の健やかな成長を祝う日。男の子のいる家庭ではかぶとや武者人形を飾ったり、鯉のぼりを屋外に立てたりする。鯉は、古くから出世魚といわれ縁起のよい魚とされている。

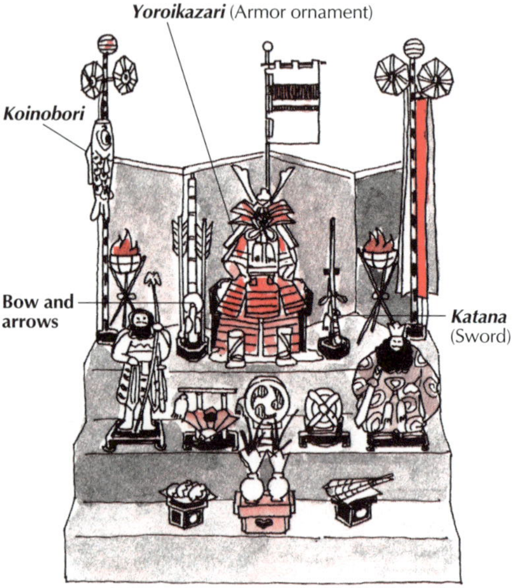

Gogatsu ningyō (Dolls for the Boys' Festival)

Chimaki (a rice dumpling wrapped in bamboo leaves) and *kashiwamochi* (rice cakes wrapped in an oak leaf with sweet adzuki beans inside) are the special treat on this day.

もち米を笹の葉で巻いて蒸したちまきや、柏の葉で包んだあんこ入りのかしわもちなども子供の日のごちそうである。

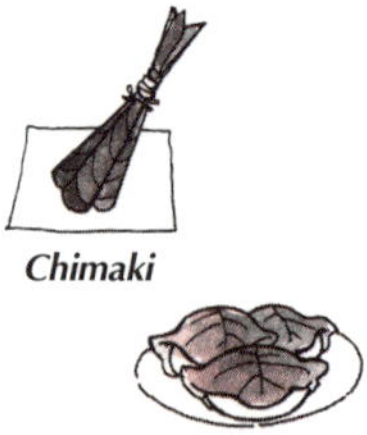

Chimaki

Kashiwamochi

MOTHER'S DAY
母の日

On the second Sunday of May, many people present red carnations and gifts to mothers with love and thanks, praying for their health and happiness.

5月第2日曜日には、日頃の感謝の気持ちと母の健康を願い、赤いカーネーションやプレゼントを贈ることが多い。

FATHER'S DAY
父の日

The third Sunday of June is Father's Day. Presents are given to fathers to express thanks and respect.

6月第3日曜日は、父への感謝と尊敬の気持ちを込めてプレゼントを贈る。

TANABATA (STAR FESTIVAL)
七夕

Tanabata is the Star Festival held on July 7. It is based on a Chinese legend in which Altair (the star of the herdsman) and Vega (the star of the weaver-princess), though separated on opposite sides of the Milky Way, meet once a year on this day. Children write their wishes on strips of fancy paper, which they put on displays made of the branches of bamboo trees.

7月7日に行われる星祭りで、牽牛（けんぎゅう）星が、織女星と、天の川をはさんで年に一度会うという中国の伝説からきたものである。笹に、願い事を書いた短冊や、飾りをつけたりする。

CHŪGEN (MID-YEAR SUMMER GIFT)
中元

Chūgen is the custom in which presents are given in mid-July to acquaintances, company supervisors, relatives, etc., to express appreciation and gratitude for help.

7月の中旬頃までに、世話になった知人や会社の上司、親戚などに、夏に贈り物をする習慣。

SUMMER FESTIVALS
夏祭り

As summer arrives, festivals are held at local shrines. Young men wearing headbands and *happi* coats carry *mikoshi* on their shoulders, shouting "*Wasshoi, wasshoi.*"

夏がくると地域の神社で祭りが行われる。「わっしょい、わっしょい」のかけ声で、はちまきをしめたはっぴ姿の若者が御輿（みこし）をかついだりする。

BON FESTIVAL
盆

A Buddhist event to hold memorial services for ancestors, from August 13 to 15 (July in the lunar calendar) in which ancestors' souls are welcomed with sacred fire and seen off with a bonfire for escorting the spirits of the dead. During the *bon* period, vegetables and fruit are offered at *bon* shelves, and in certain regions, people enjoy the *bon* dance, performed around a drum set on a scaffold. In other regions, small lanterns on floats are set adrift on rivers, symbolizing ancestors' souls (*shōrō nagashi*). Many city-dwellers go back to their home towns in the countryside over the summer holidays.

8月（旧暦では7月）13～15日に先祖の霊を供養するために行う仏教的な行事。迎え火によって霊を招き、送り火で霊を見送る。その間、盆棚に野菜や果物などを供える。やぐらにのせた太鼓を囲んで盆踊りをしたり、精霊流しをしたりする地域もある。この時期には夏休みをかねて故郷に帰省する人も多い。

TSUKIMI (MOON-VIEWING)
月見

A festival held at full moon in September (August 15 by the lunar calendar) to enjoy viewing the full moon and to celebrate the harvest. The seven flowers of autumn, and eulalia, *tsukimi dango* and vegetables are displayed.

9月の十五夜（旧暦8月15日）に満月を鑑賞しながら収穫を喜ぶ祭り。秋の七草、すすき、月見団子、野菜などを飾る。

SHICHIGOSAN
七五三

November 15 is the day parents take their sons (three or five years old) and daughters (three or seven years old) in exquisite kimono or suits to shrines to pray for their health and growth.

11月15日に、3、5歳の男の子、3、7歳の女の子が晴れ着を着て、神様に健やかな成長を祈りに神社に行く。

Chitoseame • 千歳飴

Red and white candy sticks. *Chitose* means "a thousand years," so eating the candy expresses a wish for longevity.

紅白の細長い飴。千歳は千年の意味で長生きの思いが込められている。

SEIBO (YEAR-END GIFT GIVING)
歳暮

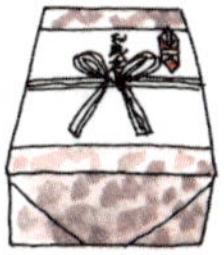

It is customary to give a present at the end of the year to those who have assisted one. The year-end present should be given by mid-December.

世話になった人に贈り物をする習慣。12月の中旬頃までに贈る。

BŌNENKAI (YEAR-END PARTY)
忘年会

A party where people gather to share and shake off the hardships they underwent during the past year and to prepare for the coming year with renewed resolve. Most parties are held at restaurants among office colleagues or friends.

年末にその年の苦労を慰めあったり、新年を新たな気持ちで迎えたりするための区切りの宴会。仕事仲間や友達同士がレストランなどに集まって行うことが多い。

CHRISTMAS
クリスマス

Christmas is not a national holiday in Japan. However, people have increasingly begun to decorate trees, eat Christmas cakes, and exchange presents with family and friends on this day.

日本では休日ではないが、近年、宗教に関係なく、クリスマスツリーを飾り、クリスマスケーキを食べ、プレゼントを交換して、友達や家族でこの日を祝う人が増えてきた。

ŌSŌJI (YEAR-END CLEANING)
大掃除

The large-scale, year-end cleaning conducted in order to welcome in the New Year with a clean house.

新年を迎えるために年末にする大がかりな掃除。

MOCHITSUKI (MAKING RICE CAKES)
もちつき

With the New Year drawing near, people traditionally pounded steamed rice to make New Year's rice cakes. These days most people buy pre-made rice cakes at stores.

正月が近づくと正月用のもちをついていたが、最近では、店で買ったりする。

ŌMISOKA (NEW YEAR'S EVE)
大晦日

Ōmisoka is the last day of the year (December 31). On the last night people enjoy music variety shows or marathon programs on TV.

大晦日は年の最後の日（12月31日）を意味する。大晦日の夜には、家族そろってテレビで歌謡番組や長時間番組などを見て過ごす。

Toshikoshi soba (New Year's Eve Buckwheat Noodles) • 年越しそば

People pray for longevity by eating long thin noodles, hoping for the health of the whole family in the coming year.

大晦日に細長いそばを食べることによって、長寿を願い、新しい年も家族が健康に暮らせるように願う。

Joya no kane (New Year's Eve Bells) • 除夜の鐘

Buddhist temples start ringing their bells late on New Year's Eve and continue into the early hours of New Year's Day—108 times in all. 108 symbolizes the casting away of 108 earthly desires.

大晦日の夜もふけてきた頃から元日にかけて、多くの寺では108回の鐘を打ち鳴らし始める。108の煩悩を除去する意味がある。

PART 2

A Glimpse of Life in Japan

日本人の生活をかいま見る

CLOTHING
衣服

Some people wear kimono on special occasions, such as on New Year's Day, Coming-of-Age Day ceremonies, wedding receptions, etc., but most Japanese wear Western-style clothing in daily life.

正月や成人式、結婚式などの特別な儀式では着物を着る人も見かけられるが、現代の日本人の多くは日常、洋服を着て生活している。

WESTERN-STYLE CLOTHING
洋服

People choose attire appropriate for each season, and usually change their wardrobes with the seasons.

四季に応じた服を選んで着用し、季節の変わりめには衣替えをする。

Spring • 春

Between-season clothes such as light-weight, light-colored suits, shirts, blouses and dresses are worn.

合い着、薄手で淡い色のスーツやシャツ、ブラウス、ワンピースなどを着る。

Summer • 夏

Cool fabrics that breathe well are preferred. Sleeves should be short as well.

汗を吸い取り、風通しのよい素材。袖は短いものが好まれる。

Winter • 冬

Heavy sweaters, jackets, and other pieces that can be layered are preferred. Coats, gloves and scarves are worn, too.

厚手のセーターやジャケットなど重ね着のできるもの、コートや手袋、マフラーなどをつける。

Autumn • 秋

Between-season clothes are worn but the colors are darker and more conservative compared to spring clothes.

合い着、春にくらべ色合いの濃い、落ち着いたものを好む人が多い。

KIMONO
和服

Women's Kimono • 女性用着物の種類

Furisode • 振り袖

Formal kimono with long sleeves worn by unmarried young women on Coming-of-Age Day, for example.

若い未婚の女性が成人式などで着る袖の長い盛装用の着物。

Tomesode • 留め袖

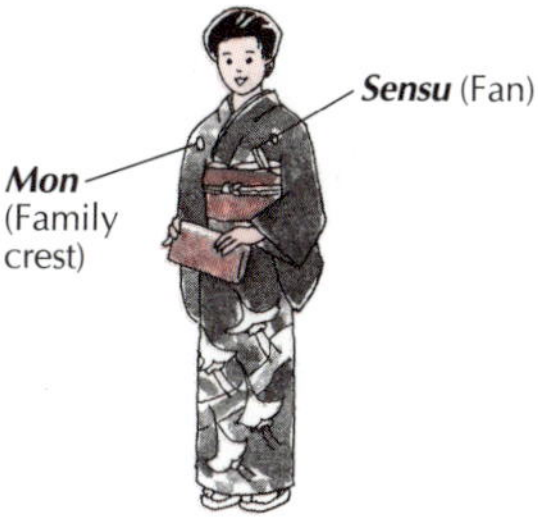

Kimono worn by married women at celebratory events such as weddings. Usually they are black with a family crest.

婦人が結婚式などの儀式に着る黒地の紋付き着物。

Hōmongi • 訪問着

A semi-formal kimono worn on New Year's Day or for a formal visit.

略式の礼装で、正月や改まった訪問の時に着る。

How to Wear a Kimono • 着物を着るために

① **Under the kimono** • 着物の下に

② **How to tie the obi** • 帯を結ぶために

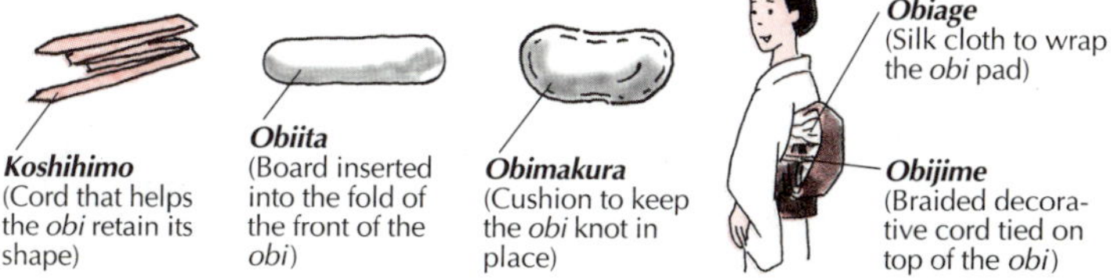

Variations in Obi Knots • 帯の結び方いろいろ

The *obi* is an important element that enhances the beauty of the kimono. It is wide and long (sometimes 4m in length), and usually made of very thick woven silk fabric, making it very hard to tie. Basically, it is knotted very tightly at the back without fastenings.

美しい着物姿の一要素である帯は幅が広く、長さが4mのものもある。布地もかたいため結ぶのが大変難しい。ふつう留め具はいっさい使わず、しっかりと締めて結ぶだけである。

Fukurasuzume

Bunko

Otaiko

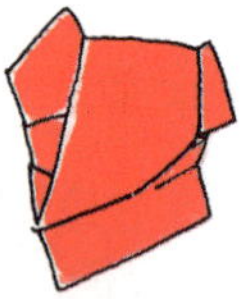
Kainokuchi

Obijime • 帯締め

Worn on top of the *obi* in order to keep the knotted *obi* in shape. There are different ways of knotting according to the occasion.

帯のくずれを防ぐために帯の上から締める。目的によって締め方が異なる。

① **For celebratory occasions**

② **For informal wear**

③ **For mourning**

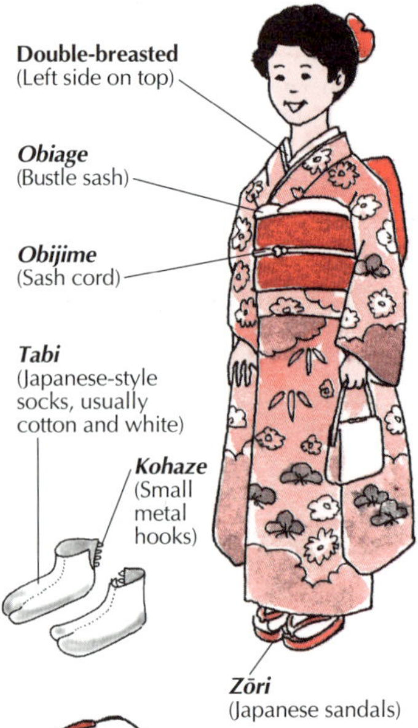

Footwear • 履物

Zōri or *geta* are footwear that go with the kimono. They should be worn so that the *hanao* (thong) comes between the big toe and the second toe. The left and right shoes of both the *zōri* and *geta* are of the same shape.

和服には必ず草履や下駄を履く。鼻緒を親指と次の指の間にはさむ。左右の区別はない。

Zōri

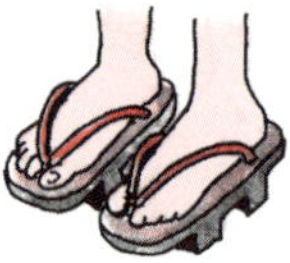
Geta

Wearing Yukata Is Easy
かんたん！　浴衣を着よう

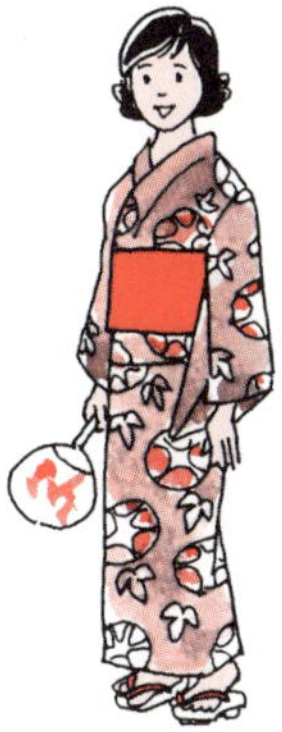

The *yukata* is a single-layered cotton kimono. It is worn after taking a bath, or during the summer.

浴衣は入浴後や夏に着る、木綿で作ったひとえの着物。

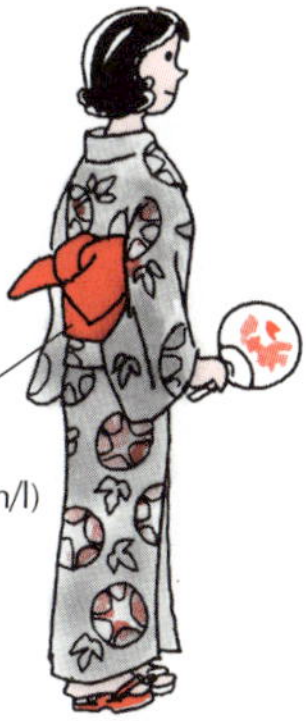

Hanhaba-obi
(Half-width *obi*)
(20cm/w x 360cm/l)

Wear *geta* on bare feet.
素足に下駄を履く。

①

Wear *yukata* in such a way as to leave a two-finger space at the back of the collar.

背中と着物の中心線の間を指2本分をあける。

②

Pull the left-side collar over the right side in front, and tie with a cord around the waistline.

左衿(えり)が外に出るよう重ね、腰ひもで締める。

③

Tie the *datejime* around the waist on top of the cord.

次に、伊達(だて)締めを締める。

④

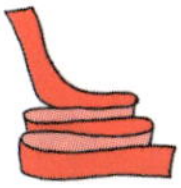

Fold like a folding screen.
びょうぶ風

Wrap the *obi* around the waist twice. Bundle the excess fabric by folding it like a folding screen.

帯を腰にしっかり2回巻きつけた後、残りは前でびょうぶ風に束ねていく。

⑤

Tie like a ribbon's bow. Tuck the ends inside the *obi* around the waist.

リボンに仕上げる。端は帯の中に入れる。

⑥

Turn the *obi* around to the right and bring the *obi* knot to the center of the back.

着物の流れと同じ方向に帯を回し、後ろで整える。

Men's Kimono • 男性用着物

Kuromontsuki (Formal kimono) **Wool kimono** (Informal kimono) ***Yukata***

On formal occasions, men wear *haori* decorated with the family crest, and *hakama*. The *haori* is a short coat worn over the kimono. The *hakama* is worn over the kimono on the lower part of the body tied at the waist with a cord. Men's informal kimono are made from wool or *ōshima* pongee and are tied with a *hekoobi* (soft *obi*) or *kakuobi* (stiff *obi*).

男性は礼装の際には紋付き羽織、袴（はかま）を着用する。羽織は着物の上に着る丈の短い上着で袴は着物の上から下半身につけて腰でひもを結んで着る。普段、町着としてはウールや大島つむぎを着用し、兵児（へこ）帯や角帯を締める。

FAMILY CRESTS
家紋

Each family has a crest as its symbol. Crest designs are mostly plants, flowers such as chrysanthemum, animals, Chinese characters, etc. Crests are printed on formal kimono or sometimes on shop curtains.

家々がその印としてつける紋章である。菊などの植物や、動物、文字などを表したものが多い。儀式の時に紋付きの礼装をしたり、店ののれんに染め込んだりする。

Three *aoi* leaves encircled

Chrysanthemum

Mt. Fuji in the mist

Four squares with eyes

PEOPLE WHO WEAR KIMONO AS PART OF THEIR WORK
着物を着て働く人々

Maiko • 舞妓

Maiko are young women entertainers who dance or play the *shamisen* at banquets.

酒宴で舞を舞ったり、三味線を弾いたりする若い女性を舞妓という。

Kannushi • 神主

The *kannushi* (Shinto priest) serves deities and recites prayers at shrines.

神主は、神社で神様にお仕えし、供え物をしたり祝詞(のりと)をあげたりする。

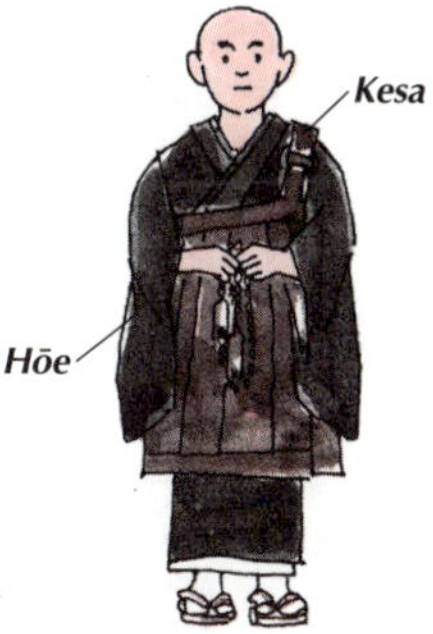

Sōryo • 僧侶

Sōryo are Buddhist priests who leave behind the material world and practice asceticism. They wear *hōe* kimono with *kesa* over them.

出家して仏門に入って修行をしている人。法衣(ほうえ)の上に袈裟(けさ)をかける。

Rikishi • 力士

Sumō wrestlers wear kimono in everyday life as well as when on wrestling tours.

力士は巡業中はもちろん、普段の生活においても着物を着ている。

Rakugoka • 落語家

Rakugoka are professional storytellers and tell humorous stories at variety theaters.

落語を寄席で演じる人。

Nakai • 仲居

Nakai are women who carry and serve food at restaurants or at Japanese inns.

旅館や料亭で、料理を運んだり客の応接をする女性。

DIET
食生活

The modern Japanese diet is full of variety. In addition to Japanese food, Western, Chinese and other ethnic dishes from around the world are popular. Bread and noodles are enjoyed in Japan, too, but most people eat rice as a staple food.

近年の日本人の食生活は変化に富み、欧米のスタイルはもちろん、中華料理やエスニック料理など、世界の味を楽しむことができる。パンやめん類が普及しても主食を米とする人が大半である。

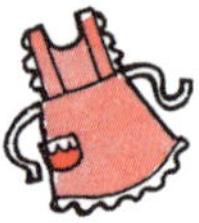

Cooking Rice on the Stove
鍋でご飯を炊こう

①

Rinse the rice, straining it in clean water. Change the water a couple of times. 1/2 a cup of rice (150g) is sufficient for one person. (1cup=180ml)

水で米を数回とぐ。1人分、1/2カップ。

②

Soak the rice in the water at a ratio of (1:1.2/rice:water) for more than 30 minutes.

（米：水）＝（1：1.2）の割合で30分以上つけておく。

③

Cook over high heat until it boils. Then turn down to medium heat and keep cooking for 7–8 minutes. Then, simmer for 12–15 minutes.

沸騰するまで強火で、それ以後中火で7～8分、弱火で12～15分炊く。

④

When the rice is cooked, remove the pot from the stove and leave it sitting for 10 minutes to steam. Lightly fluff the rice with a rice scoop, then cover with a dry cloth.

ガスからおろして、10分間蒸らす。しゃもじで軽くまぜ、乾いたふきんをかけておく。

A VARIETY OF RICE DISHES
ご飯ものいろいろ

Sekihan • 赤飯

A rice dish made by steaming glutinous rice and boiled red beans which turn the rice red. This is a special celebratory dish for happy occasions.

もち米にゆでた小豆を加え蒸して作るので、小豆の赤い色がつく。祝い事の時に食べる。

Takikomi Gohan (Japanese Paella) • 炊き込みご飯

A rice dish cooked with seafood and vegetables. (Ex. *gomoku gohan*, or chestnut rice)

魚介類や野菜などを加えて、味をつけて炊いたご飯(五目ご飯、栗ご飯など)。

Porridge • かゆ

Rice cooked with a large amount of water until the rice becomes sticky. Seasoned with salt, the porridge is easy to digest and is recommended for those suffering from illness.

水の分量を多くしてねばりがでるまで米を煮て、塩で味つけする。消化がよいので病気の時によい。

Domburimono • 丼物

This rice dish is served in a bowl with a bottom layer of rice; the top layer is covered with tempura, pork cutlet, broiled eel, etc. with *tare* sauce.

丼のご飯の上にてんぷらやトンカツ、うなぎのかば焼きなどをのせ、たれをかけた料理(天丼、カツ丼、うな丼)。

Onigiri (Rice Balls) • おにぎり

These are extremely popular as a take-out lunch. Make a rice ball with lightly salted rice. Put either pickled plum, roasted cod roe, or salted salmon into the center of the ball. Take the ball of rice into the palm and squeeze it into the shape of a triangle. Wrap with *nori* (laver). It is easy to eat with the hands.

携帯食として昔から人気がある。塩味のついたご飯の中に、梅干し、焼きたらこ、塩鮭などを入れ、手で三角に握りかため、のりで巻く。そのまま手でつまんで食べる。

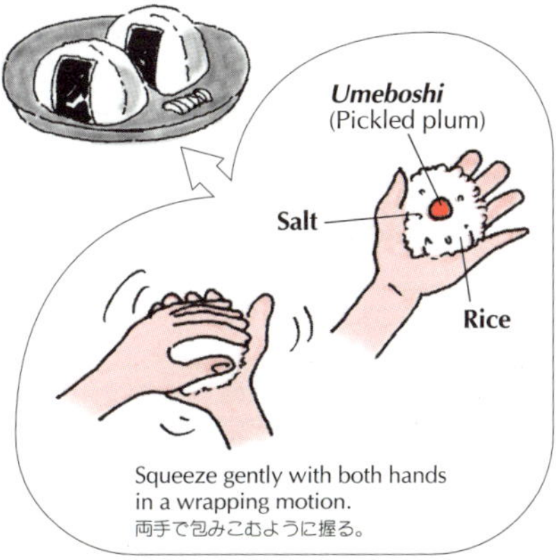

Squeeze gently with both hands in a wrapping motion.
両手で包みこむように握る。

MISO SOUP
みそ汁

Miso is made from fermented steamed soybeans with malted rice and salt. Miso soup is an integral part of the Japanese diet.

みそは蒸した大豆に、こうじと塩をまぜて発酵させて作る。みそ汁は日本人の食生活には欠かすことのできない一品である。

Making Miso Soup, a Taste of Home (4 servings)
おふくろの味、みそ汁にチャレンジ（4人分）

① Preparing the ingredients：実を用意する　(1C=200ml　Tbsp=tablespoon)

Wash 40g of *wakame* (seaweed) thoroughly to rinse out saltiness. Soak it in water for a while. Cut into small slices.

わかめ：40gを水につけ、もどして小さく切る。

Cut *tōfu* (1/2 block) into dice-sized pieces.

豆腐：1/2丁をさいの目に切る。

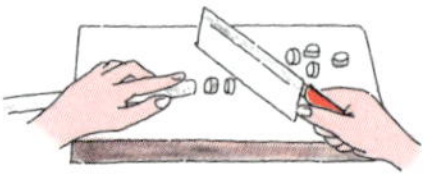

Mince a stalk of green onion.

ねぎ：少々、小口切りにする。

② Making the broth：だしをとる

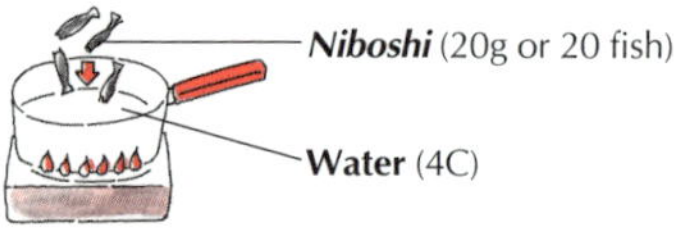

→

Clean dried sardines by removing the heads and innards, then put them into boiling water. Cook for 5–6 minutes.

水の中に頭わたを取った煮干しを入れて5～6分間煮る。

Then run the broth through a fine filter. When using powdered broth, sprinkle a teaspoonful into boiling water.

目の細かいこし器で静かにこす。市販の「だしの素」を使う場合は、沸いた湯に小さじ1を入れる。

③

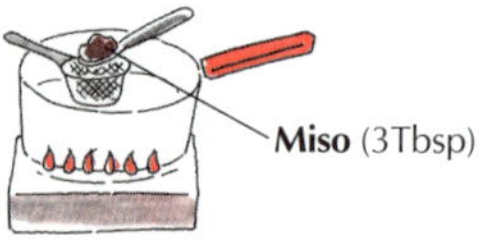

Boil the filtered broth again and blend the miso paste in. After the miso is put in, turn down the heat so as not to boil the broth again.

だし汁を火にかけひと煮立ちしたら、みそを溶き入れる。その後は煮立たせない。

→

④

Add *wakame* and *tōfu*. When the ingredients rise to the surface, sprinkle the onion on top and turn the heat off.

わかめ、豆腐を入れ、浮き上がってきたらねぎを入れて火を止める。

SEASONING
調味料

Soy sauce is an indispensable element of Japanese food. It is said that these condiments enhance the flavor of Japanese food in the order of *sa, shi, su, se, so*—representing the first phonemes of the Japanese words meaning sugar, salt, vinegar, soy sauce and miso, respectively. Sake and *mirin* (sweet rice wine) are also used in tasty dishes.

しょうゆは、日本料理には欠かせないものである。日本料理には調味料を「さ・し・す・せ・そ」の順に入れるとよいといわれている。酒やみりんも煮物に使われる。

Sa	→	**Shi**	→	**Su**	→	**Se**	→	**So**
Satō (Sugar)		***Shio*** (Salt)		***Su*** (Vinegar)		***Shōyu*** (Soy sauce)		***Miso*** (Miso)

Spices • 薬味

Spices are used in traditional Japanese dishes. They enhance the flavor and smell of the food as well as stimulate the appetite.

伝統的な日本料理には香辛料である薬味を使う。これらは味や香りを引きたて食欲をそそる役目をしている。

Seven-spice Pepper • 七味唐がらし

Sprinkle over hot *udon* or hot *soba* noodles.

うどんやかけそばにふりかける。

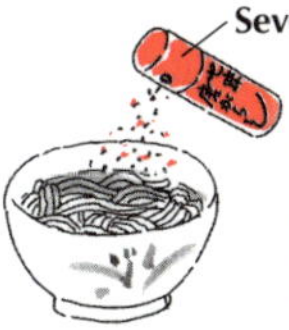

Seven-spice mixture

- Red pepper powder
- *Sanshō*
- Sesame
- *Asa no mi* (hemp seeds)
- Dried orange peel
- Dried green seaweed
- *Keshi no mi* (poppy seeds)

Wasabi (Japanese Horseradish) • わさび

A fresh *wasabi* stalk is grated for serving; powdered *wasabi* is blended with water. *Wasabi* is an accompaniment to sashimi, *zaru soba* (cold *soba* noodles), and *chazuke* (cooked rice in a broth of green tea).

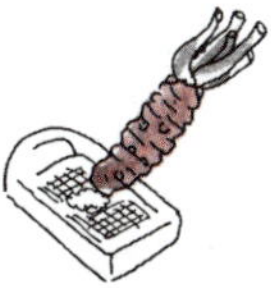

生わさびの根茎はすりおろし、粉わさびは水で溶いて使う。刺身やざるそばのつゆ、茶づけなどに使われる。

Sanshō • 山椒

Sprinkle over broiled eel or *yakitori*.

うなぎのかば焼きや焼き鳥にふりかける。

Shōga (Ginger) • 生姜

Minced ginger is used when cooking fish and meat. Grated ginger is used for bonito sashimi or barbecued meat.

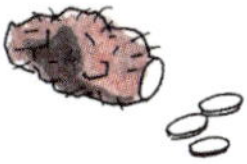

きざんで魚、肉の煮物に、すりおろしてかつおの刺身や肉のしょうが焼きに使う。

Yuzu (Chinese Lemon) • ゆず

The zest of *yuzu* adds a refreshing smell when used as a topping for soup or a stew cooked in a table-top pot.

皮を小さく薄く切り、汁物や鍋物に入れるとさわやかな香りがする。

Wakame (Seaweed) • わかめ

This greenish-brown seaweed is used in miso soup or a vinegared dish. When soaked, salted *wakame* expands three times in size, while dried *wakame* expands ten times.

わかめは緑褐色の海藻で、みそ汁や酢の物の料理に使う。水でもどすと、塩づけのわかめは3倍、乾燥ものは10倍になる。

Konnyaku • こんにゃく

Add a water/calcium-hydroxide mix to powdered *konnyaku* starch; boil and let it congeal, to make *konnyaku*.

粉末にしたこんにゃく芋に石灰乳を混ぜ、煮溶かして固めたもの。

Chikuwa • ちくわ

White fish paste is put on a bamboo skewer and steamed to make *chikuwa*.

白身の魚肉をすって、竹串に棒状に塗りつけ蒸したもの。

Tōfu (Bean Curd) • 豆腐

Tōfu is soy milk curdled by bittern. There is a variety of *tōfu* dishes, such as *hiyayakko* (chilled *tōfu*), *yudōfu* (simmered *tōfu*), etc.

大豆の豆乳をにがりで固めたもの。冷や奴や湯豆腐など食べ方はいろいろある。

Nattō • 納豆

Nattō is made from fermented soy beans with *nattō* fungus. It has a unique smell and viscosity. Add chopped green onions and soy sauce, mixing well. Serve on top of hot rice. Delicious!

大豆を納豆菌で発酵させたもので、独特のにおいと粘りがある。ねぎ、しょうゆをかけてしっかり混ぜてごはんの上にのせると、ああおいしい！

Oden • おでん

This is a stew cooked for hours in kelp broth and soy sauce.

昆布のだし汁としょうゆで何時間も煮て味をしみ込ませる。

TSUKEMONO (PICKLES)
つけもの

Vegetables such as radishes, Chinese cabbage, and cucumbers are pickled in salt, rice bran, or miso for preservation. By pickling for a long time, the vegetables ferment, adding a special flavor.

和風ピクルス。白菜、大根、きゅうりなどの野菜を塩、ぬか、みそなどに漬け込んで保存したものである。長時間漬け込むことによって発酵し、独特の風味がでる。

Takuan-zuke • たくあん漬け

Dried Japanese radishes are pickled in rice bran and salt.

乾燥させた大根を、米ぬかと塩を混ぜたものに漬け込む。

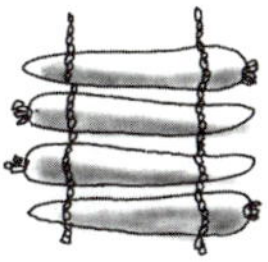

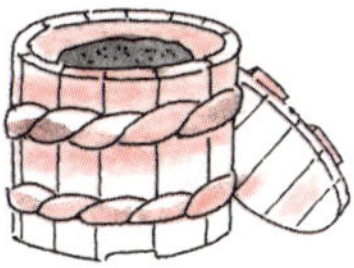

Umeboshi (Pickled Plums) • 梅干し

Green plums are pickled in salt, dried and mixed with red *shiso* leaves. The plums are very tart.

梅の青い実を塩漬けにし、干したあと赤じその葉で染めたもの。酸味がきつい。

Quick and Delicious Chinese Cabbage Tsukemono
すぐに楽しめる、白菜漬け

①

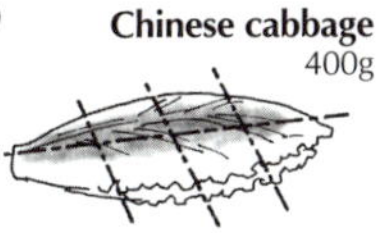

Cut the leaves.

白菜400gをざっくり切る。

②

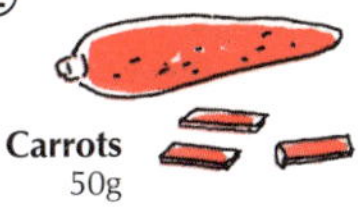

Cut into match-stick shapes.

にんじん50gを短冊か線切りに。

③

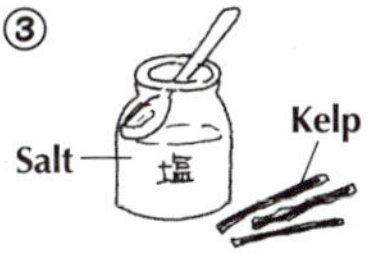

Cut a small amount of *kombu* (kelp) into match-stick shapes.

昆布を少し、細く切る。

④

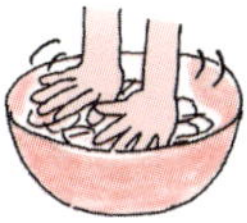

Put cabbage, carrots, sea kelp and salt (1/2Tbsp) in a bowl. Mix ingredients together with the hands, pushing strenuously.

ボールに白菜、にんじん、昆布、塩(大さじ1/2)を入れ、しんなりするまで押しながら混ぜる。

⑤

Put ingredients in a bowl, fitting a plate over them. Use a 400–500g stone on top of the plate to weigh it down. Let mixture sit for 2–3 hours.

上に皿をしいて400～500gの石をおき、2～3時間おく。

⑥

Pour off water and arrange the *tsukemono* in a bowl and serve.

水気をしぼって器に盛りつける。

SASHIMI
刺身

The Japanese eat a lot of fish. One favorite is sashimi—thinly sliced, fresh raw fish served with soy sauce and *wasabi*. Sashimi is loved as a typical Japanese dish, but fish is also eaten cooked or broiled.

日本人は魚を食べることが多い。特に新鮮な魚を生のまま薄く細く切り、しょうゆとわさびをつけて食べる刺身は典型的な和食として好まれている。ほかに魚は煮つけや焼き魚として食べる方法もある。

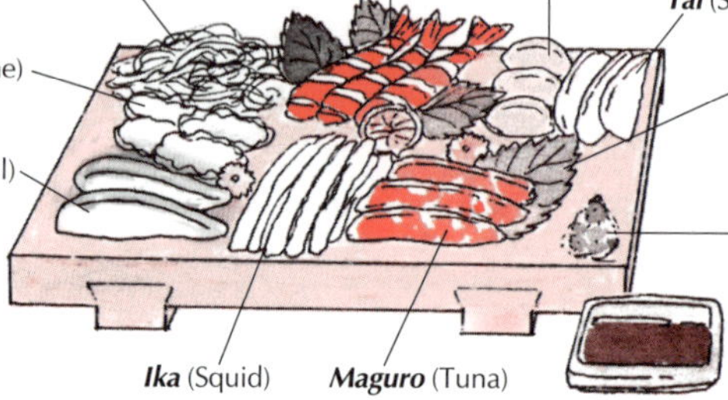

Dip sashimi in soy sauce that has been mixed with a little *wasabi*, and eat.
少量のわさびをしょうゆに溶かして、身をひたして食べる。

SUSHI
寿司

Nigirizushi • 握り寿司

A kind of sushi in which *wasabi* paste and raw fish are placed on top of a rice ball and served with soy sauce.

すし飯を握り、わさびをつけて魚介類のねたをのせたもの。しょうゆをつけて食べる。

Inarizushi • いなり寿司

Aburaage cooked in soy sauce, sugar, and sake becomes the outer wrapping for sushi rice.

しょうゆと砂糖、酒などで味つけした油揚げにすし飯をつめて形を整えたもの。

Oshizushi • 押し寿司

Square-shaped sushi made in a wooden box. Sushi rice is laid on the bottom of the box and fish such as broiled conger or marinated mackerel is placed on top of the rice.

長方形の木箱にすし飯をつめ、その上に、あなごやしめさばなどの具をのせて、ふたで押したもの。

You Too Can Be a Sushi Chef
今日からあなたも寿司職人！

●Prepare the sushi rice • すし飯をつくる

(tsp=teaspoon)

① 

Cook the rice so that it is a little hard. (3C uncooked rice, 3C water, 1C=180ml)

ご飯はかためにに炊く（米：3カップ、水：3カップ）

② 

Vinegar mix
4Tbsp vinegar
2Tbsp sugar
3/4tsp salt

合わせ酢
酢一大さじ4
砂糖一大さじ2
塩一小さじ3/4

③ 

While the rice is still hot, add vinegar mix. Stir rice well with a wooden scoop in a slicing motion, cooling the rice off by doing so.

ご飯が熱いうちに合わせ酢を入れ、さましながら切るように混ぜる。

●Norimaki • のり巻き

① 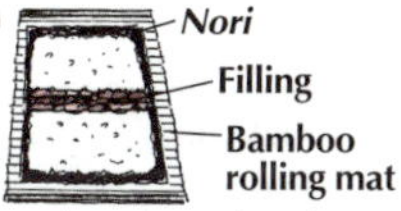

Spread *nori* on a bamboo rolling mat, then spread the sushi rice over it. Place filling in the center.

まきすの上にのりを広げ、すし飯を広げる。その中央に具をのせる。

② 

Roll so that the front end of the *nori* will align evenly with the back end when touching.

手前ののりの端を向こう側の端につけるように巻き、形を整えていく。

③ 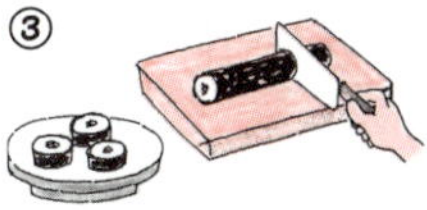

Slice the rolled *norimaki* with a knife. Wet the knife after each cut using a vinegar-moistened cloth.

酢水でぬらしたふきんで包丁をふきながら切る。

●Chirashizushi • ちらし寿司

(Tbsp=tablespoon)

① 

Mince carrots, lotus root, and *shiitake* mushrooms. Cook in 2/3C fish broth, 3Tbsp soy sauce, 1Tbsp *mirin* , 1Tbsp sake and 2Tbsp sugar, then drain. (1C=200ml)

にんじん、れんこん、しいたけなど具は細かく切って、だし汁2/3カップ、しょうゆ大さじ3、みりん大さじ1、酒大さじ1、砂糖大さじ2で煮、煮汁を切る。

② 

Mix ingredients, thinly cut boiled snow peas, and roasted sesame into the sushi rice and stir well.

①の具、ゆでて細かく切った絹さや、いりごまをすし飯と混ぜ合わせる。

③ 

Put the sushi rice in a dish and arrange raw tuna, salmon, prawns and *kinshi-tamago* over the rice.

器に②のご飯を盛り、上にまぐろ、サーモン、えびなどの刺身と金糸卵をちらして飾る。

TEMPURA
てんぷら

Fried vegetables, fish or shellfish dipped in dough and batter-fried in high-temperature oil. Serve with dipping sauce.

野菜や魚介類に衣をつけ高温の油で揚げた食べ物。てんつゆにつけて食べる。

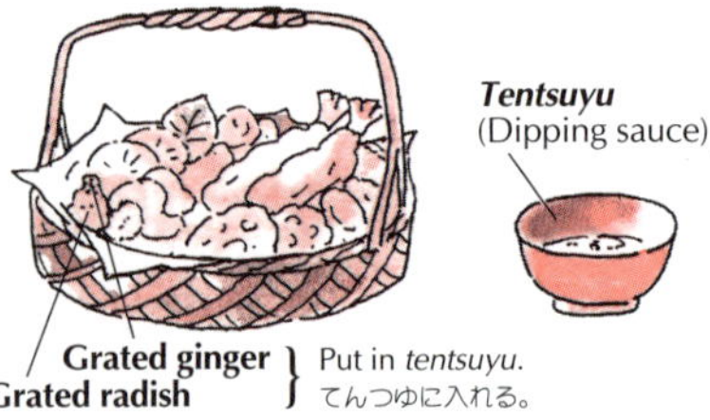

Making Crispy Tempura (4 servings)
からっと揚げたい、てんぷら（4人分）

●Prepare the batter • 衣をつくる

1C (200ml) of 1 egg and cold water
1C + 2Tbsp flour

卵1個と冷水で1C（カップ）
薄力粉　1Cと大さじ2

→ Mix using a slicing motion.

切るように混ぜる。

① 

Cut vegetables thinly. Towel-dry the seafood and soak in the batter.

野菜類は薄く切る。魚介類は水分をふき取り、衣をつける。

② 

Deep-fry in 170–180°C (338–356°F) oil until batter turns a light brown.

170～180°Cに熱した油で揚げる。

③ 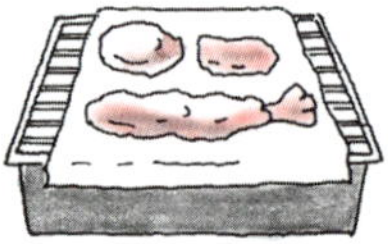

Drain the oil and arrange the tempura on a plate.

油を切ったあと、皿に盛りつける。

●Prepare dipping sauce • てんつゆをつくる

1/4C *mirin*
1C broth
1/4C soy sauce

みりん　1/4 C
だし汁　1 C
しょうゆ　1/4 C

Boil *mirin*. Add broth and soy sauce and boil again.

みりんを煮立て、だし汁としょうゆを入れて再び煮る。

Prepare grated Japanese radish (1C) and ginger (2tsp).

大根おろし（1C）を作り、しょうが（小さじ2）をする。

NABEMONO
鍋物

This dish is cooked right at the dining table. People sit around the pot to enjoy eating and talking. A particularly nice meal for wintertime.

食卓にこんろを置いて鍋を囲み、楽しく語らいながら食事ができる。特に冬場には体も暖まり喜ばれる。

Sukiyaki • すき焼き

A representative Japanese dish of made by cooking thinly sliced beef with vegetables in a sukiyaki iron pot. The dish is served with beaten raw egg.

浅いすき焼き用の鍋に肉や野菜を入れて煮る、日本の代表的な料理。溶きほぐした生卵につけて食べる。

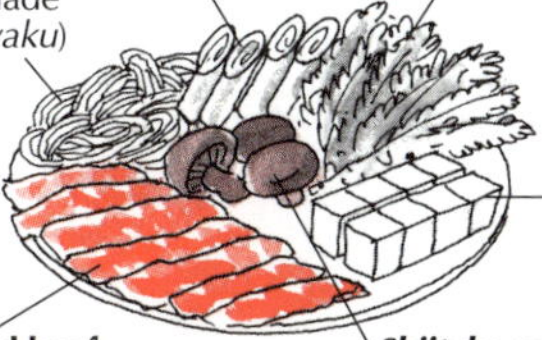

Seasoning • 味つけ

soy sauce, sugar, sake, *mirin*

しょうゆ、砂糖
酒、みりん

Shabushabu • しゃぶしゃぶ

Soak the thinly sliced beef and vegetables in boiling water and eat with either a citron-flavored sauce or a sesame-flavored sauce.

薄切りの牛肉や野菜を、火にかけた鍋の湯にくぐらせ、ポン酢かごまだれをつけて食べる。

Yudōfu • 湯豆腐

Tōfu simmered in a kelp broth. Served with soy sauce and seasoning such as green onions, ginger, *yuzu* orange, etc. Vegetables are sometimes cooked together.

豆腐をだしで煮たもので、しょうゆに薬味（ねぎ、しょうが、ゆずなど）を添えたつゆで食べる。野菜を添えたものもある。

NOODLES
めん類

Udon • うどん

Noodles made from wheat dough. Usually served with a hot, soy-sauce-based broth.

小麦粉を塩水でこねてのばしたものを、細長く切ったもの。普通は具をのせて、熱いしょうゆ味のつゆをかけて食べる。

Nabeyaki udon • 鍋焼きうどん

Udon cooked in a clay pot with vegetables and meat.

野菜や肉などといっしょに土鍋で煮込んだもの。

Tsukimi udon • 月見うどん

Topped with a raw egg.

生卵がのっている。

Yamakake udon • 山かけうどん

Topped with grated taro root.

すりおろした山芋がかかっている。

Tempura udon • てんぷらうどん

Topped with prawn tempura.

えびのてんぷらが上にのっている。

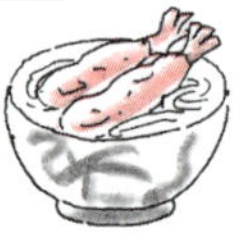

Soba • そば

Made with buckwheat noodles, taro root, egg whites, etc. These thin and long noodles are said to be a symbol of longevity and are especially nutritious. Served with hot soup, like *udon*.

そば粉に山芋、卵白などを加えて作る。栄養があり、細長いところから長寿の象徴ともいわれている。うどんと同様、熱いつゆをかけて食べる。

Zaru soba • ざるそば

After rinsing in water, arrange *soba* on the bamboo dish. Serve with dipping sauce.

水にさらしたあと竹のすに盛り、つゆにつけて食べる。

Rāmen • ラーメン

Noodles made from kneaded flour, egg, salt and soda water. Served in Chinese-style soup.

小麦粉に卵、塩、かん水を入れて練り、そばのようにしたもの。中華風のスープを注いで食べる。

CHOPSTICKS
はし

In Japan, chopsticks were originally sacred objects used to offer food to deities. That idea is still observed in some ways when using chopsticks. For example, each family member has his or her own pair. Disposable chopsticks are used for guests.

元来日本で使われるはしは、神に食べ物を捧げる神聖なものであった。現在にいたっても家庭で個人用のはしをそれぞれ決めたり、来客用には使い捨ての割りばしを出したりと、そのなごりが随所に見られる。

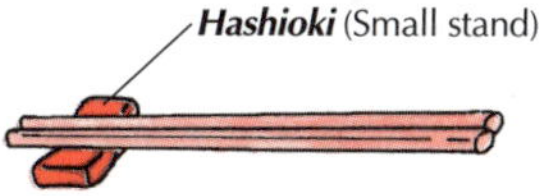

Nuribashi
(Chopsticks used for daily meals)

Waribashi
(Disposable chopsticks used for guests and at restaurants)

Toribashi
(Serving chopsticks to accompany each dish)

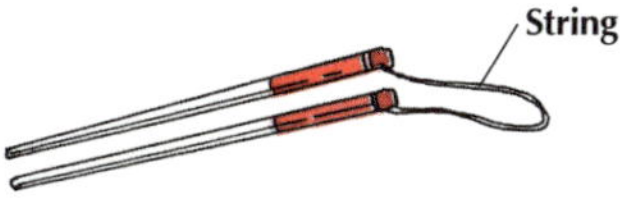

Saibashi
(Longer chopsticks used for cooking)

●DO YOU KNOW HOW TO USE CHOPSTICKS?

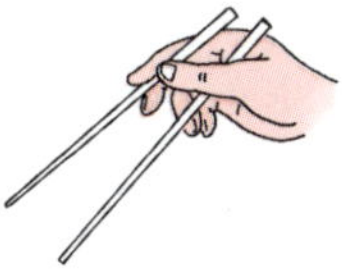

HOW TO USE • 使い方

Hold the upper chopstick between the forefinger and the middle finger, supporting it with the thumb. The lower chopstick should stay between the middle finger and the ring finger.

上のはしは、人差し指と中指の間で親指の先をそえて上下させ、下のはしは、中指と薬指の間で固定させて持つ。

BAD MANNERS • マナー違反

Tsukibashi : 突きばし

Pierce foods such as potatoes, with the chopsticks.

芋などにはしを突き刺して食べる。

Saguribashi : さぐりばし

Examine something in the dish with chopsticks.

はしで器の中のものを探す。

Mayoibashi : 迷いばし

Twirl around the chopsticks, wondering what to eat.

どれを取るか、迷って皿の上で回す。

Neburibashi : ねぶりばし

Lick food on the chopsticks.

はしについているものを、口でなめて落とす。

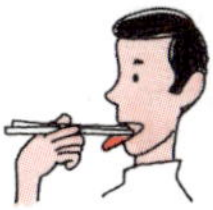

SUSHI RESTAURANTS
寿司屋

If you sit at the counter in a sushi restaurant, you will be served sushi according to your order. You can also order one of *nigirizushi* or *chirashizushi* sets at fixed price such as *tokujō* (superior), *jō* (excellent), or *nami* (standard).

握り寿司は、カウンター席に座ると注文に応じて握ってもらえる。特上、上、並と呼ばれるセットで、握り寿司や、ちらし寿司を頼むこともできる。

●SUSHI VOCABULARY CHECKLIST

Neta

Seafood on top of a sushi rice ball.

握り寿司の上にのせる魚介類。

Gari

Vinegared ginger accompanying sushi.

寿司の横に添えるしょうが。

Murasaki

Soy sauce specifically for sushi.

刺身用のしょうゆ。

Agari

Green tea served in a large cup.

緑茶が大きな湯飲みで出される。

Oaiso

The bill.

会計してもらうこと。

RYŌTEI
料亭

Very upscale restaurant where customers are served in a private room. They drink sake in a friendly atmosphere and enjoy *kaiseki ryōri* (a fixed menu of select delicacies served in order). Sometimes the dishes are served together on a dinner-tray.

客室を設けて個別に料理を出す高級な店。酒を酌み交わしながら、なごやかな雰囲気で会席料理を楽しむことができる。献立に従って一品ずつ出す場合と、料理をのせた膳を卓上に出す場合がある。

Kaiseki ryōri • 会席料理

Serving order →
出てくる順番

YAKITORIYA
焼き鳥屋

Barbecued chicken meat, giblets and leeks on a skewer. Seasoned with *tare* (sauce) or salt.

小さく切った鶏肉、もつ、ねぎなどを竹串に刺して焼いて出す店。塩やたれで味をつける。

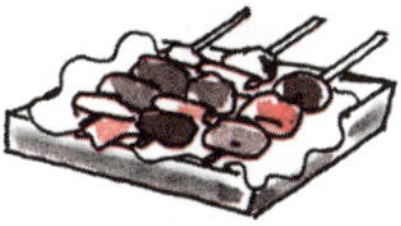

OKONOMIYAKIYA
お好み焼き屋

At an *okonomiyaki* restaurant, the customer cooks a pancake-like batter (flour, egg and water) on the hot table-top iron griddle, adding meat, seafood, and vegetables as desired. Season with sauce, green seaweed, and bonito flakes, slice and eat.

卵と水で溶いた小麦粉に野菜や魚介類などを入れ、鉄板の上で、自分で焼いて食べる。ソース、青のり、かつおぶしで味をつける。

YATAI (STALLS)
屋台（おでん／ラーメン）

In the evening, portable stalls set up shop in the streets (selling *oden* and *rāmen*). On festival days, there are stalls where fried noodles, *takoyaki* (ball-shaped pancake with octopus) and *okonomiyaki* are cooked.

夜になると車のついた屋台を引いて路上で店を出す人が現れる。縁日には、焼きそば、たこ焼き、お好み焼きなどの屋台が出る。

JAPANESE FOOD RESTAURANTS
和食レストラン

Restaurants serving only soba, broiled eel or pork cutlets are popular, but there are Japanese food restaurants that serve a variety of Japanese food.

そば屋、うなぎ屋、トンカツ屋など専門店があるが、いろいろな日本食を選んで食べることのできるレストランもある。

Noren • のれん

Shop curtains adorn the entranceways of Japanese restaurants. They usually have the shop's symbol or crest printed on them as an advertisement. They are hung outside when the shop is open and taken down when it is closed.

日本食のレストランで、店の屋号や紋が染め抜かれた看板の役もする布。開店時に店の軒先に掲げ、閉店時に取りはずす。

Oshinagaki • お品書き

A menu brought by waiters/waitresses upon being seated at the table.

店員の指示に従って席についたら、お品書きを見て注文する。

Bill Payment • 精算

The customer brings his or her own bill to the register near the exit and pays there. Tipping is almost nonexistent in Japan.

精算書を出口脇の会計窓口まで自分で持っていき、そこで払う。レストランでのチップの習慣はほとんどない。

Showcase • ショーケース

Plastic or wax models of food are displayed in outdoor glass cases, with their prices, for quick reference.

ワックス見本がショーケースの中に入っており、値段とともにひと目でわかる。

Oshibori • おしぼり

Moist towels—usually cold in summer, hot in winter—are offered for customers to wipe their hands with.

夏は冷たい手拭きタオル、冬は熱い手拭きタオルを出す店もある。

Teishoku • 定食

A popular set meal usually served with rice, soup, pickles and an entrée like roasted fish.

ご飯に汁物、香物、焼き魚など一品料理がセットになった定食メニューも人気がある。

BENTŌ SHOPS
弁当屋

Recently, there are a lot of *bentō* (take-out lunch box) shops crowded with *salarymen/women* and students during lunch hour.

近年弁当を売る店が増え、昼食時には会社員や学生が多く利用している。

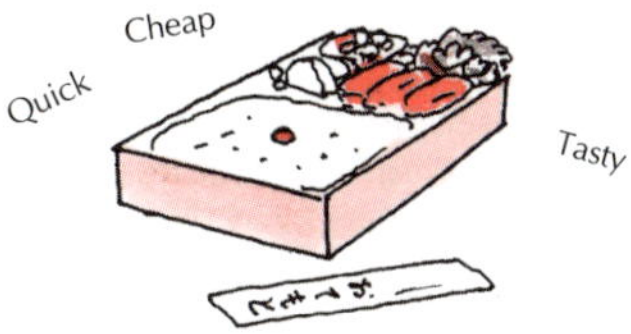

DEMAE (HOME DELIVERY)
出前

Udon, soba, rāmen and other foods are home-delivered, too. Broiled eel dishes and sushi are often delivered for entertaining guests at home. The restaurant usually sends someone to pick up the serving dishes the next day.

うどん、そば、ラーメン屋などが注文に応じて家に配達してくれる。うなぎや寿司なども来客のもてなし用に頼むことが多い。食べた後の食器も取りにきてくれる。

KISSATEN (COFFEE SHOPS)
喫茶店

People drop in at *kissaten* frequently, where coffee, tea, juice, cakes, and other dishes such as curried rice and pasta are served.

コーヒー、紅茶、ジュース、ケーキや、カレーライス、スパゲティなどの軽食を出す喫茶店は、よく利用される。

KAMMIDOKORO
甘味処

Traditional Japanese sweets like *ammitsu, dango,* and *manjū* are served with Japanese green tea. Hot *shiruko, zenzai, amazake,* etc. are served, too, according to the season.

日本古来の和菓子であるあんみつや団子、まんじゅうなどは、日本茶といっしょに出される。また季節により汁粉やぜんざい、甘酒なども用意される。

DRINKS
飲み物

Japanese Sake • 日本酒

Sake is made from brewed rice, water and malt and is around 16% alcohol. Served at a warm temperature (when the bottom of the *tokkuri* is a bit hot to the touch, is perfect), or cold. Also indispensable as a seasoning in cooking.

米に水とこうじを加えて発酵させたもの。16%前後のアルコール濃度である。人肌程度の温かさで飲んだり、冷たいまま飲んだりする。また料理用としても欠かせない。

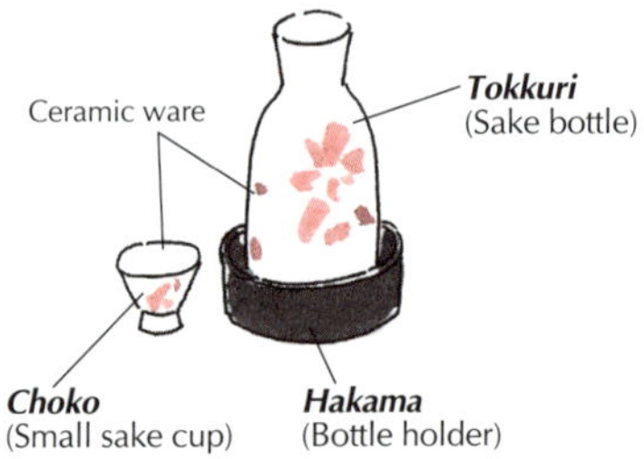

How to Warm Sake
酒のおかんの仕方

①

Boil water.

湯を沸かす。

②

Place the *tokkuri* (filled with sake) in the boiling water.

酒をついだとっくりを湯につける。

Shōchū (Coarsely Distilled Spirits) • 焼酎

Grains or potatoes are brewed with malt and distilled into *shōchū*. The alcohol content is around 25%.

穀物や芋類を原料としてそれにこうじを加えて発酵させ蒸留したもの。アルコール分は25%前後のものが多い。

Umeshu (Plum Liquor) • 梅酒

Pickled-Plum *Shōchū*.

焼酎に梅を漬け込んだもの。

Japanese Green Tea • 日本茶

Green tea is made from steamed young tea leaves. Teas differ according to processing.

若葉を摘んで蒸して作る。発酵の度合いや製造法によって味の違う茶となる。

Sencha • せん茶

Steamed and dried tea leaves. The most common green tea is *sencha*.

葉を蒸して乾燥させたもの。一番よく飲まれる緑茶は、せん茶である。

Matcha • 抹茶

New green tea leaves are pounded into powder. Used in the tea ceremony.

茶の新芽を摘み、粉末にしたもの。茶の湯に使う。

Bancha • 番茶

Made of hard leaves and stalks after the young, soft leaves have been picked for *sencha*.

緑茶用の葉を摘み取ったあとのかたい葉や茎が原料。

Mugicha • 麦茶

Made not from tea leaves but from roasted barley or rye. Served cold in summer.

茶の葉ではなく、大麦や裸麦を焙じたもの。夏、冷やして飲む。

Gemmaicha • 玄米茶

Bancha mixed with roasted brown rice.

番茶に、いった玄米を混ぜたもの。

Hōjicha • ほうじ茶

Roasted bancha. The roasting gives the tea a smoky flavor.

番茶を焙(ほう)じたもので、香ばしい。

How to Serve Fragrant Tea
おいしいお茶をいれよう!

①

After warming the pot, put well-rounded spoonfuls of *sencha* (2tsp/person) into the pot and pour hot boiled water in. Let steep for a while.

温めた急須に人数分のせん茶(1人、小さじ2)をいれ、沸騰したお湯をしばらくおく。

②

Warm the tea cups and pour the tea, alternating evenly from cup to cup. Drain the pot completely.

温めた湯飲み茶碗に少しずつ均等に注ぎ、最後の一滴まで注ぎ切る。

HOUSING
住居

In Japan, land area with a suitable living environment and convenient transportation is limited, so housing density is high. It is difficult for Japanese to own a house with a yard, consequently, many people live in high-rise apartment buildings.

土地が限られた日本では、環境のよい所や便利な所は住宅が密集している。大きな庭つきの家を持つことが大変難しく、高層のマンションやアパートに住む人が多い。

KINDS OF RESIDENCES
住居の種類

Single-Family Houses • 一戸建て

Most houses are made of wood or concrete, and there are both Japanese and Western styles. Houses have ceramic tile roofs of different designs and shapes.

ほとんどの家が木造やコンクリートでできており、純日本的なタイプと西欧風のタイプのものがある。屋根は、かわら屋根が多い。

Housing Complexes • 集合住宅

There are many rental apartments, and public and private housing complexes in certain areas. Condominiums are a more upscale kind of housing that is very expensive, particularly in the central part of the city.

賃貸のアパートや、一地域に集合的に建てられた公営や民営の団地も多い。マンションはさらに高級な集合住宅で、分譲のものも多く、都市では値段もたいへん高くなる。

FLOOR PLAN OF A TWO-STORY SINGLE-FAMILY HOUSE
一戸建て二階造り家屋の間取り

Most houses contain a mix of Japanese-style rooms with *tatami* mats and Western-style rooms with hard-wood floors.

ほとんどの家は畳敷きの部屋と、床板敷きの部屋をもつ和洋折衷スタイルである。

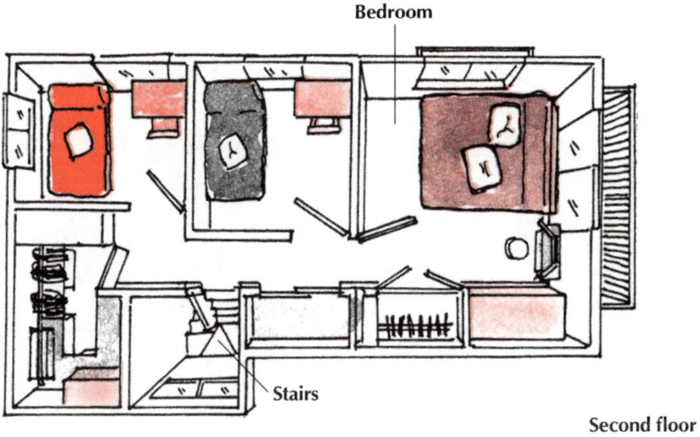

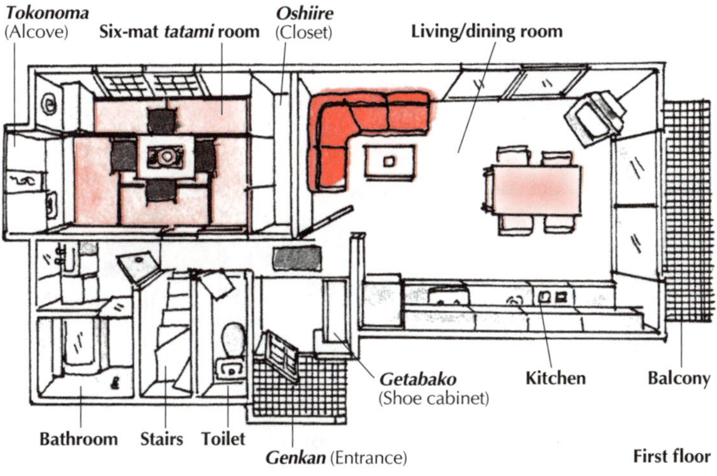

ENTRANCE
玄関

In traditional Japanese houses, entrance ways are usually sliding doors; contemporary Western-style houses have Western-style doors.

伝統的日本家屋では、玄関は引き戸のことが多いが、今日では西洋式ドアの家が多い。

In Japan, you should take your shoes off at the *genkan*. Usually, slippers are provided.

日本では屋外で履いている靴は全て玄関ホールで脱ぐ習慣がある。ここで室内用スリッパに履きかえることもある。

Getabako • 下駄箱

The family's shoes are placed inside the cabinet.

家族の靴は全てここに片付けられる。

JAPANESE ROOMS
日本間

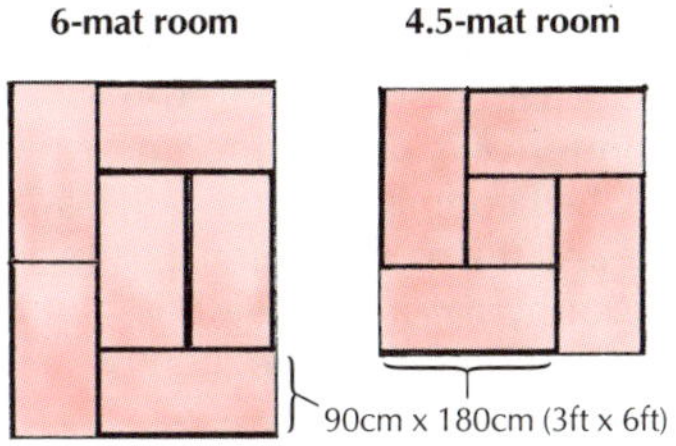

The size of a Japanese-style room with a *tatami* mat floor is measured according to how many mats there are. A four-and-a-half mat room is a square room with its origins in the tea ceremony.

畳の敷かれた日本風の部屋で、畳の数によって部屋の大きさを示す。4畳半は茶室の大きさである。

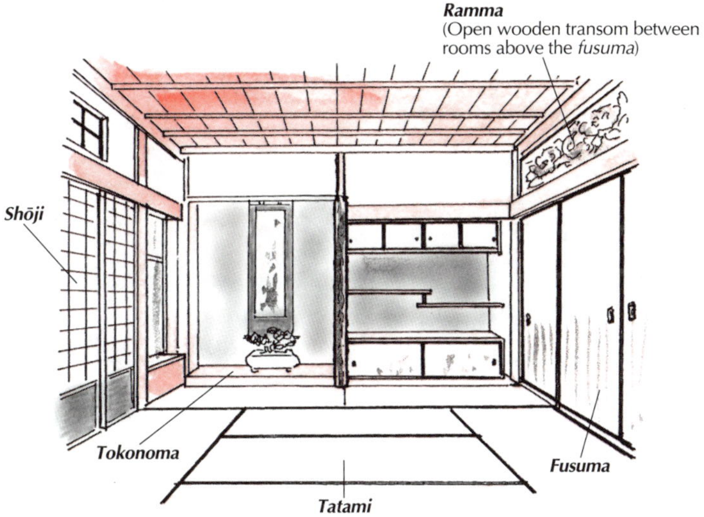

Tokonoma • 床の間

The wood-floored alcove in a Japanese room, about a one-half or one *tatami* mat size. A hanging scroll and flowers or decorations are displayed there, too.

和室の壁面が半畳か一畳へこんだ板張りの場所。掛け軸をかけたり、生け花や置物を飾ったりする。

Fusuma • 襖

Sliding doors at the *oshi-ire* or between rooms, serving as a partition. It is made of a wooden frame on which Japanese paper is first pasted, followed by a layer of *fusuma* paper.

木枠に和紙で下張りをし、その上に襖紙を貼ったもので、押し入れの戸や部屋の間仕切りに使う。

Shōji • 障子

A sliding door made of a wooden frame on which white Japanese paper is pasted, used as a partition between rooms or as a window shade. Soft sunlight comes through it.

格子の木枠に和紙を貼り付け、引き違い戸にしたもので、間仕切りや窓に取り付ける。明るく柔らかい光が差し込んでくる。

OSHIIRE
押し入れ

Bedding or cushions are stored inside the *oshiire*.

押し入れの中には、寝具や座布団などを収納しておく。

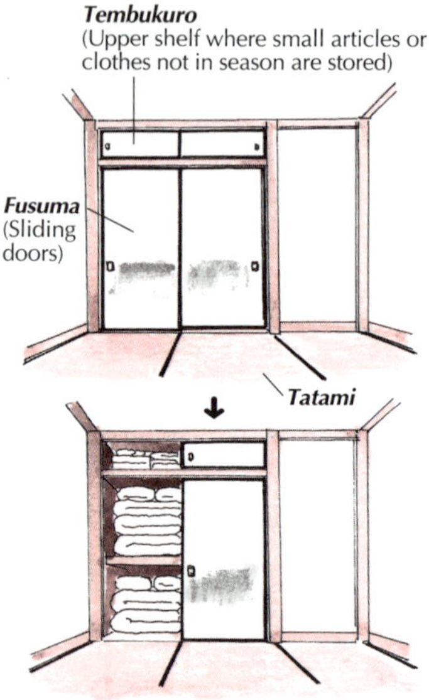

KAMIDANA
神棚

Talisman from shrines are placed on top of the lintel and prayers for the safety of the family and prosperity in business are made. Sake and rice are offered to this end.

鴨居の上に神社のお札などを祭って、家内安全や商売繁盛を祈るもの。酒や米などを供える。

FUTON
布団

At night, bed is made on the *tatami* by laying a sleeping mattress covered with a sheet on it. On top, a comforter is used. In the morning all the bedding is stored in the *oshiire* and the room is used as a living room by day. Because it is humid in Japan, *futon* are frequently aired in the sun.

毎晩、畳の上に、敷き布団、シーツを敷き、上には掛け布団を掛けて寝る。朝になるとこれらを押し入れに片付け、その部屋を居間として有効に活用する。日本は湿気が多いので、布団を日に当て乾燥させるために外に干す。

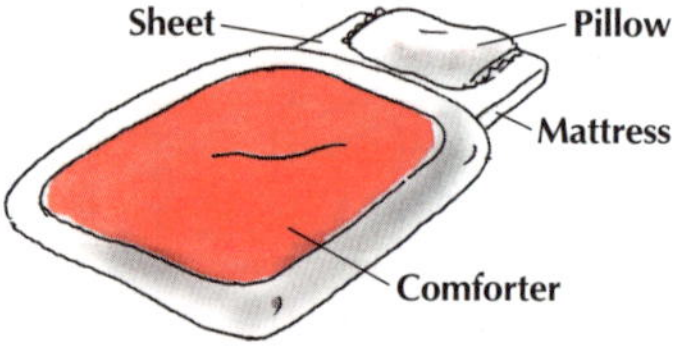

BUTSUDAN
仏壇

A family Buddhist altar used to pay respect to family ancestors. Buddhist statues, pictures and mortuary tablets are set inside. Prayers are made with candles and food offerings.

先祖を供養するための祭壇で、仏像や仏画とともに先祖の位牌を納める。家庭で灯明や供え物をして拝む。

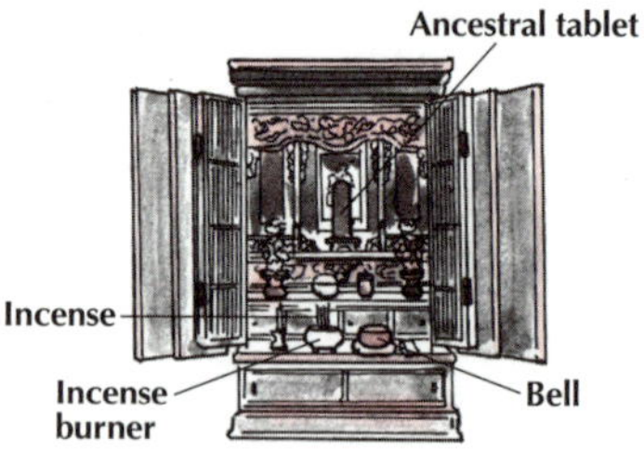

AIR CONDITIONING
冷房

Summers in Japan are hot and humid. Most houses have air conditioners or fans. But there are other ways to cool off.

日本の夏はたいへん暑く湿度も高いので、どこの家庭にも冷房機か扇風機は必ずある。また、暑い夏をしのぎやすくする工夫も欠かせない。

Sempūki (Electric Fan) • 扇風機

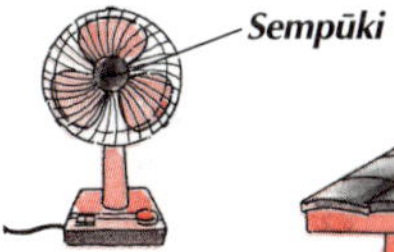

Circulates and cools the air down.

風を送って涼しくする器具。

Fūrin • 風鈴

Hangs outside under the roof. When the wind blows, this bell makes an enjoyable soothing sound.

軒先につり下げ、風に吹かれた時の涼しげな音を楽しむ。

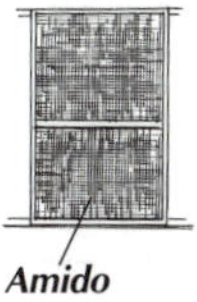

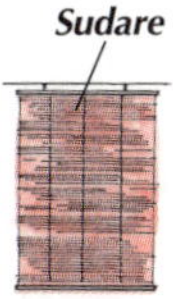

Amido / Sudare (Screens) • 網戸／すだれ

The *amido* is fixed to the window and the *sudare* hangs from it. The *amido* lets cool air come in but prevents insects from flying through and the *sudare* prevents people on the outside from seeing in.

窓にはめたり、垂らしたりして使う。暑い時に、窓を開けても虫が入らず、外からも見えにくく、風通しをよくすることができる。

HEATING
暖房

Most houses use *kotatsu* (foot warmers) and oil, gas, and electric heaters. These days *irori, hibachi* or *horigotatsu* (foot-warmers fixed in a sunken floor) are seldom found in most Japanese houses.

炬燵(こたつ)や石油・ガス・電気ストーブ等の需要が多く、最近では囲炉裏(いろり)や火鉢、掘り炬燵などはほとんど見られなくなった。

Kotatsu • 炬燵

A portable low table with an electric foot-warmer underneath, covered with a quilt.

ヒーターのついた低いテーブルを布団で覆い、上に台を乗せる。

Irori • 囲炉裏

The floor is cut in a square at the center of the room for the hearth, which is used for heating and cooking.

部屋の中央の床を四角く掘り、そこで火をたき、暖をとったり、煮炊きもする。

Hibachi • 火鉢

A ceramic brazier with charcoal inside, used for heating.

陶器製の暖房器具で、灰を入れ炭火をおこして暖まる。

KITCHENS
台所

Some houses have Western-style kitchens with modern appliances, but most kitchens are very uniquely Japanese.

近年、システムキッチンを取り付ける家庭が増えてきたが、従来のスタイルの台所も数多く見られる。

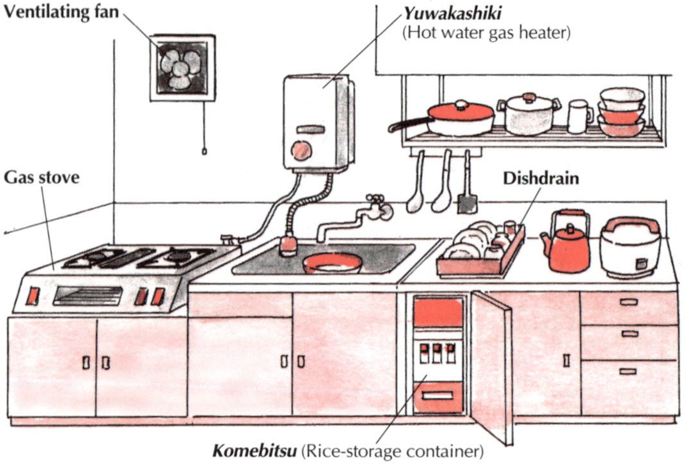

Gas Stove • ガステーブル

Gas stoves are preferred to electric ones, as they provide higher temperatures for frying and stir-frying. The stove includes a broiler beneath the burners, for fish only.

揚げ物、炒め物などには電気より火力の強いガスが好まれるため、ガスこんろを使う家庭が多い。魚専用のグリルがついている。

Komebitsu • 米びつ

A rice-storage container that has a measuring device.

米を入れて保存しておく容器。必要量のレバーを押すとその分量だけ米を取り出せる。

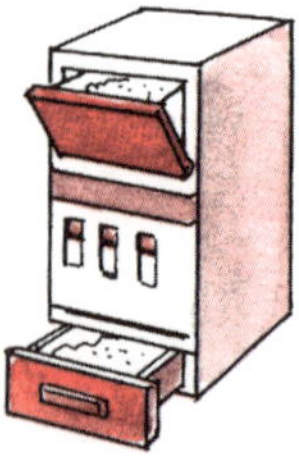

Rice Cooker • 炊飯器

Each family has an electric or gas rice cooker, which also keeps the cooked rice warm.

電気かガス炊飯器は必ずどこの家庭にもある。そのまま保温できる。

TOILETS
便所

There are two types of toilets: Western and Japanese. Toilets are usually separate from bathrooms.

日本では和式のトイレと洋式のトイレがあり、家庭では風呂場から独立している。

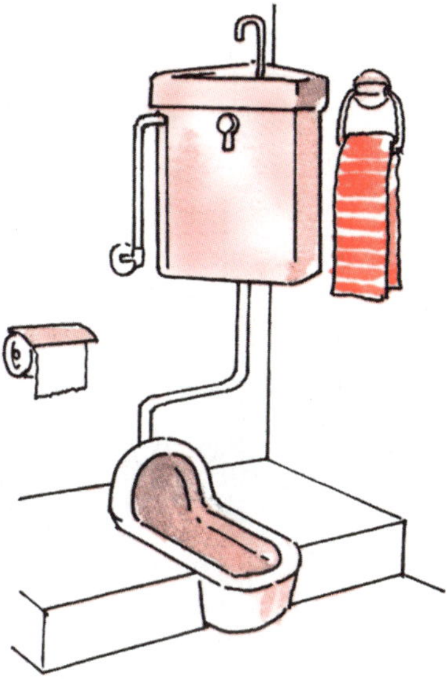

Japanese Toilet • 和式トイレ

Some prefer Japanese-style toilets since they do not have to sit directly on the seat. Men stand; women squat to use them.

和式のトイレは肌が直接便器に触れることがないため、これを好む人も多い。男性は手前に立ち、女性は便器をはさんでしゃがみ、用を足す。

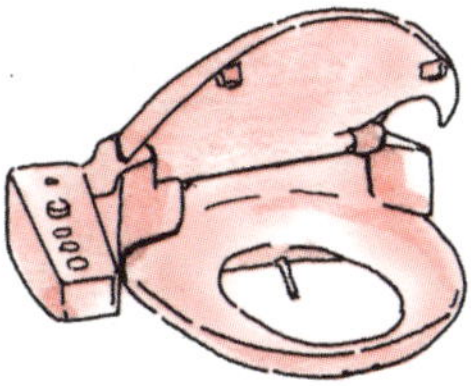

Toilet with Warm-water Bidet • 温水洗浄便座

Some toilets have warm-water bidets which spray warm water from under the seat and dry with air. Some have seat warmers, too.

洋式のトイレに温水洗浄便座を取り付けている家庭も多い。下から洗浄のためのシャワーが出たあと、温風が吹き出す仕組み。便座を温めることもできる。

Public Toilet • 公衆便所

There are many public toilets. Not all of the toilets, however, have toilet paper or paper towels.

街のいたる所にあるが、その全てにトイレットペーパーやペーパータオルが完備されているとは限らない。

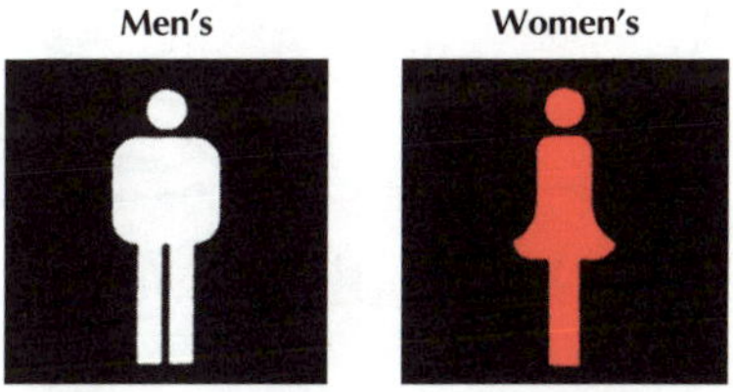

BATHS
風呂

Next to the bathroom, there is an area for changing clothes. The bathtub holds a lot of hot water for soaking, getting warm and relaxing. Washing should be done outside the tub.

浴室の外側には脱衣用の場所があり、そこで衣服の着脱をする。浴槽に湯をためてつかり、体を暖め、体は浴槽の外側で洗う。

Small apartments and hotels usually have module-style bathrooms which contain tubs, washstands and toilets in a small space.

せまいマンションやホテルなどでは、洗面所、風呂、トイレをコンパクトにまとめたユニットスタイルもある。

SENTŌ (PUBLIC BATHS)
銭湯

For those who have no bathtub at home or who want to try special baths like Jacuzzis, or a sauna, the *sentō* is ideal. Men and women bathe separately.

家庭に風呂がない人や、ジェットバス、サウナバスなどを楽しみたい人々に親しまれている。男性用、女性用に分かれている。

CEREMONIES
儀式

There are traditional customs and specific ways to conduct Shinto and Buddhist ceremonies in each local district, as well as celebration and condolence ceremonies. These traditions are passed on to succeeding generations.

神事や仏事、慶弔の礼などにおいて、各地方に古くから伝わる独特の作法や習慣があり、若い世代の人々にも受け継がれている。

CONGRATULATIONS
祝い事

Maternity Belt Celebration • 帯祝い

The day of the dog (according to the traditional calendar) in the fifth month of pregnancy is celebrated. People pray for a smooth delivery by wrapping the pregnant woman's belly with a white sash. A dog's delivery is thought to be smooth.

妊娠5ヵ月目の戌(いぬ)の日に、白い腹帯を巻いて安産を願う。(犬の出産は安産であるため。)

Shrine Visits • 宮参り

Parents take the newborn baby to a shrine and pray for the child's healthy growth. They are accompanied by the father's mother on this visit.

生後、父方の祖母と両親が赤ん坊を連れて神社に参り、元気に成長することを祈願する。

Shichigosan • 七五三

→P.28

Coming-of-Age Ceremonies • 成人式

→P.18

School Entrance / Graduation Ceremonies • 入学式／卒業式

Children and their parents attend school entrance/graduation ceremonies, which are very solemn.

学校への入学、卒業時には父母も参加し、学校で厳粛な式が行われる。

Kanreki (60th Birthday) • 還暦

At sixty years of age, the sexagenarian cycle is completed and we return to the zodiac sign of the birth years. People celebrate their sixtieth birthdays and wear a red vest on this day. There are other customs for celebrating the 70th birthday (*koki*), 77th (*kiju*) and 88th (*beiju*) birthday.

60年で生まれた年の干支に再び戻り、また新しい暦が始まるので、赤いちゃんちゃんこを着て、60歳の誕生日を祝う。70歳の古稀や77歳の喜寿、88歳の米寿など長寿を祝う習慣もある。

WEDDINGS
結婚

Traditionally, marriage has been considered a matter between families rather than individuals, and wedding ceremonies and receptions are conducted as such under the family names.

昔から結婚は家同士がするという意識が強く、結婚式や披露宴も○○家といった姓で表されることが多い。

Miai • 見合い

Matchmakers deliver photos and simple self-introductory notes to a prospective man's and woman's family. If they are interested in each other, a *miai* meeting will be arranged. Usually they are introduced at a hotel lobby or restaurant, and if they are interested in each other, they start dating.

仲人は、簡単な自己紹介文と写真を双方の家に届け、互いに気に入れば見合いが成立する。ホテルやレストランなどで会い、気に入れば交際が始まる。

Yuinō (Betrothal Gifts) • 結納

As a token of engagement, both families and the matchmaker gather on an auspicious day to exchange betrothal money and give gifts composed of nine lucky items. The money is usually given by the man's family to the woman's. Recently, some people exchange rings instead of money.

婚約の成立の証として、大安の日に両家と仲人が集まり、結納金や縁起のよい九品目の結納品を取り交わす。結納金は普通、男性の家から女性の家へ贈る。代わりに指輪などの記念品を交換する傾向がある。

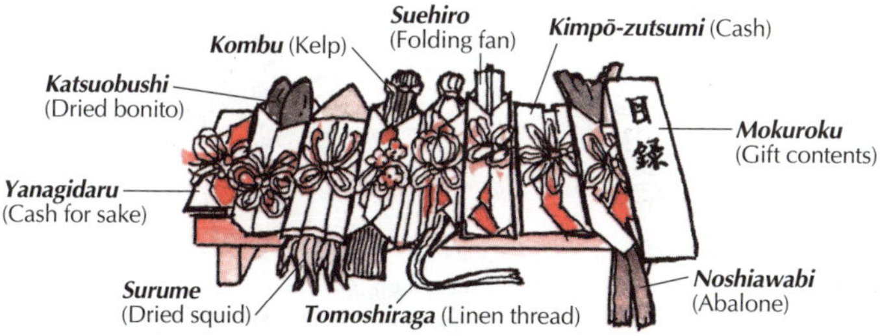

Wedding Ceremonies • 結婚式

There are Shinto, Buddhist and Christian ceremonies conducted at shrines, temples and churches, respectively. Many couples have both the wedding ceremony and banquet at the same time on a chosen lucky day at a hotel or other wedding hall.

神前式、仏前式、キリスト教式があり、それぞれ神社、寺、教会で式を挙げる。縁起のよい大安の日に、ホテルや専門の式場で、式と披露宴をまとめて行う人も多い。

Shinto Weddings • 神前結婚式

- Purification by the priest
  神主による清めのおはらい
- Report and prayer at the altar
  神前への報告と祈念
- Three-times-three exchange of nuptial cups
  三三九度の杯
- Oath by bride and groom
  新郎、新婦の誓い
- Exchange of rings
  結婚指輪の交換
- Offering of sprigs of sacred tree to the gods
  神前へ玉串を供える
- Relatives' pledge over cups of sake
  親族の固めの杯

Three-times-three Exchange of Nuptial Cups • 三三九度

Both bride and groom exchange nuptial cups three times, pledging marriage.
3つ重ねられた杯を、新郎新婦がそれぞれ3回ずつに分けてお神酒(みき)を飲んで結婚を誓う。

Wedding Receptions • 披露宴

After the wedding ceremony, a reception is held to which company colleagues, supervisors, respected teachers and friends of both sides have been invited.
式が終わるとそれぞれの会社の上司、恩師や友人を招いての披露宴が行われる。

Nakōdo (Machmakers)

- Greetings by the matchmaker
  仲人の挨拶
- Congratulatory address by the main guest
  主賓の祝辞
- Toast
  乾杯
- Cutting the wedding cake
  ウエディングケーキ入刀
- *Oironaoshi* (The bride and groom both change their garments to *furisode*, evening dress, tuxedo, etc.)
  お色直し（新郎新婦も振り袖やドレス、タキシードなどに着替える。）
- Congratulatory addresses by the guests
  来賓の祝辞
- Candle service
  キャンドルサービス

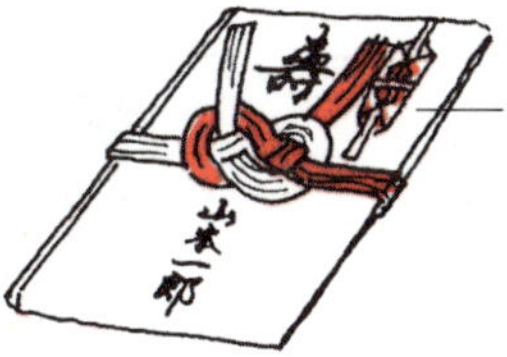

Shūgibukuro
(Envelope for gift money tied with red/white or gold/silver cords called *mizuhiki*)

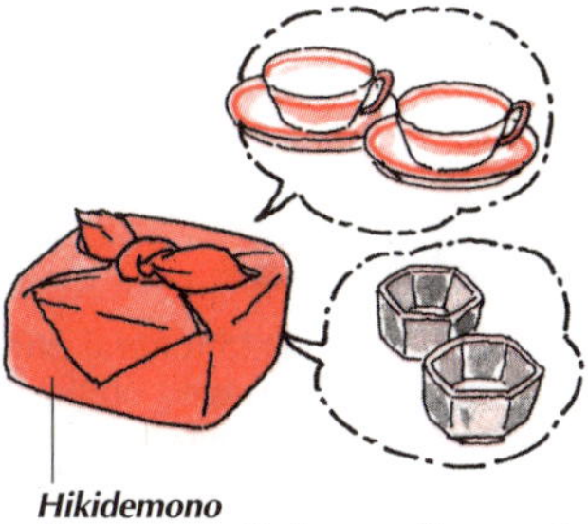

Hikidemono
(Souvenir or gifts for reception guests: tablewares, sweets, sugar, etc.)

Wedding Profile of the Average Japanese Couple Today • 今日の結婚像

- Age: man 28.3, woman 26.1　結婚時の年齢：男性28.3歳、女性26.1歳
- Betrothal gift money: ¥738,000　結納金：73.8万円
- Cost of ceremony and reception: ¥3 million　挙式、披露宴の費用：約300万円

(Sanwa Bank Home Consultant 三和銀行ホームコンサルタント 1995)

FUNERALS
葬儀

Most Japanese funerals are conducted nowadays in Buddhist style, consisting of prayers for the souls of the departed, and bidding farewell. The ceremonies are mostly arranged by professional undertakers. Buddhist priests attend, recite sutras, and give the deceased a posthumous Buddhist name.

亡くなった人の冥福を祈り、別れを告げる葬式は、現在ほとんどが仏式で行われ、葬儀屋の手によって段取りがととのえられる。僧侶を呼んで、読経してもらい、死者の死後の名前である戒名をつけてもらう。

Participants wear black mourning clothes.
参列者は黒い喪服を着る。

Funeral Signs • 葬式の標示

Used to give directions to funeral participants, funeral signs are posted on the way. Some signs carry more detailed information, like "funeral at Yamada Family at 2:00 P.M."

初めて訪れる人にもわかりやすいよう道案内の標示や、「2時より山田家葬儀」といったポスターが貼られる。

Kōdenbukuro • 香典袋

Funeral money contribution offered at the ceremony. New bills should not be used in the donation envelope, which is tied with black and white cords.

霊前に供えるお金。新札は避けて、黒と白の水引でくくられた封筒に入れる。

Tsuya (The Wake) • 通夜

The night before the funeral, relatives and friends of the departed gather and spend time together. Offerings such as a mound of rice in a bowl with chopsticks standing upright are left on the altar and a sacred light should be left on the entire night.

亡くなった人を葬る前夜に親類や友人が集まり一夜を過ごす。祭壇には山盛りのご飯に、はしを垂直に立て、一晩中、火をともし続ける。

Funeral Ceremonies • 告別式

While the priests chant the sutras, participants go to the altar one by one, place their hands together praying, burn incense, pray and bid farewell to the deceased.

僧がお経をあげるなか、参列者が一人ずつ祭壇の前で合掌と焼香をして死者の冥福を祈り、別れを告げる。

Shōkō (Incense) • 焼香

Pick the incense up with the thumb, forefinger and middle finger, raise the hand up to the height of your forehead, place the incense in the burner.

香を右手の親指、人差し指、中指の3本でつまみ、額の位置まで持ってきたあと、香盆にくべる。

Reikyūsha (Hearse) • 霊柩車

At the end of the ceremony, the coffin is taken to the crematorium in a hearse.

告別式が終わると柩(ひつぎ)は霊柩車で火葬場へ運ばれる。

After returning from the funeral and before entering the house, those who attended the funeral are sprinkled with a pinch of salt.

葬式から戻った人は、家に入る前に、塩を一つまみ体にかけてもらい清める。

Hōyō (Memorial Services) • 法要

After the funeral, ceremonies are held in memory of the deceased on the 7th, 49th, 100th day, and a year after death. While in mourning, surviving family members avoid happy celebrations and refrain from sending New Year's greeting cards for a year.

故人の死後、成仏を願って行う追悼の儀式。死後7日目の初七日、四十九日、百箇日、一周忌などがある。遺族は喪中といって、一年以内は祝い事を避けたり、年賀状での挨拶を控える。

GREETINGS
挨拶

Universally, good human relations begin with pleasant greetings. When meeting for the first time on a particular day, Japanese exchange different greetings in accordance with three time periods.

どこの国でも同じように、人との出会いはまず気持ちのよい挨拶から始まる。時間帯によって変わる下記の挨拶は、その日、最初に出会った時のみ使われる。

Ohayō gozaimasu

Good morning.
おはようございます。

Konnichiwa

Hello.
Good afternoon.
こんにちは。

Kombanwa

Good evening.
こんばんは。

Arigatō gozaimasu / Sumimasen

Thank you.
ありがとうございます。／すみません。

Sayōnara

Good-bye.
さようなら。

Gomennasai / Sumimasen

I'm sorry.
ごめんなさい。／すみません。

Sumimasen

Excuse me.
すみません。

Oyasuminasai

Good night.
おやすみなさい。

Hai

Yes.
Here./Present.
Here it is.
はい。

Dōmo

Thank you.
Hello.
Pardon me.
どうも。

BOWING
お辞儀

Instead of shaking hands, the Japanese bow. They also express gratitude, apologies, and requests by bowing. There are different ways of bowing depending on the situation, shown by how deeply you bend forward.

日本人は握手の代わりにお辞儀をする。また、感謝、おわび、お願いなどの気持ちをお辞儀で表す。場合に応じてその深さも変わる。

In a *tatami* room, you move to the side of the cushion to show respect to the others present, and then bow with your hands placed in front of you.

座敷では、座布団からおり、手前に両手をついてお辞儀をする。

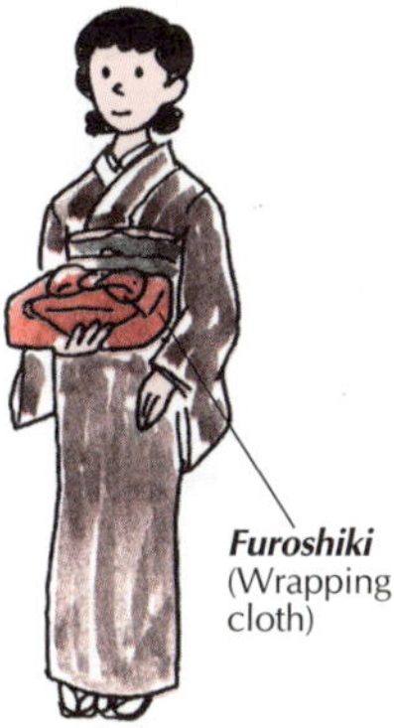

GIFTS
手土産

It is customary to bring a gift, such as a box of sweets with you, when you visit your acquaintances or those to whom you feel some obligation. When offering a gift, Japanese will usually say, "This is a trifle," which simply expresses a self-effacing attitude.

知人やお世話になった人の家に訪問する時には菓子折りなどの手土産を持参する習慣がある。手土産を渡す時に「つまらないものですが…」ということもあるが、これは謙虚な気持ちを表している言葉にすぎない。

MEISHI (NAMECARDS)
名刺

In business, people exchange namecards when they are introduced. This card is printed with the name of the person, the company and his/her title on it.

仕事において初対面の人とは、会社名、役職名の入った名刺を交換する。

GESTURES
いろいろなしぐさ

The Japanese often use unique hand gestures.
日本人のコミュニケーションには、手や指を使ったユニークなしぐさもある。

Three-Banzai Cheer • 万歳三唱

On happy occasions, people call out *banzai* three times with both hands raised in the air, expressing their wish for a blessing.
めでたい時に両手を挙げて、万歳を3回叫ぶ。

Hand Clapping • 手締め

On completion of some special project or event, etc., participants rhythmically clap their hands together.
物事が無事終了した時の祝いに、締めくくりとして全員で手を打つ。

To Beckon Someone • 人を呼ぶ

The hand is extended palm down and fingers moved in a beckoning motion from front to back.
手を前後に振り手招きする。

Saying "No" • 断る／否定する

The hand is held vertically in front and moved from left to right.
顔の前で手を左右に振る。

To Drive Something Away • 追い払う

The hand is moved from back to front in a sweeping motion.
「あっちへ行け」と手の甲を相手に向け前後に振る。

Saying Good-bye • 別れる

The hand is waved from left to right with the palm facing the other person.
てのひらを相手に向け左右に振る。

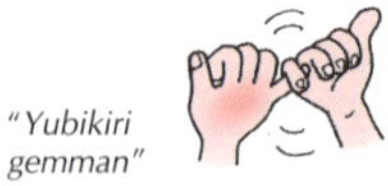

Promise • 指きり

Children, particularly, make a pact by hooking each other's pinky fingers.
互いの小指をからめて約束を守ることを誓い合う。

Rubbing or Touching One's Own Head with a Hand • 頭をかく／頭に手をやる

One attempts to hide embarrassment when scolded or even praised.
叱られたり、ほめられたりした時、照れや恥じらいを表す。

Money • お金

A circle made with forefinger and thumb touching means money.

人差し指と親指でまるを作る。

I • 私

Pointing to the nose with the forefinger means "I."

自分の人差し指で鼻を指す。

Anger, Jealousy • 怒り／嫉妬

Hold the pointed forefingers up over the head like horns.

両人差し指で角を作る。

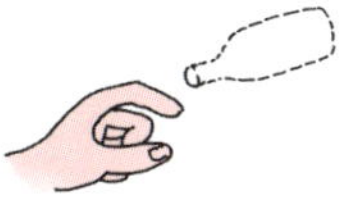

Let's Have a Drink • 一杯行こう

Make a round shape with fingers as if holding a small sake cup.

指の間におちょこをはさんでいる様子。

Lovers • 恋人

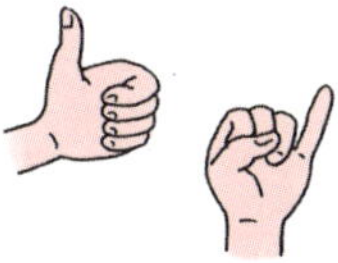

A upraised thumb means a boyfriend; an upraised pinky finger means a girlfriend.

親指を立てるとボーイフレンド、小指を立てるとガールフレンドを意味する。

Quarrel • けんか

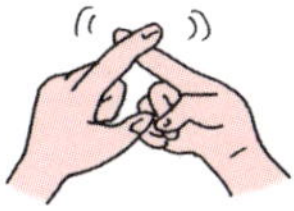

Cross and crisscross forefingers alternately.

両手の人差し指どうしを交互に合わせる。

COUNTING AND SHOWING FIGURES
数の数え方・示し方

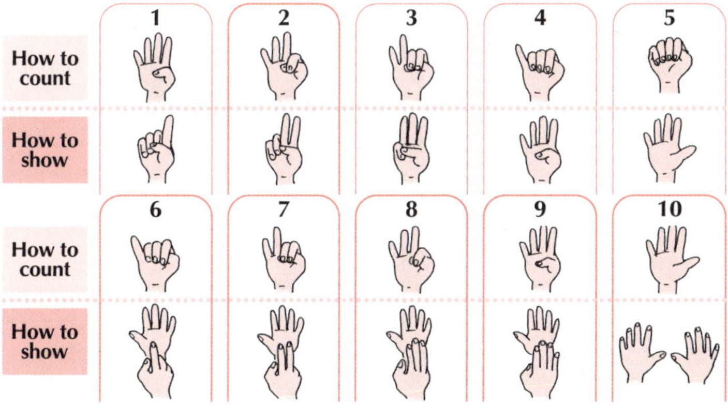

TRANSPORTATION
交通

Japan's transportation system is so well developed that it is very easy, and safe, to travel in the country.

交通の発達した日本では、日本国内はもとより世界の各地に速くしかも安全に行くことができる。

COMMUTER TRAINS / SUBWAYS
電車／地下鉄

Many people take commuter trains and subways to their offices and to school. Big cities have particularly well developed railroad networks and the trains run punctually, which makes city life very convenient.

通勤、通学の足として多くの人々に利用されている。特に大都市では路線網が発達しており、列車も頻繁に運転されているのでたいへん便利である。

Station Platform

Let's Take a Train
電車に乗ってみよう

① Buying tickets：切符を買う

First check the fare to your destination on the chart and buy a ticket at the automatic ticket-vending machine.

目的地までの切符の金額を調べ、自動券売機で切符を買う。

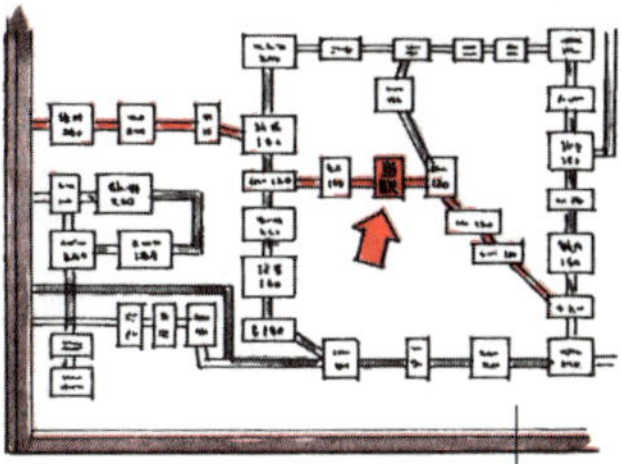

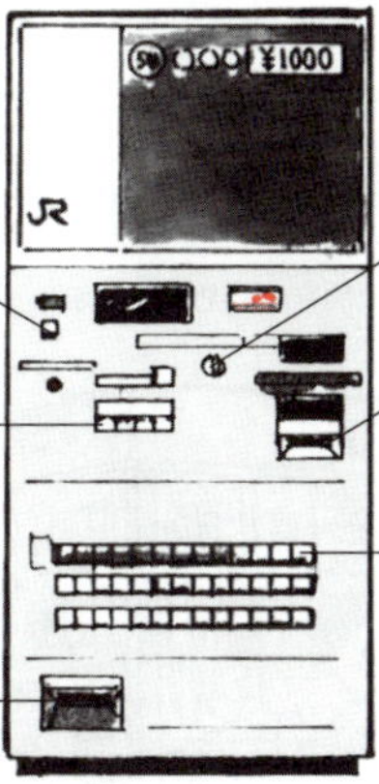

Put the money in and push the button corresponding with your destination. A ticket will be ejected and any change returned.

お金を入れ、ボタンを押すと切符とおつりが出てくる。

② Automatic wicket：自動改札機

Put your ticket in the entrance slot, which opens the gate to let you in. The ticket comes out from the other end of the slot automatically.

手前にある投入口に切符を入れるとゲートが開き、反対側から切符が出てくる。

③ Platform：プラットホーム

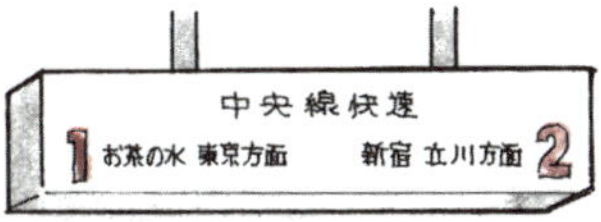

At the larger stations, there are many platforms, each of which has a different destination. It is best to confirm your platform.

大きな駅では、行き先別にプラットホームが分かれているので確認する。

④ Announcement：アナウンス

An announcement is made in the train before the next stop.

車内では、次の停車駅の案内のアナウンスがある。

Ticket Reservation Office • みどりの窓口

Major JR (Japan Railway) stations have a ticket reservation office where you can buy tickets for the *shinkansen* (bullet train), long-distance train tickets, etc.

大きなJRの駅にはみどりの窓口があり、ここでは新幹線の切符や長距離列車の切符などが買える。

Kiosk • 売店

In the train and subway stations, there are kiosks where you can buy magazines, newspapers, drinks and sweets.

地下鉄や電車の駅構内には売店があり、雑誌、新聞をはじめ、飲み物や菓子類も買える。

Some stations even have noodle stands or coffee counters on the platforms.

立ち食いうどんの店やカウンターのコーヒーショップなどがある駅もある。

BUSES
バス

City buses play an important role in city transportation. There are other types of buses like long-distance or tour buses as well.

路線バスは市民の足として大切な役割を果たしている。また、旅行者のための長距離バスや観光バスもある。

In one-man operated buses, passengers board from the front door, pay the fare, and get off at the back door.

ワンマンカーでは前から乗車し、料金を払い、後ろから下車する。

In buses which require different fares, passengers board from the back door, pick up an automatic ticket coupon there, and pay in front when they get off.

料金が一律でないバスは、後ろから乗車しチケットを取り、前から下車する時にチケット番号に応じた料金を支払う。

Tape-recorded announcements are made before each coming stop. Passengers signal the driver to stop by pushing the button on the side of the window or on the ceiling of the bus.

次の停車駅の案内がテープで流れる。降車の合図はバスの壁や天井にあるブザーで知らせる。

TAXIS
タクシー

Catching a taxi at the taxi stands of train stations or hotels is easy. In order to stop a taxi in the street, just raise your hand. The taxi's left rear door is automatic.

駅やホテルの前のタクシー乗り場では、簡単にタクシーをつかまえることができる。道でタクシーを止めるには、片手を挙げるだけでよい。左後部ドアは自動ドアである。

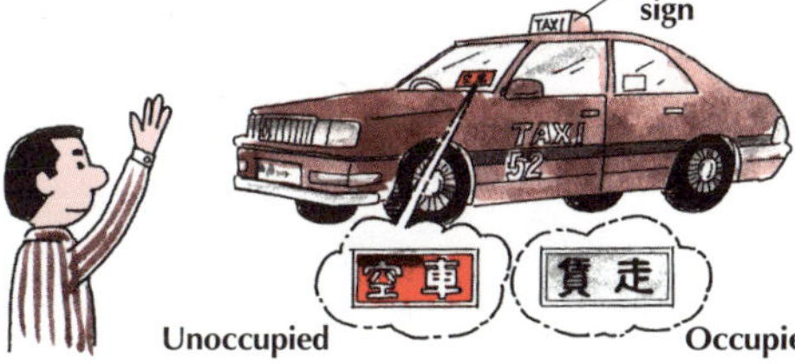

SHINKANSEN (BULLET TRAINS)
新幹線

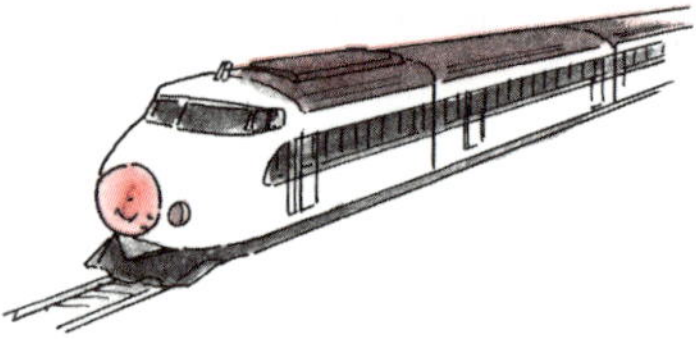

The *shinkansen* started in 1964, the year of the Tōkyō Olympics, and attracted attention as the fastest train in the world. A plan to connect most of the major cities in Japan with this system is steadily progressing.

1964年、東京オリンピックの開催と同時に開通した新幹線は、世界一速い列車として注目をあびた。全国の主要都市を結ぶ計画も着実に進行中である。

LINE	TERMINI	ROUTE LENGTH	TRAVEL TIME OF FASTEST TRAIN	NAME OF TRAINS
TŌKAIDŌ	Tōkyō—Shin-Ōsaka	552.6km	2hr 30min	Nozomi, Hikari Kodama
SAN'YŌ	Shin-Ōsaka—Hakata	623.3km	2hr 17min	
TŌHOKU	Tōkyō—Morioka	535.3km	2hr 36min	Yamabiko, Aoba
JŌETSU	Tōkyō—Niigata	333.9km	1hr 40min	Asahi, Toki
YAMAGATA	Tōkyō—Yamagata	359.9km	2hr 27min	Tsubasa
AKITA	Tōkyō—Akita	222.4km	3hr 49min	Komachi
HOKURIKU	Tōkyō—Nagano	662.6km	1hr 30min	Under construction

(Ministry of Transport 運輸省 as of April 1997)

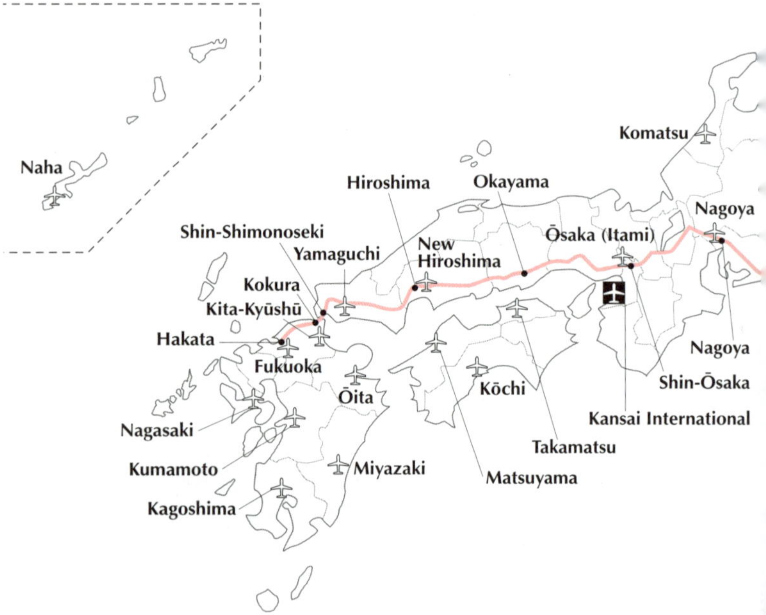

AIRPLANES
飛行機

The three major domestic airlines are JAL (Japan Air Lines), ANA (All Nippon Airways), and JAS (Japan Air Systems). Flight time to major cities is as follows:

現在、JAL、ANA、JASの3社による国内便がほとんどである。主な地域の飛行時間は次の通り。

Tōkyō (Haneda)–Sapporo ➢ **1hr 30min**

Tōkyō (Haneda)–Ōsaka ➢ **1hr**

Tōkyō (Haneda)–Fukuoka ➢ **1hr 45min**

Tōkyō (Haneda)–Okinawa ➢ **2hr 45min**

TELECOMMUNICATIONS
通信

Generally, telephone, telegraph and postal services are used for communication. Digital data communication using fax and computers has recently become popular.

電話や郵便を使ったコミュニケーションが一般的に利用されているが、最近ではファクシミリやパソコンによるデータ通信が盛んになってきている。

PUBLIC TELEPHONES
公衆電話

Public telephones are everywhere: at stations, shopping malls, parks. There are two types of telephones: green for public phones; gray for digital data communications.

駅やショッピングエリア、公園など、いたる所に公衆電話がある。緑色の公衆電話とデータ通信もできる灰色のデジタル公衆電話がある。

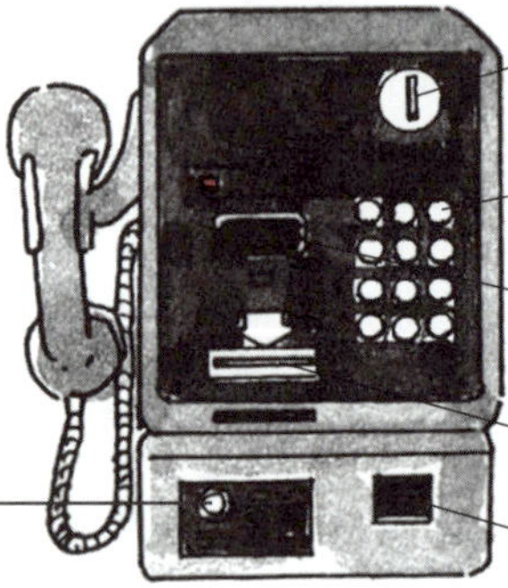

EMERGENCY BUTTON
110 ➢ Police
119 ➢ Fire & Ambulance
(Free)

Digital Public Phones • デジタル公衆電話

Portable terminal equipment, such as computers, can be plugged in for data transmission.

パソコンやデーターターミナルなど携帯用端末装置をつないでデータ通信ができる。

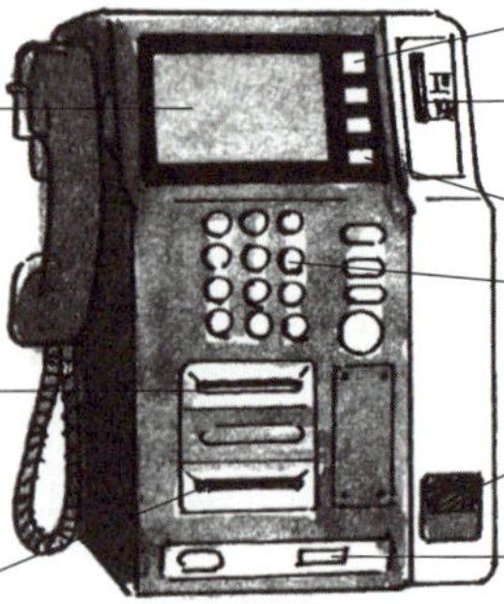

POSTAL SERVICE
郵便

Post offices with 〒 mark are all over Japan, providing quick and assured delivery of domestic and overseas mail. Besides postal service, utility payments, money deposits & savings are handled at the Post Office. (Open Monday–Friday 9:00A.M.–5:00P.M.)

〒のマークの郵便局は日本全国にあり、国内郵便だけでなく外国郵便も迅速かつ確実に届けてくれる。このほか、公共料金の支払いから、預貯金の業務まで行っている点が大きな特徴である。(月〜金：9:00〜17:00)

Delivery • 配達

A mailman delivers mail to each household once a day.

郵便配達員は1日に1回、郵便物を各家庭に配達して回る。

Mailbox

Kinds of Mail • 郵便の種類

Postcards
(special New Year's postcards with lottery numbers are sold at year's end)

Registered-mail envelope for sending cash

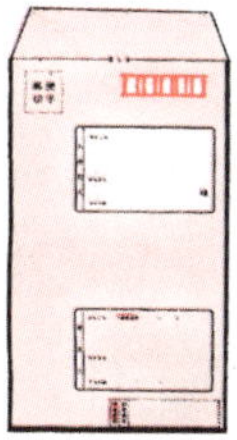

Japanese-style vertical envelope

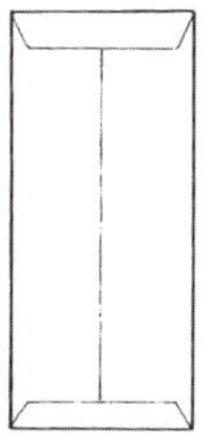

Express mail

Parcels

Other delivery services called *takuhai* are handled at nearby tobacco shops, cleaners, etc.

小包を送るのに宅配便を利用する人も多い。宅配便は、たばこ屋、洗濯屋など近所の店で取り扱う。

BANKS

銀行

Banks are usually open Monday–Friday from 9:00A.M. to 3:00P.M. ATM's are open on weekdays till 7:00P.M.; many are also available on Saturday and Sunday.

通常、銀行は月～金の9:00～15:00が営業時間である。自動支払い機は店舗により異なるが、平日19時まで、土・日曜日も使用可能なところが多い。

Japanese Currency • 日本の通貨

Three notes and six coins are in use. Checks are not popular in Japan.

主に3種類の紙幣と6種類の硬貨が使われている。小切手は日常生活の支払いにはあまり使われない。

¥1,000
(portrays Natsume Sōseki, a literary figure)

Amount / material
(decoration)

¥1 / aluminum
(Sapling)

¥50 / nickel
(Chrysanthemum)

¥5,000
(portrays Nitobe Inazō, an educator)

¥5 / copper
(Rice stalk)

¥100 / nickel
(Cherry blossom)

¥10,000
(portrays Fukuzawa Yukichi, a Meiji-era educator)

¥10 / bronze
(The Byōdōin Temple)

¥500 / nickel
(Paulownia blossom)

Banking Facilities • 銀行の業務

Many banks have deposit & saving, utility payment, and wire & transfer, and foreign currency exchange services.

預貯金、公共料金の支払い、送金や振替、両替、外貨の交換などの業務をしている。

Bank Accounts • 銀行口座

You can open a bank account by bringing a name seal, ID, and money for deposit directly to the bank counter. By registering secret code numbers, you can have an ATM bank card made.

銀行口座を開く時は、印鑑、身分を証明する物、入金したいお金を持参すると窓口で簡単に手続きをしてくれる。暗証番号を届け出ると、キャッシュカードを作ることができる。

●HOW TO USE THE ATM

①

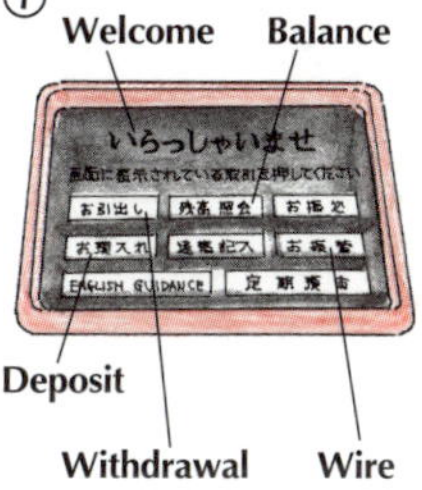

Push the desired transaction button.

画面の取引の種類のボタンを押す。

②

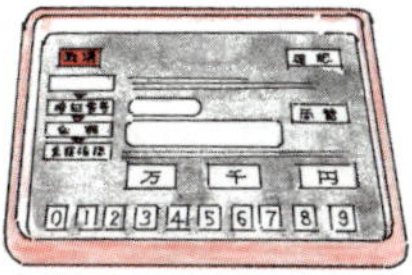

Insert your card and input your secret number and the amount of money desired in the transaction. Push "confirm" button if the encoding is correct.

カードを入れ自分の暗証番号と金額を押す。正しければ確認ボタンを押す。

③

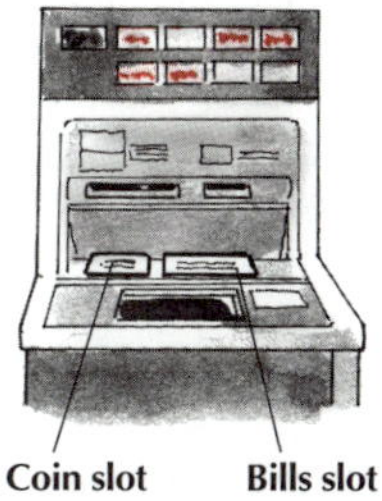

Use the slots for depositing and receiving cash.

入金時は入金口に現金を入れる。出金はここから現金が出てくる。

Seals • 印鑑

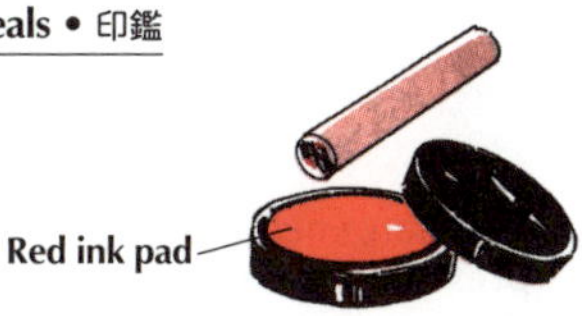

Instead of using a signature, Japanese use a seal. The *mitomein* (personal seal), which is sold at shops, is used for informal documents at the office or home.

サインの代わりに印鑑が使われる。認め印は職場や家庭での簡単な書類に使われ、市販されていることが多い。

A *jitsuin* is the legally recognized seal of the individual, which is used in official documents or contracts such as real estate contracts.

実印は個人の印章として法的に大きな効力をもち、土地売買などの公的契約書に使われる。

HOSPITALS
病院

Every Japanese is covered by some kind of medical insurance and can receive modern medical treatment under this system.

日本国民は誰もがなんらかの形で医療保険に加入しており、進んだ医療制度のなか、安心して診察が受けられる。

Health Insurance Cards • 健康保険証

Issued by the insurance organization to which one belongs, this insurance card should be submitted at the doctor's or hospital's reception desk at the time of examination. The card-holder pays only 10–30% of the total expense, with the monthly premium determined by the income of the individual.

加入している団体から発行される。診察を受ける時に病院の窓口に提出すると費用の1～3割を支払えばよい。毎月の掛け金は所得に応じて決定される。

●HOW TO GET A MEDICAL EXAMINATION

① Fill in the form at the reception desk and submit it with the insurance card at the counter. Wait until your name is called.

開業医や病院の窓口で受付用紙に記名し、健康保険証を出す。名前を呼ばれるまで待つ。

② Get medical examination.

診察をしてもらう。

③ Pay at the cashier.

窓口で精算をする。

④ Medicine is prescribed at the doctor's office. It might be filled at the hospital dispensary or at an outside pharmacy.

窓口で薬をもらう場合（開業医）と病院内の薬局や外部の調剤薬局でもらう場合がある。

- In Japan, medicine is mostly prescribed and given at the doctor's office.

  ほとんどの場合が医薬分業ではない。

- Over-the-counter medicine can be bought at drugstores.

  地域の薬局で、処方箋の必要でない薬は買うことができる。

POLICE
警察

Japan maintains exceptionally good public order. The Japanese police have a high arrest ratio, protecting citizens for a peaceful and safe life.

世界の中でも有数の治安のよい国である日本の警察の検挙率はたいへん高く、市民の平和で安全な生活を日夜守っている。

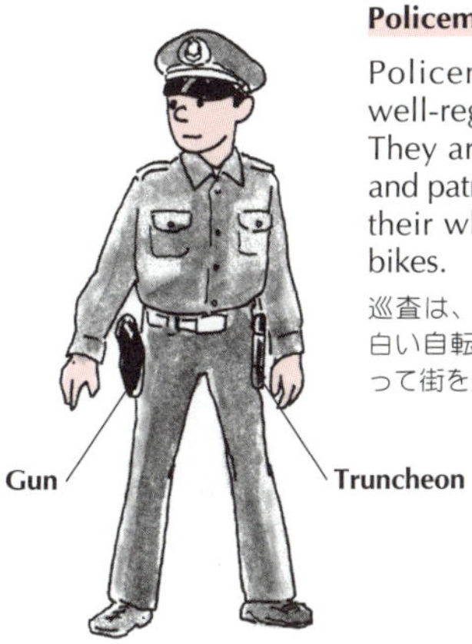

Policemen • 警察官

Policemen or patrolmen are well-regarded among citizens. They are called *"omawarisan"* and patrol the neighborhood on their white bicycles or motorbikes.

巡査は、「お巡りさん」とも呼ばれ、白い自転車、バイクやパトカーに乗って街を巡回する。

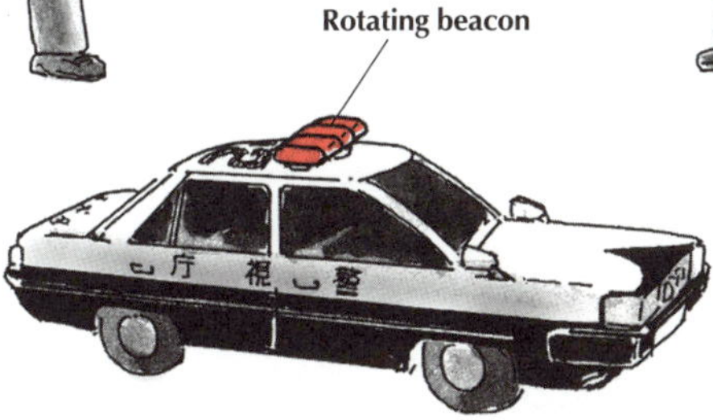

Police Boxes • 交番

Police boxes are called *kōban* or *hashutsujo*, and are located in many places. Policemen are on duty in shifts and handle such things as lost & found objects, giving directions, and major criminal cases.

交番(派出所・駐在所)は街のいたる所にあり、巡査が交代で勤務にあたっている。落とし物、道案内から、大きな事件の対応までかかわる。

VENDING MACHINES
自動販売機

Vending machines are ubiquitous in town: at shops, in the streets, hospitals, stations and other public places, which operate 24 hours a day, 365 days a year.

自動販売機は店先はもちろん、道路上、病院内、駅構内などの公共の場のいたる所で365日、24時間利用することができる。

Drink vending machine

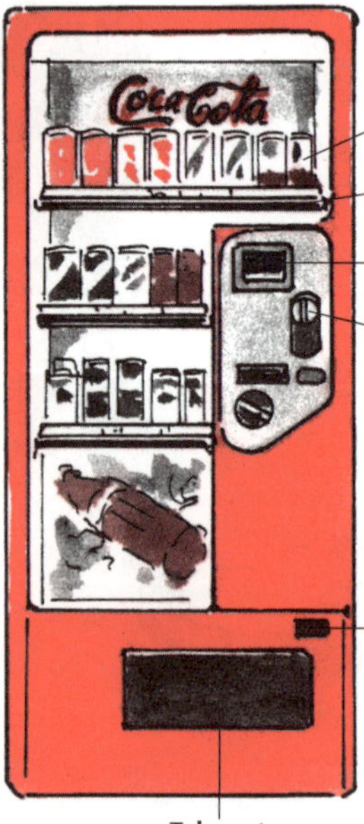

You can buy almost anything—postcards, stamps, magazines, sweets and even flowers—at vending machines.

葉書や切手類、雑誌、菓子、花にいたるまで自動販売機で買い求めることができる。

Telephone card vending machine

Installed near public phones.
公衆電話機の近くに設置されている。

To avoid the inconvenience of using coins at vending machines, some people use prepaid cards like the Orange cards (for JR tickets) or telephone cards, which are also sold at certain vending machines.

小銭の使用のわずらわしさを省くため、前もってカードを買い、そのカードを使用してサービスを受ける人も多い。オレンジカード(JR線の切符)、テレホンカードは所定の自動販売機で買うことができる。

PART 3

An Introduction to Japanese Culture

日本の文化にふれる

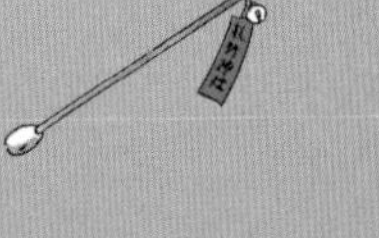

TEA CEREMONY

茶の湯

Chanoyu, tea ceremony, originated in China and was refined by Sen no Rikyū in 16th-century Japan. It incorporates Zen customs and promulgates *wabi* aesthetics, that is, simple beauty. After Rikyū's death, tea ceremony schools such as Omote Senke, Ura Senke, and Mushanokōji Senke, were created by his descendents.

茶の湯は中国から伝えられ、16世紀に茶人、千利休によって大成されたものである。禅の礼法をとり入れ、わび（簡素な美しさ）の心を研究した。流派として、利休の子孫により表千家、裏千家、武者小路千家ができた。

TEA UTENSILS
茶道具

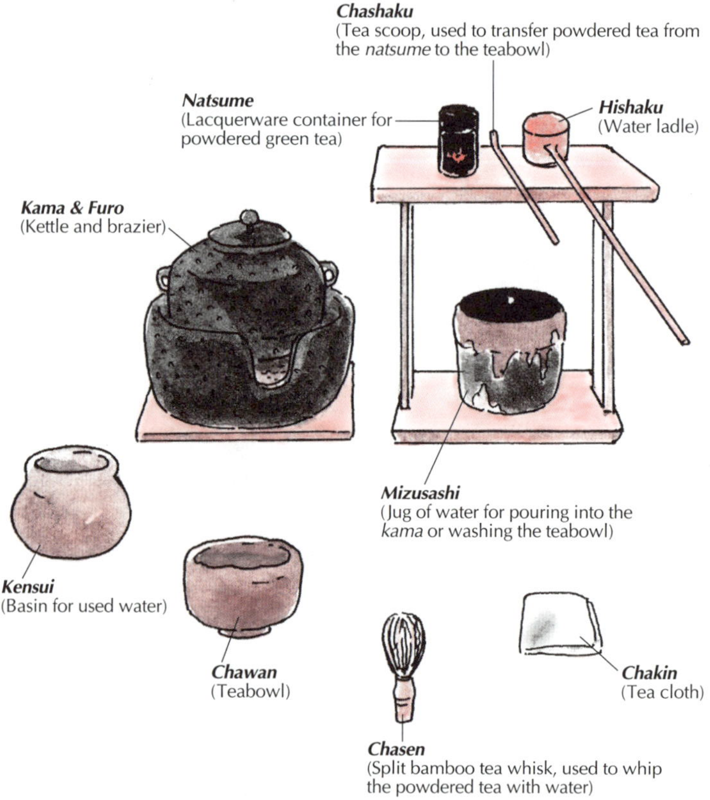

CHASHITSU (TEAROOM)
茶室

The tearoom is basically a 4.5-mat *tatami* room. The decorative elements of the tearoom are minimal, reflecting *wabi* aesthetics. The entrance to the room, called the *nijiriguchi*, is small. Guests must crouch to make themselves as small as possible to get through it, which reflects a "humble" spirit.

茶室の基本は四畳半である。部屋の装飾を最小限に抑えたところに「わび」の精神がある。また狭いにじり口を姿勢を低くして入るところに「敬」の心があるといわれる。

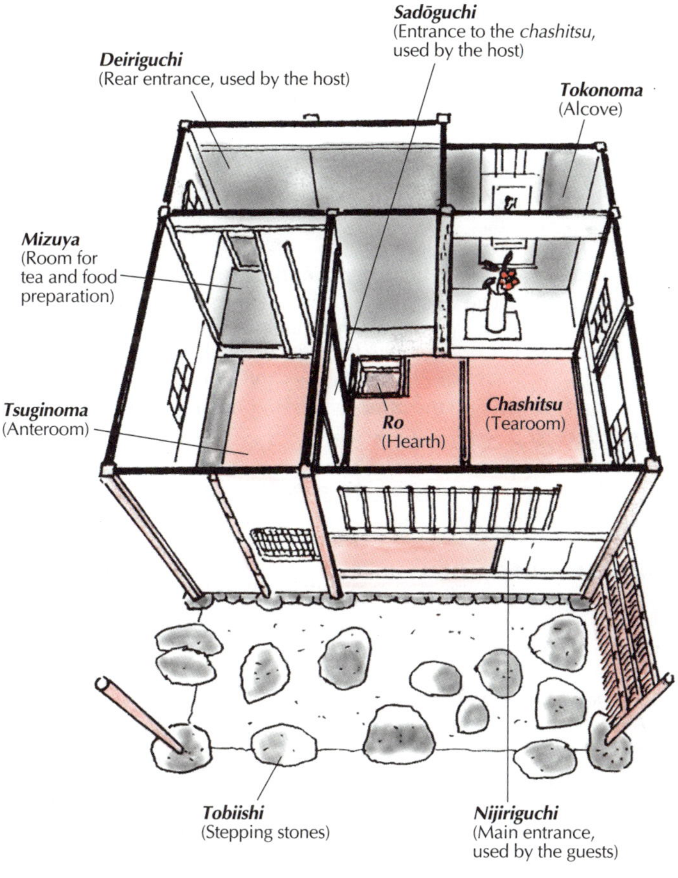

BONRYAKU-TEMAE (SIMPLIFIED TEA CEREMONY ON A TRAY)
盆略手前

Prepare the *chawan, chakin, chasen, chashaku* and *natsume* on a tray, and the *kensui*, so that tea can be made easily and enjoyed simply. You can use the hot water from the pot.

お盆に茶碗、茶巾、茶筅(ちゃせん)、茶杓(ちゃしゃく)、棗(なつめ)をのせ、建水を用意すれば手軽にお茶を楽しむことができる。ポットのお湯を使ってもよい。

USUCHA AND KOICHA (THIN TEA AND THICK TEA)
薄茶と濃茶

Usucha is made by pouring hot water over powdered tea in a bowl, then whisking it quickly. The host makes a bowl of *usucha* for each guest. *Koicha* preparation, on the other hand, begins with making a thick tea with the whisk moved slowly. *Koicha* is then served in a big bowl, with each guest having a sip. *Koicha* symbolizes the spirit of sharing through its communal teabowl and the atmosphere among the guests.

抹茶に湯を注いで茶筅で泡立てたものを薄茶(うすちゃ)といい、亭主は、客一人ずつに対してたてる。一方、一碗のお茶を練り、数人の客で飲み回す濃茶(こいちゃ)がある。これは、一碗の茶を囲み心を寄せ合うという精神からきている。

HIGASHI AND OMOGASHI
干菓子と主菓子

Higashi (dry sweets) or *omogashi* (fresh sweets) are served with *usucha*; *omogashi* are served with *koicha*. Guests place the sweets on a *kaishi* (special paper napkin the guests bring with them) and eat them with *kaishi* in hand.

薄茶には干菓子か主菓子(おもがし)(生菓子)を、濃茶には主菓子を使う。自分の懐紙に取り、そのまま懐紙ごと取り上げて食べる。

How to Drink Tea
お茶のいただき方

①

Place the sweets on your *kaishi* and eat them at the host's signal.

お菓子を懐紙に取り、亭主からの合図でお菓子を先にいただく。

②

When the tea is served, bow to the host and the other guests, take the teabowl with your right hand and place it in your left palm.

お茶が出されたらお辞儀をして、茶碗を右手で取り上げ左手にのせる。

③

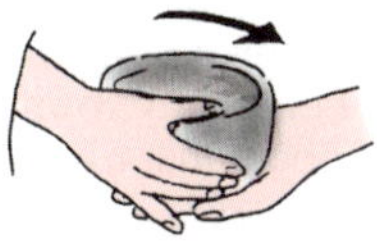

Turn the teabowl in your palm 2-3 times clockwise. Avoid having the front of the bowl face you.

茶碗を手前へ時計方向に2、3回、回し、正面を避ける。

④

Drink three and a half sips, approximately. The last sip is a kind of slurping action to remove any remaining tea.

3口半ぐらいでいただく。最後は音をたてて吸い切る。

⑤

Wipe the area of the bowl where you sipped from with your fingers. Clean the fingers with the *kaishi* (pre-inserted between your kimono collar).

飲み口を指でふき、胸元の懐紙の先でぬぐう。

⑥

Turn the bowl counterclockwise until the front of the bowl faces you.

茶碗を逆の方向に回し、自分に正面を向けるようにして戻す。

●How to make tea • 茶のたて方

Spoon 1.5 *chashaku* scoops of powdered green tea into the teabowl. Ladle hot water over the tea in 3.5 pourings, then whisk with the *chasen* to create a fine froth.

茶杓に1杓半ほどの抹茶を入れ、熱湯（3口半ほど）を注ぎ、細かい泡がたつように茶筅を振る。

FLOWER ARRANGEMENT

生け花

Ikebana is the art of traditional Japanese flower arrangement, originally related to religious ceremonies. Flowers were originally arranged where gods were welcomed or used as offerings at Buddhist altars. When the tea ceremony became popular in the 16th century, flowers were arranged in tea ceremony rooms. There are now three major *ikebana* schools: Ikenobō, Ohara, and Sōgetsu.

日本独自の伝統的な挿花(そうか)の技法。本来は信仰行事の一つとして始まり、神を迎え入れる場所に飾ったり、仏前に献じて供養したりした。16世紀には、茶の湯の流行に伴い、茶室の花として生けられるようになった。現在、池坊、小原、草月の3流派が中心である。

STYLES
様式

Rikka • 立花

Originally a style used on religious occasions, *rikka* arrangements later became *tokonoma* or alcove displays.

信仰のための花として生まれ、その後も床の間に飾られた。

Nageire (Slanting Style) • 投入れ

A modern style of arrangement which became popular with the introduction of Western flowers. At first, it was used for tearoom flower arrangements, showing the natural shape of the flowers.

茶室用に自然のままの姿で生けたのが、洋花の普及に伴い、近代的な「投入れ」となった。

Moribana (Upright Style) • 盛り花

Arrangement in the shape of three points of *shin* (center), *soe* (support), and *hikae* (overall balance), which indicate heaven (leader), earth (subordinate), and man (one to keep harmony in between) respectively. These three elements are called *sansai* (harmony between nature and man).

真・副・控が三角形を描くようにに生ける。これは、天(導くもの)、地(従うもの)、人(中間で調和を保つもの)の三才(自然と人間の調和)を表している。

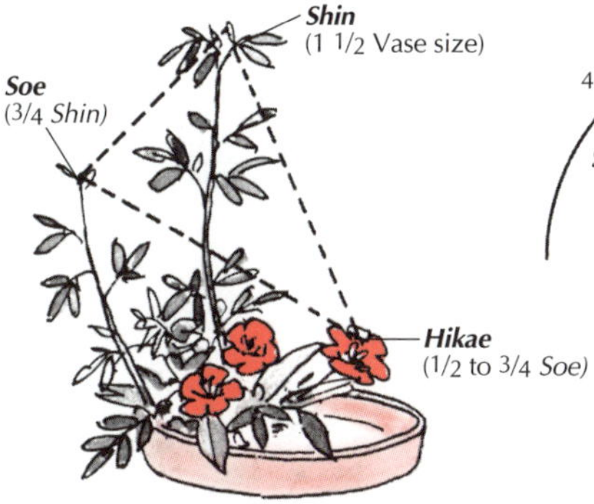

Vase size=Diameter of mouth of vase + Height of vase

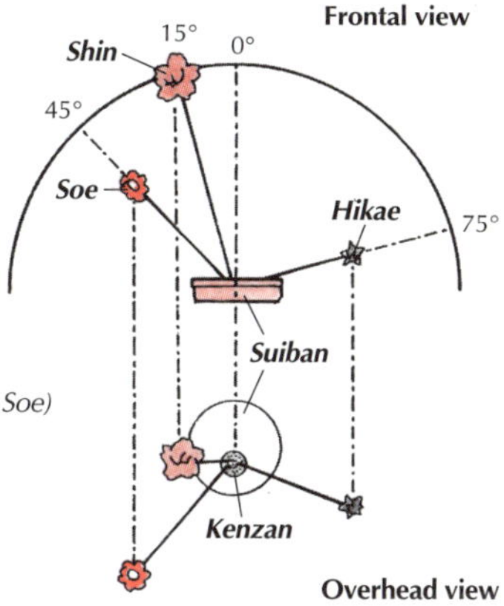

UTENSILS AND FLOWER VASES
道具と花器

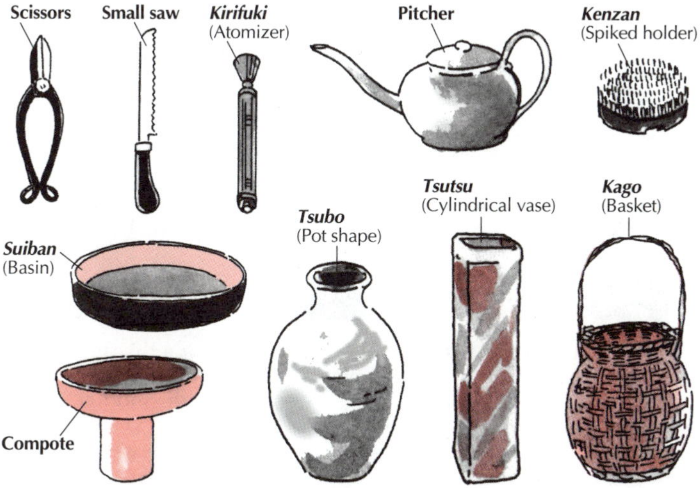

BASIC TECHNIQUES
基本の技術

How to Cut • 切り方

Remove all unnecessary leaves. Cut the branches in oblique sections. Cut stalks at a right angle under water to increase water absorption.

余分な枝葉を落とし、枝ものは斜めに切り、草ものは水中で輪切りにして、水揚げをよくする。

How to Bend • ため方

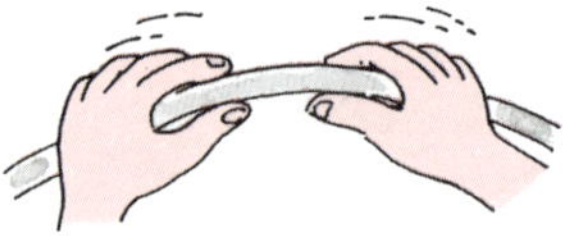

Use the thumbs to bend a branch to create a better shape.

枝ものは形よく、両手の親指の腹でためながら曲げる。

How to Fix • 留め方

Using Support Devices • 留め木を仕掛ける

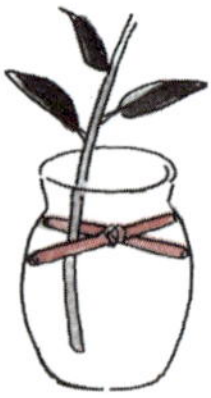

Cross bar holder.

十文字に留める。

Single bar holder at the base of the stalk.

花材の根元に横木を仕掛ける。

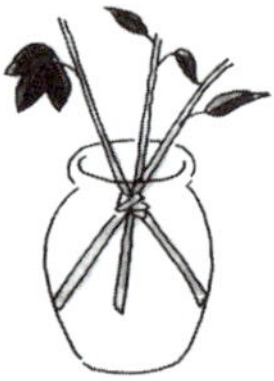

Bundle flowers together and fasten them.

花材を束ねて留める。

Using Kenzan • 剣山を使って生ける

For branches, pierce them vertically and then tilt them.

枝ものは、垂直にさして傾斜させる。

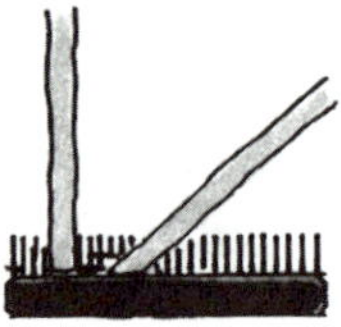

For stalk flowers, insert them at the desired angle.

草ものは、生ける角度に合わせて安定させる。

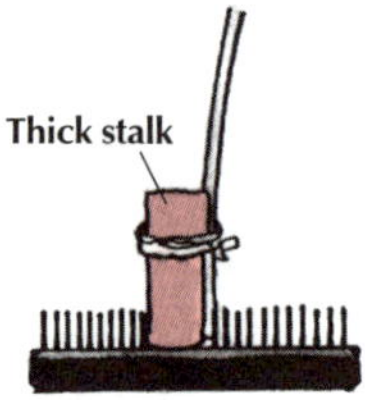

For a thin branch or stalk, make a support with another thick stalk.

細い枝や茎は、添え木をする。

Let's Arrange the Flowers from Your Garden
庭の花で生け花を楽しもう！

①

Pick a couple of different kinds of flowers; remove unnecessary leaves.

2、3種類の花を選び、よぶんな葉を落とす。

②

Use any vessel with an attractive shape for a flower vase. Add water to it and then put in a green styrofoam block that has been soaked in water.

しゃれた器に水を入れ、水を含ませたオアシスを入れる。

③

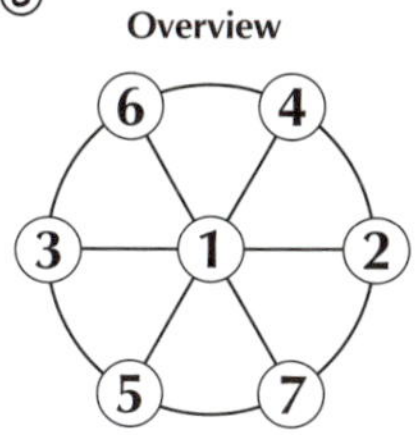

Arrange big flowers in the numbered order and fill the empty space with small flowers.

①～⑦の順に大きな花をさし、その間に小花をさす。

②

Put a crumpled wire in a vase and arrange the flowers along the wire from the tallest in order.

まるめた針金に長い茎のものから、順にさす。

③

Arrange small flowers and leaves with balance.

小花や葉を間にバランスよくさしていく。

Arrange small flowers in a coffee cup.

Arrange wild flowers in a basket.

BONSAI
盆栽

Bonsai is a horticultural art whereby trees and grasses are transplanted into small containers and are trained to grow into the shapes of naturally grown trees or grasses in the earth. Evergreen trees such as pine or cedar are highly preferred for *bonsai*, but deciduous trees like maple, or fruit trees like plums are also used. The average height of a tree is approximately 54cm (21in).

盆栽は、小鉢に草木を植えこみ、樹形や枝ぶりが自然の姿を保つように育てる園芸である。松や杉などの常緑樹が主流だが、もみじなどの落葉樹や、梅などの花もの、実ものも使われる。樹高54cm前後が標準である。

TOOLS
用具

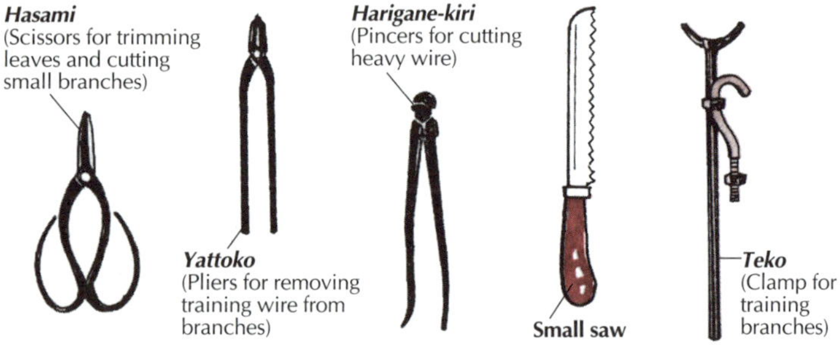

HOW TO CULTIVATE BONSAI
仕立て方

Wiring • 針金かけ

Wind the wire around a crooked branch to make it grow straight, or to train the shape of the tree.

針金を巻いてやや曲がった幹をまっすぐにしたり、枝ぶりを整えたりする。

Pruning • 剪定

Prune unnecessary branches or branches that have grown too dense.

剪定(せんてい)して、不要の枝や密生した枝を切り取る。

Transplanting • 植え替え

Transplant *bonsai* if necessary. *Bonsai* take many years to become properly shaped.

植え替えなどして、何年もの年月をかけて美しいものに仕上げていく。

BONSAI TREE SHAPES
盆栽の樹形

Chokkan (Upright Style) • 直幹

Basic *bonsai* shape. The branches should be symmetrically balanced.

盆栽の基本の形。枝ぶりは、左右対称である。

Shakan (Slanting Style) • 斜幹

The shape of a trunk, at an angle, that has been affected by wind or other natural conditions.

風などの影響で幹が斜めに傾いた形。

Ishizuki (Rock Planting) • 石付き

The shape that reflects a tree surviving on the edge of a precipice, made with stones.

崖や島の石の上で、樹木が生存する姿を表現した形。

Kengai (Cascading Style) • 懸崖

The shape of a *bonsai* tree grown out from a precipice, with the edge of the tree hanging down over the container's edge.

崖から乗りだした木の先端が鉢の上端より垂れ下がっている形。

POINTS OF APPRECIATION
観賞のポイント

Roots 根張り

Whether or not the roots have grown properly, spreading in all directions.

太根が四方八方に張っているか。

Trunk 幹

Whether or not the trunk expresses the strength of growing upward, reflecting its natural beauty.

地上に立ち上がる姿の力強さと、大自然の美しさを表しているか。

Branches 枝ぶり

How healthy and thick the branches are and how well-balanced their curves or contours are.

枝のこみ具合い、曲がり具合いのバランスはよいか。

CALLIGRAPHY
書道

Calligraphy, which originated in China, is the art of writing pictographic characters with an ink-drenched brush and a focussed mind. It is taught in elementary and junior high schools as part of Japanese language class. Writing with a brush is not common these days except on New Year's cards, or writing one's name on special envelopes for monetary gifts given on celebratory or condolence occasions.

毛筆に墨を含ませ、精神統一して文字を書く、中国から伝わった芸術。わが国では「習字」とも呼ばれて、小・中学校の国語科の一分野となっている。しかし、日常生活においては年賀状や祝儀、不祝儀袋の名前を書くなどの改まった場合以外、毛筆はあまり使われない。

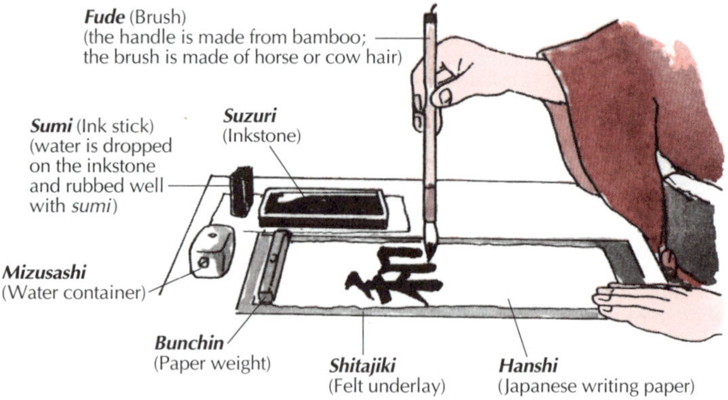

●POSTURE AND HOW TO HOLD THE BRUSH

- Straighten your back and sit deeply into the chair.
  背筋をぴんと伸ばし、椅子は深く腰かける。

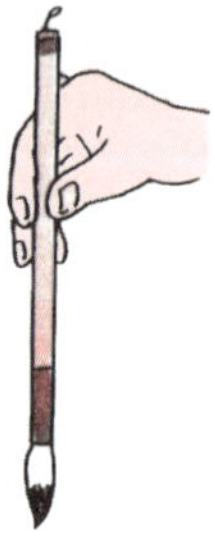

- Place the hand which is not holding the brush on the corner of the *hanshi* to support it.
  筆を持っていない手は、必ず半紙の端を押さえる。
- Hold the brush lightly, leaving a space the size of a ping-pong ball in your palm.
  筆はてのひらにピンポン球がすっぽり入るくらいに軽く持つ。

Let's Write the Character for "Friend"
「友人」を書こう

① Preparation : 準備

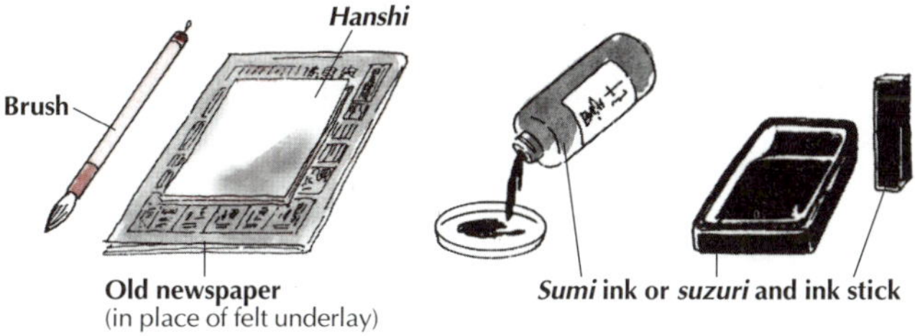

② Soak the brush in the ink. Let the excess ink run off at the end of the brush to prevent the ink from splattering onto the paper.
筆に墨をつける。ぽたぽた落ちないよう、先のほうの墨はしっかり落とす。

③ Practice *tome* (stop), *hane* (sweep up), and *harai* (brush).
「とめ」、「はね」、「はらい」の練習。

Calligraphy is artistic "writing," not painting.
書道は「書く」のであって、黒く塗る絵画ではない。

④ Practice the stroke order of the character : 書き順の練習

- Trace the character with your finger on the paper, before actually writing on the desired paper.
  指で実際に、紙の上に書いてみたり、お手本の上からなぞってみたりする。
- Now let's do it.
  そして本番！
- Put your name at the bottom left corner.
  名前を左下に書く。

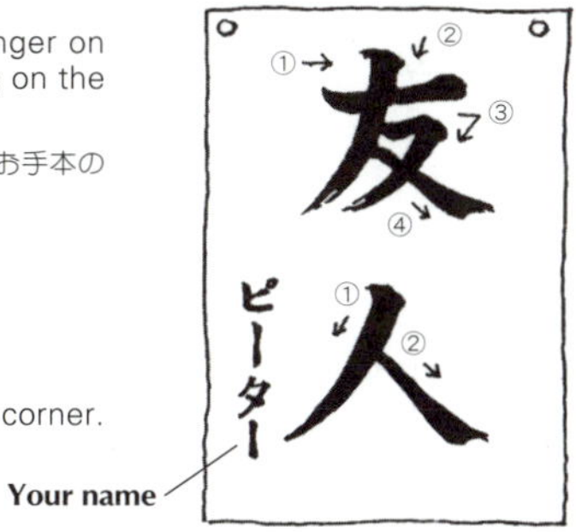

JAPANESE LANGUAGE

日本語

Japanese language consists of three alphabets: *kanji* (pictographic characters imported from China), *hiragana* and *katakana* (phonetic alphabets developed in Japan). To read a newspaper, one must know 1,945 commonly used *kanji*, *hiragana* and *katakana*, which are taught in elementary school and junior high school, along with the English alphabet.

日本語は中国から入ってきた漢字、日本独自につくられた平仮名、片仮名の3種類の文字が使われている。現在、新聞を読むために必要とされているのは、1,945字の常用漢字、平仮名、片仮名、アルファベットで、これらはだいたい小・中学校で習得される。

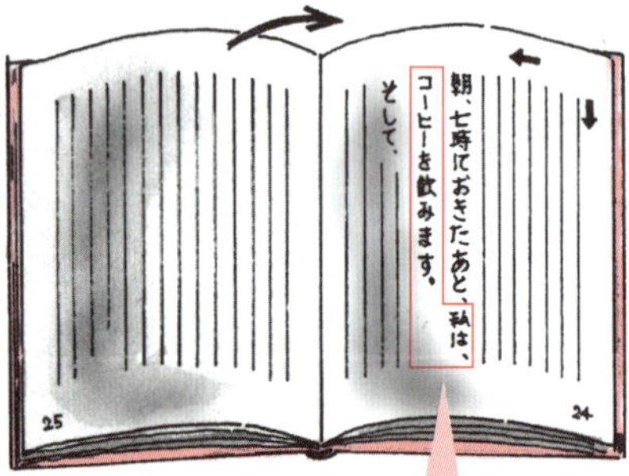

- Vertically written sentences should be read from top to bottom and from the right line to the left line.
  縦書きを上から下へ、右の行から左の行へ読む。
- Pages should be turned from left to right.
  ページを右にめくる。
- Horizontally written sentences should be read from left to right.
  横書きで左から右へ読む場合もある。

私は、コーヒーを飲みます。

Watashi wa, kō hī o no mi ma su.

I coffee drink.

Kanji • 漢字

An ideographic character. Each letter has a meaning.

それぞれの字に意味をもつ表意文字である。

Katakana • 片仮名

Used to describe a word of foreign origin or onomatopoeia.

外来語、擬音語、擬声語などに用いられる。

Hiragana • 平仮名

Like *katakana*, *hiragana* letters are phonetic symbols.

片仮名同様、音のみを表す表音文字である。

ROOTS OF KANJI
漢字の成り立ち

Kanji Developed from Hieroglyphics • 象形から発達した例

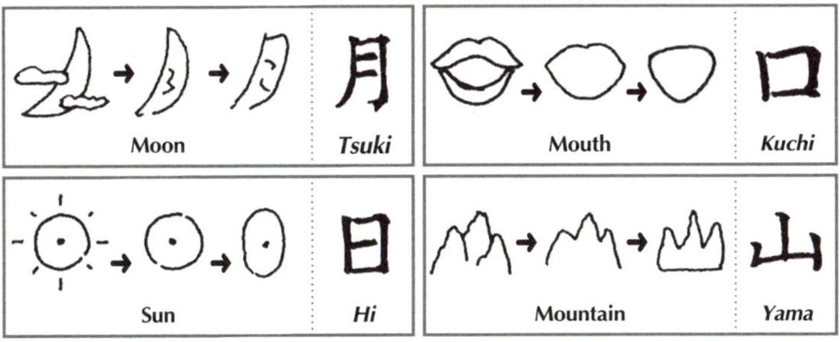

Kanji Developed from Notation • 指示から発達した例

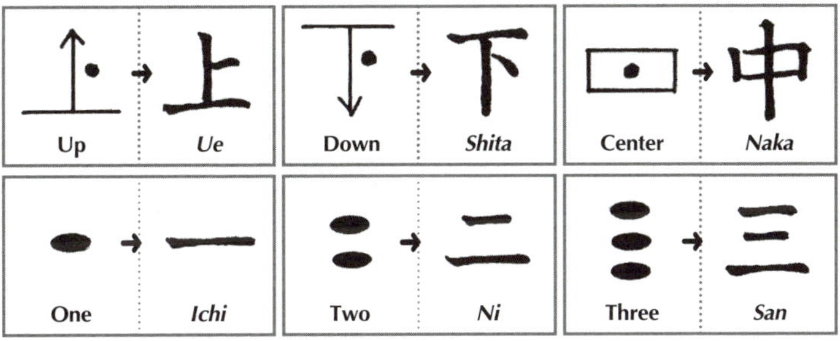

ROOTS OF KATAKANA AND HIRAGANA
片仮名／平仮名の成り立ち

Katakana was made by deleting a part of *kanji* and symbolizing it. *Hiragana* was made from the cursive style of writing *kanji*, particularly as used in the ancient poetry anthology, the *Man'yōshū*.

片仮名は漢字の一部を略して記号化した。また平仮名は、万葉仮名の漢字をくずした草書体からできた。

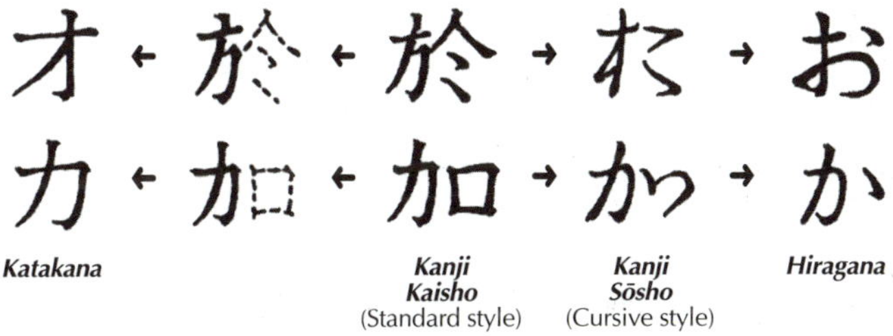

HIRAGANA AND KATAKANA
平仮名と片仮名

あ ア a	い イ i	う ウ u	え エ e	お オ o
か カ ka	き キ ki	く ク ku	け ケ ke	こ コ ko
さ サ sa	し シ shi	す ス su	せ セ se	そ ソ so
た タ ta	ち チ chi	つ ツ tsu	て テ te	と ト to
な ナ na	に ニ ni	ぬ ヌ nu	ね ネ ne	の ノ no
は ハ ha	ひ ヒ hi	ふ フ fu	へ ヘ he	ほ ホ ho
ま マ ma	み ミ mi	む ム mu	め メ me	も モ mo
や ヤ ya	(i)	ゆ ユ yu	(e)	よ ヨ yo
ら ラ ra	り リ ri	る ル ru	れ レ re	ろ ロ ro
わ ワ wa	(i)	(u)	(e)	を ヲ o
ん ン n				

きゃ キャ kya	きゅ キュ kyu	きょ キョ kyo
しゃ シャ sha	しゅ シュ shu	しょ ショ sho
ちゃ チャ cha	ちゅ チュ chu	ちょ チョ cho
にゃ ニャ nya	にゅ ニュ nyu	にょ ニョ nyo
ひゃ ヒャ hya	ひゅ ヒュ hyu	ひょ ヒョ hyo
みゃ ミャ mya	みゅ ミュ myu	みょ ミョ myo

りゃ リャ rya	りゅ リュ ryu	りょ リョ ryo

が ガ ga	ぎ ギ gi	ぐ グ gu	げ ゲ ge	ご ゴ go
ざ ザ za	じ ジ ji	ず ズ zu	ぜ ゼ ze	ぞ ゾ zo
だ ダ da	ぢ ヂ ji	づ ヅ zu	で デ de	ど ド do
ば バ ba	び ビ bi	ぶ ブ bu	べ ベ be	ぼ ボ bo
ぱ パ pa	ぴ ピ pi	ぷ プ pu	ぺ ペ pe	ぽ ポ po

ぎゃ ギャ gya	ぎゅ ギュ gyu	ぎょ ギョ gyo
じゃ ジャ ja	じゅ ジュ ju	じょ ジョ jo
ぢゃ ヂャ ja	ぢゅ ヂュ ju	ぢょ ヂョ jo
びゃ ビャ bya	びゅ ビュ byu	びょ ビョ byo
ぴゃ ピャ pya	ぴゅ ピュ pyu	ぴょ ピョ pyo

Let's Teach Japanese to Non-Japanese Friends
外国の友達に日本語を教えてあげよう！

STEP 1

Explain the meaning of the Japanese names. Even names that sound alike have different meanings when written.

日本人の名前の意味を教えてあげよう。同じ発音の名前でも漢字のもつ意味が違う！

A delightful child
慶子（よろこばしい子供）

A respected child
敬子（尊敬される子供）

A blessed child
恵子（恵まれた子供）

STEP 2

Write the person's name in both *katakana* and *kanji*.

友達の名前を片仮名と漢字で書いてあげよう。

Maria
（マリア：真理亜）

Robert
（ロバート：路波都）

Catherine
（キャサリン：花沙鈴）

STEP 3

Teach them how to introduce themselves in Japanese.

日本語で自己紹介のしかたを教えてあげよう。

HAIKU
俳句

Haiku, a Japanese poetic form, developed from the longer *haikai* (*renga*), the first part of which became an independent unit. It comprises 17 syllables (5-7-5 syllables) and has to contain *kigo*, a word that expresses a season. Matsuo Bashō was a famous *haiku* poet in the Edo period (1600–1868). In the Meiji period (1868–1912), Masaoka Shiki revolutionized *haiku*.

俳句は、もとは俳諧と呼ばれる連歌(れんが)の第1句目が独立したもので、5・7・5の17音節から成り、季語を入れるきまりがある。江戸時代には松尾芭蕉が活躍し、明治時代には正岡子規がこれを「俳句」として完成させた。

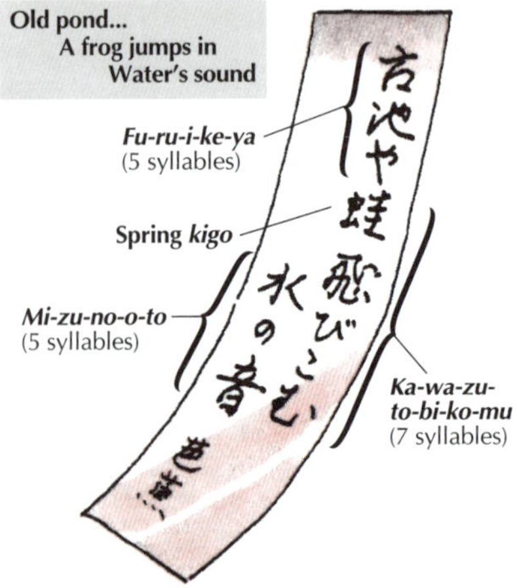

A frog jumped into an old pond at Bashō's hermitage. Even the slight sound of the water could be heard, so quiet was it there.

芭蕉庵の庭の古びた池に蛙(かわず)が飛び込んだかすかな水音さえも、はっきりと聞こえてくるあたりの静けさよ。

Let's Make English Haiku
英語で俳句をつくろう

- Pick a "season" in nature and describe it through any of the five senses.

  五感覚を活用して、自然の中から「季節」を見つける。

- Depict the moment as it is in three lines, forming a short poem.

  その瞬間を、3行の短い英詩で見たまま写生する。

What can you see?
Can you see the season?

TANKA
短歌

The *tanka* is a short poetic form consisting of a 5-7-5-7-7 syllabic structure in which the poet expresses his/her feelings. It originated in the *Man'yōshū*, an 8th century anthology, which was followed by the *Kokin wakashū* and *Shin kokin wakashū*, anthologies full of beautiful, skillful *tanka*.

5・7・5・7・7の31音の定型をもち、人々の心情を短い言葉のなかで表現している。8世紀の「万葉集」以後、「古今和歌集」、「新古今和歌集」などに多くのすばらしい作品が収められている。

The Karuta Card Game of Hyakunin Isshu
カルタ会　百人一首

Ogura hyakunin isshu (collction of one hundred *waka*) is an anthology compiled by Fujiwara Sadaie, which contains *waka* (31-syllable poems) of 100 poets from the 3rd to the 7th centuries.

小倉百人一首は、7世紀以降13世紀頃までの各時代の歌人百人の和歌を、藤原定家が選んだもの。

Reader 読み手

One person will read from the beginning of the *efuda* (picture and poetry card).

1名（絵札を持ち、上の句から読みはじめる。）

Picker 取り手

More than two persons will place *jifuda* (poetry cards) in front of themselves and quickly try to pick up the card whose verse matches that of the card being read.

2名以上（字札を並べ、読み手の読んだ上の句と一致する下の字句の札を、速く取ることを競う。）

JAPANESE LITERATURE
日本文学

NARA PERIOD (710–794)
奈良時代

Oral literature. Myths, legends, and songs began to be recorded in *kanji.*
口誦文学だった神話、伝説、歌謡などが、漢字で記録されるようになった。

- ***KOJIKI,*** Japan's oldest extant chronicle, recording myths, legends, etc.
  「古事記」神話や伝説などがおさめられている日本最古の歴史書。
- ***MAN'YŌSHŪ,*** the oldest Japanese poetry anthology.
  「万葉集」日本最古の詩集。

HEIAN PERIOD (794–1185)
平安時代

Hiragana and *katakana* were invented. Aristocratic literature flourished with women writers and poets playing important roles. Historical fiction and legends were also created.

平仮名、片仮名が創始され、女流文学中心の貴族文学が栄え、歴史物語、説話文学も現れた。

- ***TAKETORI MONOGATARI,*** *The Tale of the Bamboo Cutter*, the oldest story in Japan.
  「竹取物語」わが国最古の物語。
- ***GENJI MONOGATARI,*** *The Tale of Genji,* written by Murasaki Shikibu.
  「源氏物語」紫式部。

KAMAKURA AND MUROMACHI PERIODS (1185–1568)
鎌倉／室町時代

This was the age of civil warfare. Heavily influenced by Buddhist philosophy on the transience of life, the literature of the times was created by *samurai* and Buddhist monks.

武士の戦乱の時代となり、仏教の無常思想の濃い文学が武士や僧侶を中心に生まれた。

- ***HEIKE MONOGATARI,*** *The Tale of the Heike*, a story of the famous war recited by a Buddhist monk.
  「平家物語」琵琶法師によって語られた戦記物語。
- ***TSUREZUREGUSA,*** *Essays in Idleness,* written by Yoshida Kenkō.
  「徒然草」吉田兼好。

EDO PERIOD (1600–1868)
江戸時代

The culture of urban dwellers flourished based on their economic power. *Ukiyozōshi* (realistic novels), *dokuhon* (storybooks), and *kokkeibon* (humorous stories) became popular.

経済力のある町人の文化が中心となり、浮世草紙、読本、滑稽本が盛んになった。

- ***OKU NO HOSOMICHI,*** *The Narrow Road to the Deep North*, written by Matsuo Bashō.
  「奥の細道」 松尾芭蕉。
- ***SONEZAKI SHINJŪ,*** *The Love Suicides at Sonezaki*, written by Chikamatsu Monzaemon.
  「曽根崎心中」 近松門左衛門。

MEIJI, TAISHŌ, SHŌWA PERIODS (1868–1989)
明治／大正／昭和時代

New literature was created, focussing on individual characters under the influence of Western culture.

西洋文化の影響を受け、個性的な人間の生き方を描いた文学が生まれた。

- **NATSUME SŌSEKI 夏目漱石** (1867–1916)
  I Am a Cat, Botchan, The Three-Cornered World, Light and Darkness, etc.
  「吾輩は猫である」、「坊ちゃん」、「草枕」、「明暗」など。
- **AKUTAGAWA RYŪNOSUKE 芥川龍之介** (1892–1927)
  Rashōmon, The Nose, The Spider's Thread, Tu Tzechun, etc.
  「羅生門」、「鼻」、「蜘蛛(くも)の糸」、「杜子春」など。
- **TANIZAKI JUN'ICHIRŌ 谷崎潤一郎** (1886–1965)
  A Portrait of Shunkin, The Makioka Sisters, The Key, etc.
  「春琴抄」、「細雪」、「鍵」など。
- **KAWABATA YASUNARI 川端康成** (1899–1972)
  The Izu Dancer, Snow Country, Thousand Cranes, The Sound of the Mountain, The House of the Sleeping Beauties, etc.
  「伊豆の踊子」、「雪国」、「千羽鶴」、「山の音」、「眠れる美女」など。
- **MISHIMA YUKIO 三島由紀夫** (1925–1970)
  Confessions of a Mask, The Sound of Waves, The Temple of the Golden Pavilion, Madame de Sade, After the Banquet, etc.
  「仮面の告白」、「潮騒」、「金閣寺」、「サド侯爵婦人」、「宴のあと」など。
- **ŌE KENZABURŌ 大江健三郎** (1935–) →P.193

KABUKI
歌舞伎

Kabuki originated in the early Edo period, when a woman called Okuni of Izumo performed a Buddhist dance in an unusual costume in Kyōto. The dance was later deemed morally unacceptable, and women were prohibited from performing it. Instead, only adult men were allowed to perform. This custom has been maintained in present-day *kabuki*.

歌舞伎は江戸時代初期、出雲の阿国という女性が京都で突飛な扮装（ふんそう）で念仏踊りをしたことに始まる。その後、風俗上、女性芸人の出場が禁止され、成人男子のみが演じることを許された。現代の歌舞伎がすべて男性によって演じられているのもこのためである。

STAGE
舞台

The stage floor is made of cypress and equipped with various devices such as a revolving stage or a trap door for special effects.

舞台は檜板（ひのきいた）で張ってあり、演出効果をあげるために回り舞台やせりなど、様々な装置が工夫されている。

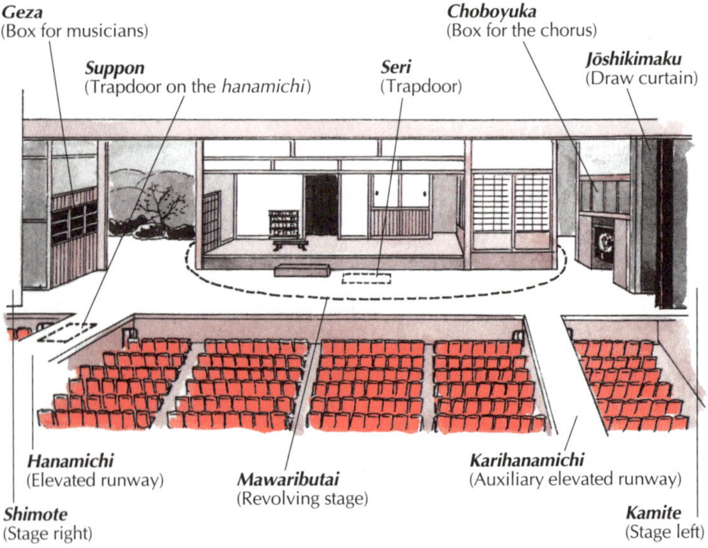

DRAMATIC PRESENTATION
演出

Mie • 見得

A pose an actor takes when emotions reach a climax, by stopping movement for an instant and gazing.

演技の中で感情が最高潮に達した時、役者が一瞬行動を停止し、にらむ。

Tachimawari • 立廻り

The fight scene, which is not realistic but formalized.

歌舞伎の闘争演技で、写実を排した、様式性が濃いものである。

Kumadori • 隈取

Make-up to shade the face along the bones and muscles.

顔の骨格や筋肉に沿って陰影をつける化粧方法。

CHARACTERS
役柄

Tachiyaku • 立役（男役）

Tachiyaku designates either male-role actors as a whole or the actors of the leading male roles.

男役の総称または、主役の男性をさす。

Aragotoshi • 荒事師

The hero fighting for justice. Wears red *kumadori* make-up.

豪傑な正義の味方。正義を強調する紅の隈取をする。

Wagotoshi • 和事師

The handsome man or lover.

色男・二枚目。

Onnagata (Oyama) • 女方（女形）

A male actor who plays women's parts.

男性が女役を演じる。

NŌ & KYŌGEN
能／狂言

Nō originated in the art of *dengaku* (ritual field music and dance) and *sarugaku* (mimic plays) in the Kamakura era; which developed as music-plays incorporating beautiful music and dances in the Muromachi era. Kan'ami and Zeami, father and son, completed *nō*, fashioning it into as a performing art. *Kyōgen*, on the other hand, is comedic drama.

鎌倉時代の田楽、猿楽から、室町時代に、優雅な歌舞と結んで音楽劇として発達したのが能である。能を芸能として大成させたのが、観阿弥、世阿弥親子である。一方、狂言は日常的な笑いを取りあげたせりふ劇である。

STAGE
舞台

At an early period in its development, *nō* was performed at shrines or temple halls; nowadays, it is performed at *nō* theaters (in major cities such as Tōkyō, Ōsaka and Nagoya).

発生当時は、社寺の拝殿や舞楽舞台を使用していたが、現在は能楽堂（東京、大阪、名古屋など）で演じられる。

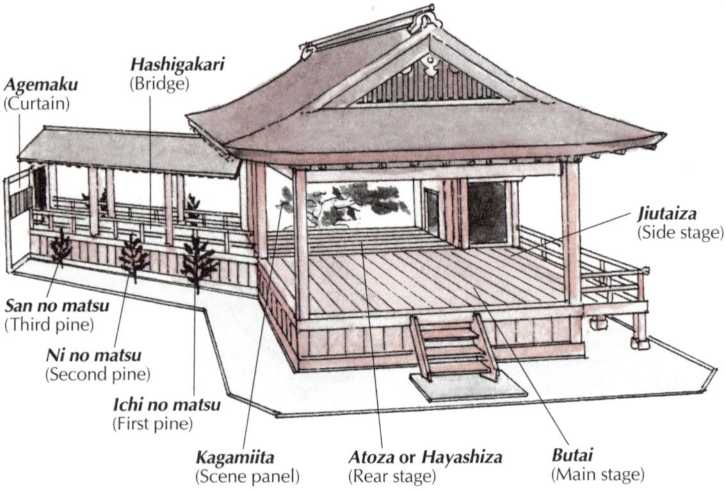

ROLES IN NŌ
能役者分担

Tsure (a companion of *shite*) and/or *waki* (a supporting character, not wearing a mask) appear in some nō dramas.

ツレ（シテの助演者）やワキ（脇役で能面はつけない）が、登場する場合もある。

KYŌGEN
狂言

There are two kinds of *kyōgen*: *hon-kyōgen*, which is performed independently; *ai-kyōgen* is performed between *nō* plays in the same program. The main role is called *shite*; the supporting role is called *ado*.

独立して演じられる本狂言（ほんきょうげん）と、能と能の間に行われる間狂言（あいきょうげん）がある。主役をシテ、助演者をアドと呼ぶ。

MEN (KINDS OF MASKS)
面いろいろ

Nō Masks • 能面

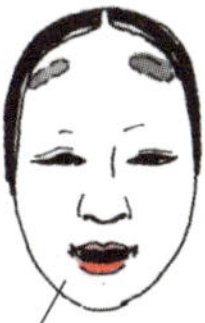

Onna-men
(for women's roles)

Jō-men
(for old men's roles)

Hannya
(for female demon's roles)

Kyōgen Masks • 狂言面

Kitsune
(Fox)

Ebisu
(God of commerce)

BUNRAKU
文楽

Bunraku is a form of puppet theater where puppets are manipulated in accordance with *shamisen* music and chants known as *jōruri*. *Gidayū-bushi* (a type of *jōruri* narrative chant) was composed by Takemoto Gidayū in the Edo period. Takemoto and the writer Chikamatsu Monzaemon revolutionized *jōruri* as a drama.

文楽は三味線の伴奏で語る浄瑠璃(じょうるり)と人形劇を合わせたものである。浄瑠璃は江戸時代に竹本義太夫が義太夫節をつくり、作家近松門左衛門と組んで戯曲として完成させた。

PUPPETS
人形

Puppets are composed of heads, bodies, hands, legs and costumes. Woman puppets have no legs, and the puppeteers' manipulation of the kimono is used to simulate leg movements. The eyes, eyebrows and mouth are moved by strings.

首(かしら)、胴、手、足、衣装からなる。女人形は足がなく、衣装のすそをさばくことにより足があるように見せる。糸で操作すると、目、眉、口が動く。

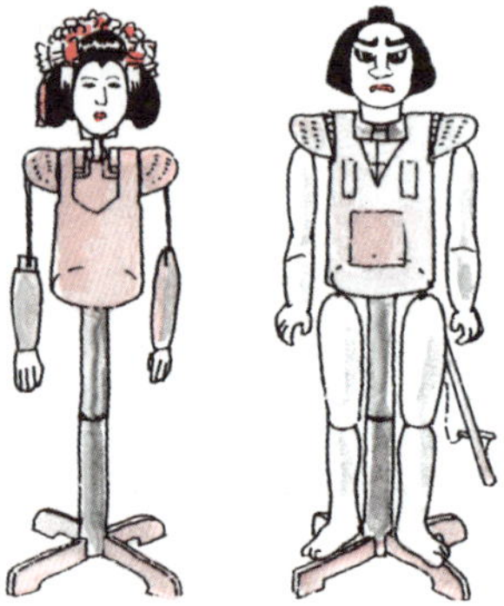

PUPPETEERS
人形遣い

One puppeteer and two assistants manipulate one puppet.

3人で一体を演じる。

YOSE
寄席

Yose literally means "a place where people gather" and is a variety show theater where popular entertainment, like *kōdan*, *rakugo*, or *rōkyoku*, is performed.

講談、落語、浪曲などの大衆芸能を上演する演芸場のことで「人寄せ場」という意味がある。

KŌDAN
講談

The art of telling stories such as tales of bravery or human relationships. The story-tellers perform holding a fan in their hand, sitting behind a small stand called a *shakudai*.

武勇伝や人情物語を語り聞かせる話芸。張り扇を使って釈台を置いて行う。

RAKUGO
落語

The art of telling comic stories, marked by audience laughter and an *ochi* ("punch-line"). The story-teller performs sitting down. He plays more than two roles, expressing action as well as atmosphere.

滑稽(こっけい)な話で聴衆を笑わせ、終わりに「落ち」をつける話芸である。座ったまま、2人以上の動作や雰囲気を表現する。

Props used are only a fan and a Japanese towel.
用具は扇子と手ぬぐいのみ。

MANZAI
漫才

Manzai is performed by two people who entertain the audience by their comic dialogue. These days popular performers are usually young, fast-moving, and full of improvisation.

2人1組の芸人が、掛け合いで観客を笑わせる。最近では、若手コンビの巧みなアドリブやテンポの速さに、人気がある。

RŌKYOKU
浪曲

Commonly known as *naniwa-bushi*, it is sung with a special tune accompanied by the *shamisen* (a three-stringed musical instrument) and narration.

一般に浪花節(なにわぶし)として親しまれ、曲師の弾く三味線を伴奏として、節をつけて謡う部分と、語りの部分がある。

JAPANESE MUSIC
邦楽

Hōgaku is the general term for Japanese music: classics such as *gagaku* (court music) or *nōgaku* (*nō* music); folk music like local performing arts or *min'yō* (country music); and contemporary music.

日本独自の音楽は、古典音楽（宮廷音楽の雅楽、能楽など）、民族音楽（郷土芸能、民謡など）、現代音楽などからなり、総称して、邦楽とよぶことがある。

JAPANESE MUSICAL INSTRUMENTS
日本の楽器

Shakuhachi • 尺八

Vertical bamboo flute with seven joints.

7節ある真竹で作られた縦笛。

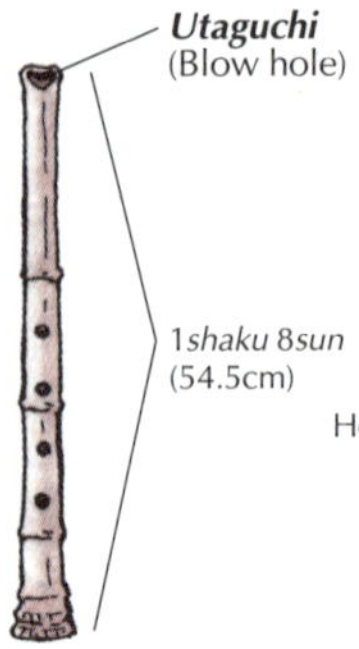

Kozutsumi • 小鼓

Played in *kabuki* and *nō*.

歌舞伎、能で演奏される。

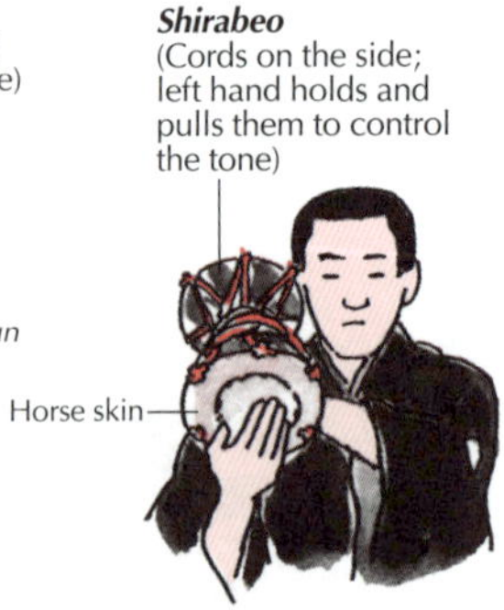

Biwa • 琵琶

Played with a plectrum hitting forcefully against the strings, while performer is also singing.

ばちをはげしくたたきつけるようにして、弾き謡いする。

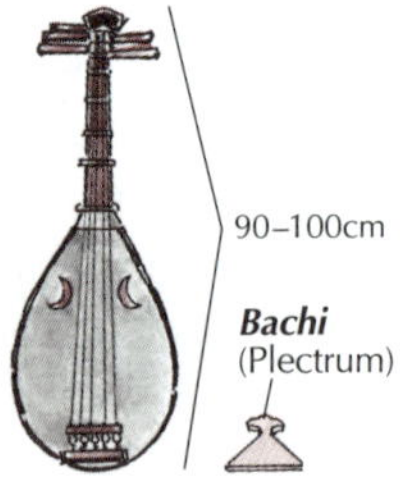

Koto • 琴

Pressing the strings and controlling the tone with the left hand, the player plays with the right hand, wearing small picks on the fingers.

左手で絃を押して音の高低を調整し、爪をはめた右手で弾く。

Shamisen • 三味線

Accompanies *bunraku*, *kabuki* and *min'yō*.

文楽、歌舞伎、民謡の伴奏に用いられる。

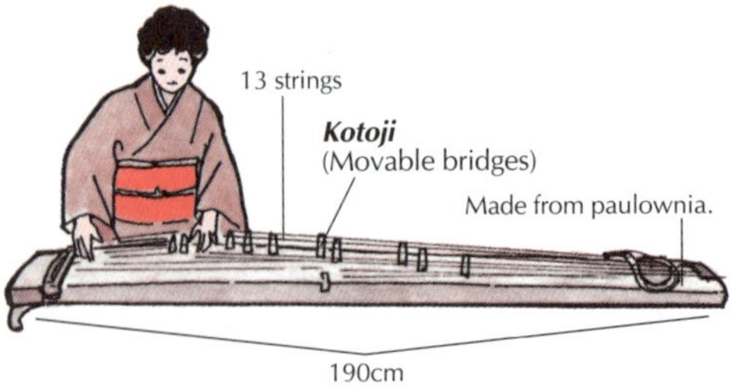

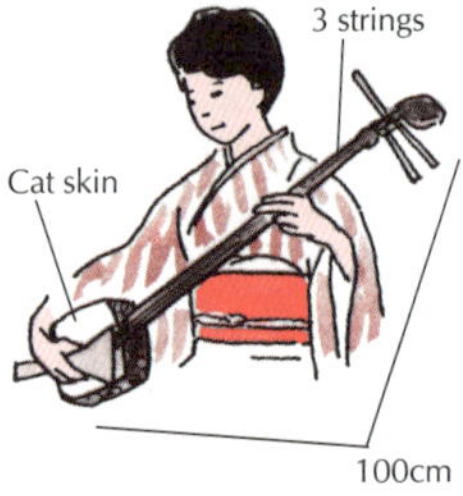

INK PAINTING

水墨画

This style of painting was brought to Japan from China by Zen monks, and became very popular in the Muromachi era—the 15th and 16th centuries. The shading of the ink color expresses depth and variety; and the subjects are frequently human figures, animals, landscapes, plants and trees.

中国から伝わった絵画形式の一つで、墨の濃淡やぼかしの度合いによって変化をもたせ、人物、動物、山川草木などを描いたもの。禅僧たちの手により伝えられ、15～16世紀（室町時代）には盛んに描かれるようになった。

Sesshū: *Haboku sansui-ga*
(Landscape picture in splashed ink style)

Ogata Kōrin: a part of *Chikubai-zu*
(Bamboo and plum trees)

●TECHNIQUES OF INK PAINTING

Ink Color Shading : 濃淡のだし方

Rub *sumi* well in a little water.
墨をよくする。

Dilute some of it with water.
水でうすめる。

Put the brush in the ink.
墨をふくませる。

Draw in one stroke.
一気に描き上げる。

The Aesthetics of Ink Blurring : にじみの味

The paper quality, proportion of water to ink, and the speed of brush movement comprise the aesthetics. For example, the soft outline of a mountain.

紙の質、水と墨の分量、筆運びの速さで決まる。例えば、山のやわらかい輪郭線など。

UKIYO-E

浮世絵

A genre painting popular among the common people during the Edo period (1600–1868). *Ukiyo* means "pleasure-seeking," or "sensual" in Japanese, and this world was actually the subject of paintings called *ukiyo-e*. Most *ukiyo-e* were prints that could be mass-produced. Drawings were rare.

江戸時代（1600～1868）、庶民の間で栄えた風俗画の一種である。享楽的、好色的の意味をなす「浮世」が題材であったので、「浮世絵」と呼ばれた。量産の可能な木版画が主流で、肉筆画は少ない。

Portraits of Beauties • 美人画

The major subject of *ukiyo-e*; models were usually courtesans or *geisha*.

浮世絵の中心で、遊女や芸者が多い。

Kitagawa Utamaro:
Takigawa from *A Collection of Beauties at the Height of Their Popularity*

Portraits of Actors • 役者絵

Portraits of *kabuki* actors.

歌舞伎役者のスターの似顔絵。

Tōshūsai Sharaku:
Ichikawa Ebizō *as Takemura Sadanoshin*

Landscape Pictures • 風景画

Andō Hiroshige:
the Shinagawa print from the *Fifty-Three Stations of the Tōkaidō Road*

●HOW UKIYO-E ARE MADE

①

Eshi (painter) draws a draft and a block copy.

絵師：下絵と版下を描く。

→ ②

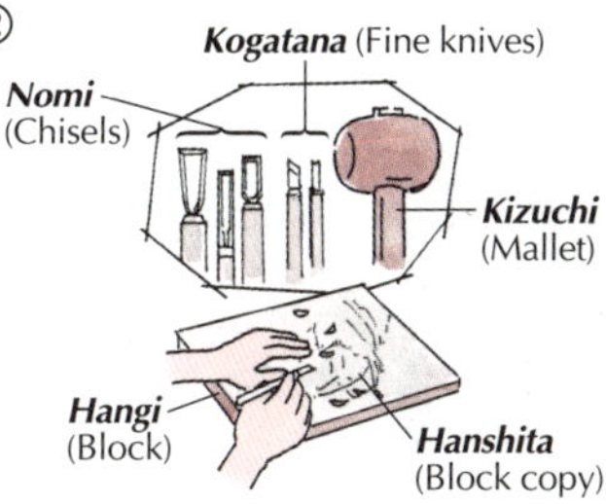

Horishi (carver) pastes the block copy on the block, engraves the block and makes prints, using ink only.

彫師：版木に版下を貼り、彫る。墨1色で摺(す)る。

③ →

Eshi designates colors to be used on the print.

絵師：墨で摺ったものに色の指定をする。

④ →

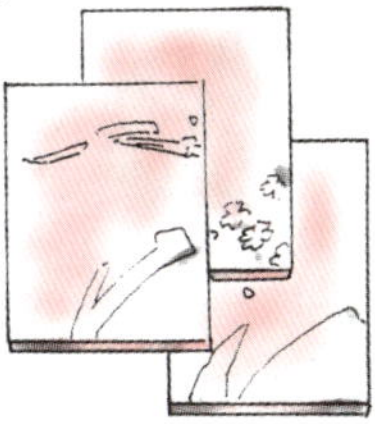

Horishi carves a block per color.

彫師：1色ごとに1枚の版木に彫りおこす。

⑤ →

Surishi (printer) applies paint over the carved block with a brush.

摺師：版木にはけで顔料を塗る。

⑥ →

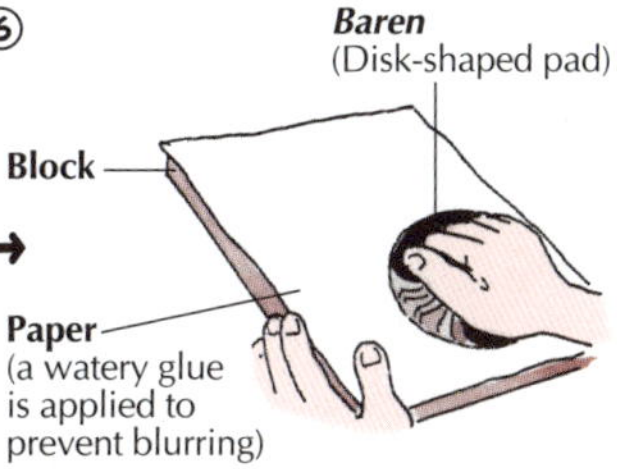

Surishi scrubs the back of the paper with *baren* to transfer the paint onto the paper.

摺師：ばれんで裏からこすり、顔料を紙に移す。

⑦ →

Surishi prints color by color.

摺師：1色ずつ色を重ねて摺りあげる。

TRADITIONAL CRAFTS

伝統工芸

There are many locally manufactured Japanese products that utilize local materials and the natural environment. These arts and techniques have been passed down from generation to generation. Most of the production is handicraft manufacturing.

昔から、その土地特有の原材料をもとに、地域の自然条件を生かし、技術を伝え受け継がれてきた手工業製品がたくさんある。

The mark symbolizing "traditional craftwork," as designated by the Minister of International Trade and Industry
通産大臣指定の「伝統的工芸品」マーク

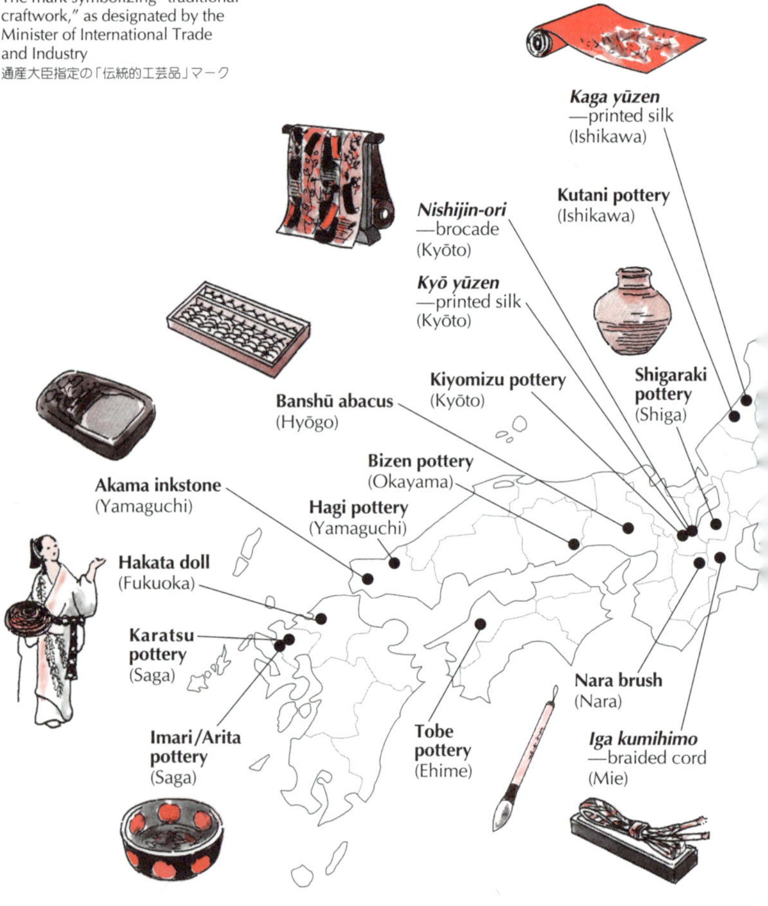

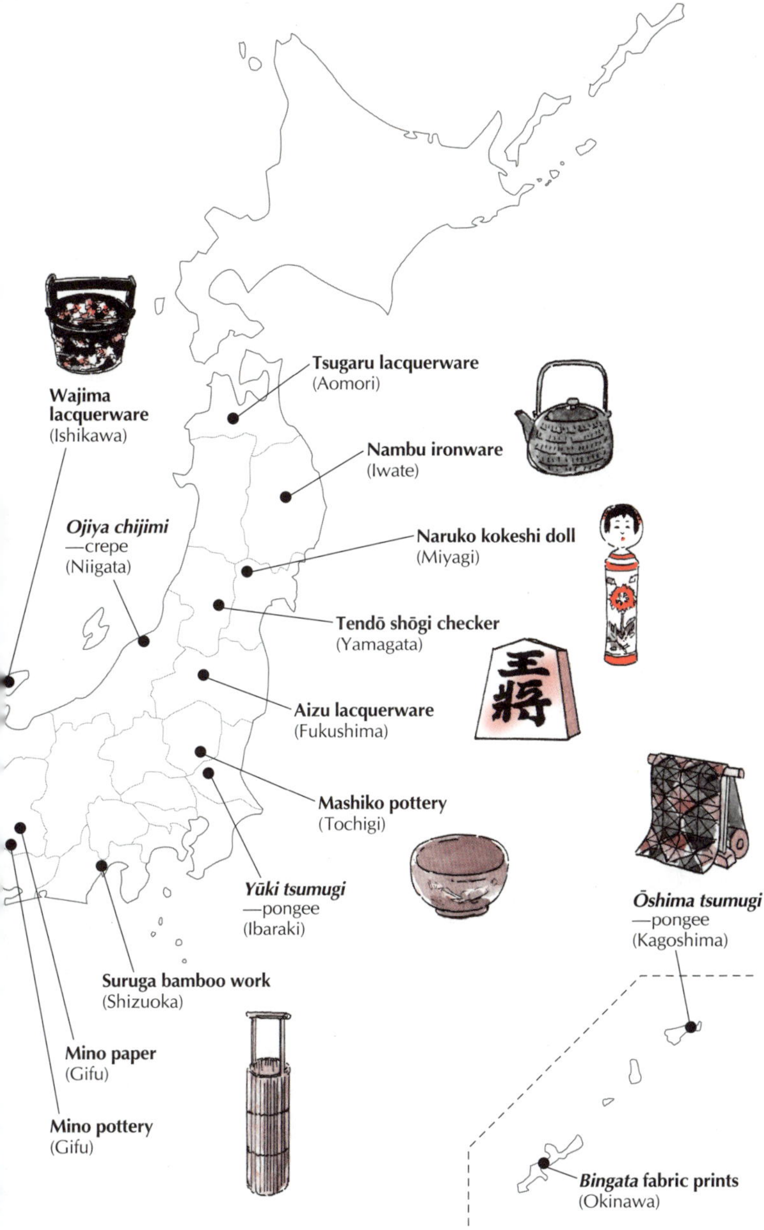
Wajima lacquerware (Ishikawa)
Tsugaru lacquerware (Aomori)
Nambu ironware (Iwate)
Ojiya chijimi —crepe (Niigata)
Naruko kokeshi doll (Miyagi)
Tendō shōgi checker (Yamagata)
王将
Aizu lacquerware (Fukushima)
Mashiko pottery (Tochigi)
Yūki tsumugi —pongee (Ibaraki)
Ōshima tsumugi —pongee (Kagoshima)
Suruga bamboo work (Shizuoka)
Mino paper (Gifu)
Mino pottery (Gifu)
Bingata fabric prints (Okinawa)

ARITA WARE
有田焼

Arita pottery is a craft that has been handed down for many generations in Arita, Saga Prefecture. Local *tōseki* (stone which becomes clay) is used for the material.

有田焼は有田町（佐賀県）で採れる陶石（とうせき）を利用した古くから伝わる産業である。

●HOW ARITA WARE IS MADE

①

Tōseki is broken into pieces, mixed with and kneaded some 200 times to make into clay.

陶石を砕き、水を混ぜ、数百回こねて粘土にする。

②

The clay is put on a potter's wheel and a shape created.

ろくろにのせて、器の形を作る。

③

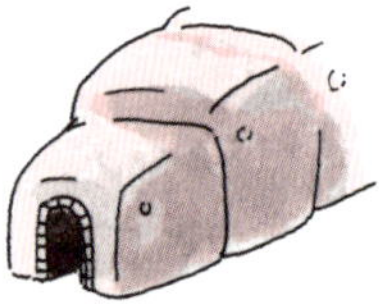

After it dries, the shaped prototype is put into a 800–900°C kiln and fired. (*Suyaki*)

乾燥させたあと、800～900℃の窯に入れて焼く。（素焼き）

④

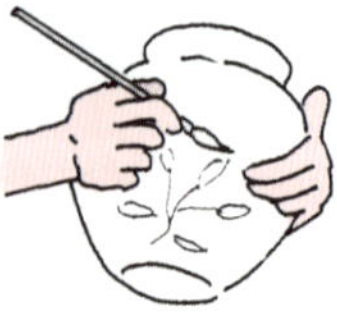

A rough drawing is made on the fired prototype. Glaze is applied and the piece is fired again, at 1,300–1,400°C. (*Hon'yaki*)

下絵を書いたあと、うわ薬を付け、1300～1400℃で焼く。（本焼き）

⑤

Paint is applied and the piece is fired again at 700–800°C.

絵の具で色付けをし、さらに700～800℃で焼き上げる。

⑥

The finished product.

完成。

WAJIMA LACQUERWARE
輪島塗

The discovery of *jinoko* (powder obtained from a special soil) in Wajima City, Ishikawa Prefecture, triggered the development of a revolutionary technique for making durable lacquerware. The technique has brought a major industry to this region.

輪島市(石川県)で採れる地の粉(じのこ)の発見は、丈夫な漆器作り技術をもたらし、地域の重要な産業となっている。

●HOW WAJIMA LACQUERWARE IS MADE

①

Forming wood : 木地づくり

Wood, which has been left and dried for many years, is carved and formed into a bowl.

何年もねかせ乾燥させた木を、お椀などの形にする。

②

Nunokise : 布着せ

A piece of fabric is pasted onto the fragile, breakable parts of the bowl.

木地の欠けやすい部分に、布を張り付ける。

③

Jizuke : 地付け

Lacquer, mixed with *jinoko*, and applied to the bowl, which is then polished. This process is repeated.

地の粉を混ぜて漆を塗り、磨く作業を繰り返す。

④

Uwa-nuri : 上塗り

Good-quality lacquer is applied with a brush.

上質の漆をはけで塗る。

⑤

Chinkin / Maki-e : 沈金/蒔絵

The lacquerware is drawn on with a brush, engraving with a chisel is done, and gold or silver is embedded in the lacquer.

筆で絵を描いたり、のみで模様を彫ったりして、金銀を入れる。

⑥

Roiro : ろ色

The finish is created by polishing with charcoal or by applying more lacquer.

炭で磨いたり、さらに漆を塗って仕上げる。

MINO HANDMADE JAPANESE PAPER
美濃和紙

Japanese paper has been made for more than 1,000 years from local plants like *kōzo* (paper mulberry) and *mitsumata*, mixed with pure river water.

千年以上も前から作られてきた和紙は、原料のこうぞ、みつまたなどの植物と、良質の川の水を生かして作られ続けている。

●HOW MINO WASHI IS MADE

①

The bark of *kōzo* and *mitsumata* is soaked in water to soften it.

こうぞやみつまたの木の皮を水に入れてやわらかくする。

→ ②

The softened bark and water are placed in a pan. It is boiled with soda ash.

釜に移しかえ、ソーダ灰を入れて煮る。

→ ③

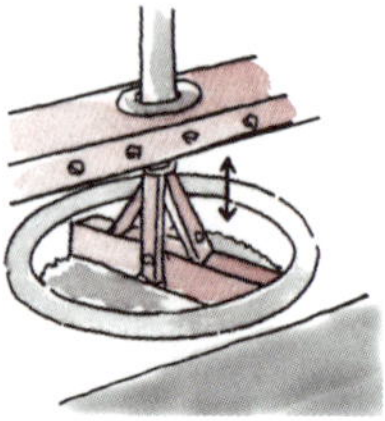

The bark is struck to break down the fibers into small pieces.

たたいて繊維をほぐし、細かくする。

→ ④

The fibers and *tororo-aoi* (a suspension agent made of grated yam) are put into a water tank and mixed.

水槽に繊維ととろろあおいを入れ、混ぜる。

→ ⑤

Sukigeta (Paper mold)

Paper is made sheet by sheet by using a paper mold.

すきげたで1枚ずつすいていく。

→ ⑥

The water is drained from the paper. Paste paper which is brushed onto the board to dry.

すいた紙の水をしぼり、1枚ずつ乾燥機に張る。

KOKESHI DOLLS (TŌHOKU DISTRICT)
こけし（東北地方）

Kokeshi are traditional wooden dolls for children inspired by the climate and culture of the Tōhoku district. The *kokeshi* doll is deeply related to the faith of the people living there.

東北地方の風土、生活文化の中から生まれてきたもので、庶民の信仰とも関係が深く、子供に作り与えた木の人形である。

●HOW KOKESHI ARE MADE

① 

Wood is cut and left to dry.

原木を乾燥させる。

② 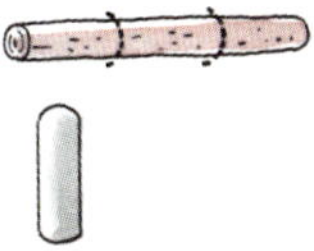

Six months after the wood is cut down, it is then cut into small pieces (the size of the *kokeshi*). The edges are then shaved and rounded off.

伐採して半年後に、玉切りにし、木取りをする。

③ 

The wood is roughly shaped into a doll with a plane on the lathe, and further shaped with a smaller plane.

ろくろにかけて、かんなで荒く削ったあと、細かいかんなで仕上げる。

④ 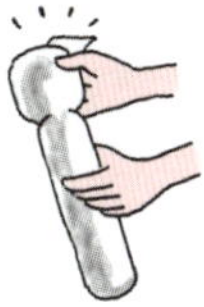

The surface is filed with a paper file.

紙やすりなどで磨きあげる。

⑤ 

The face and the body are drawn on and painted with a brush.

顔や胴の模様などを筆で描く。

⑥ 

White wax or silicon wax is applied on the lathe and the surface is polished.

さらにろくろにかけて、白ろうやシリコンワックスなどで磨く。

⑦

The finished product.

完成。

Many *kokeshi* are painted with girls' faces, and floral designs on the body.

胴体に花模様が描かれ、少女の顔をしているこけしが多い。

ARMOR & WEAPONRY
武具／武器

Armor, helmets, and swords worn by *samurai* were not only used during battle, but also were time-honored crafts, to be appreciated for their workmanship and the dedication of their makers.

武士が戦う際使用した、鎧(よろい)、兜(かぶと)、刀などは単なる武具や武器としてだけでなく、しだいに精神のこもった工芸品へと発達した。

ARMOR
甲冑（かっちゅう）

This style of armor known as *ōyoroi* came into use in the 9th century. It was armor for *samurai* (cavaliers).

大鎧(よろい)とよばれる武具は、9世紀から使われ、騎馬武者が着用した。

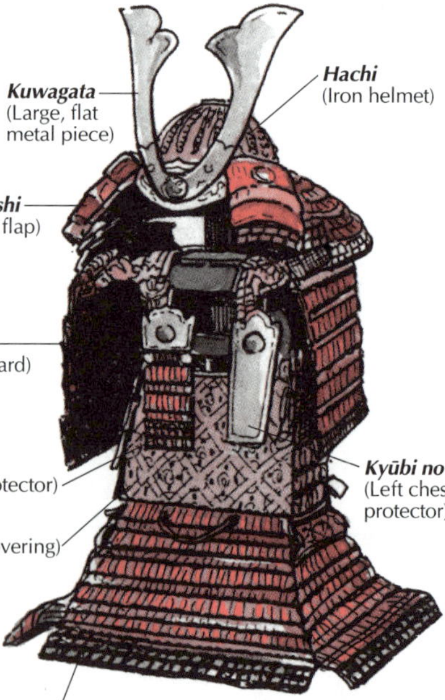

JAPANESE SWORD
日本刀

The Japanese sword is made distinctly for cutting, so it is single-edged and curved. Generally the hilt is long and made to be held with both hands.

日本刀は「切る」を目的としているので片刃で反りがある。一般に柄が長くて、両手で使用する。

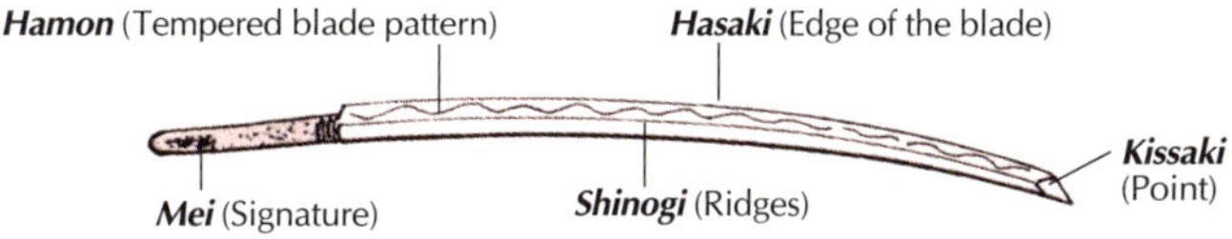

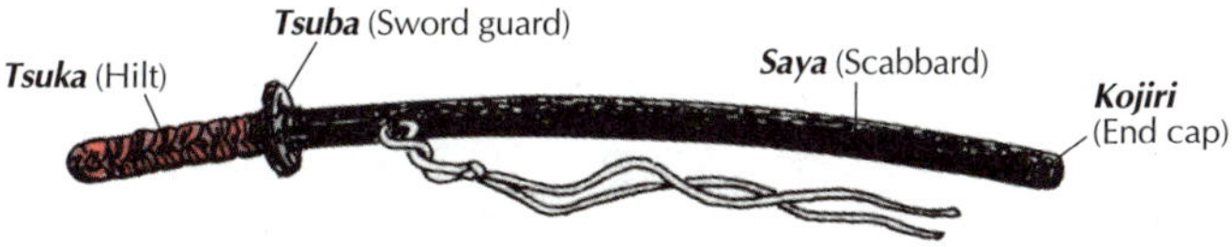

NINGU (NINJA WEAPONS AND TOOLS)
忍具

Ninja were engaged in espionage activities during periods of civil war. They used special tools and weapons with which to carry out their missions.

敵方の動静や機密をさぐるため、武士の手先として、戦国時代には忍者が活躍し、忍具を使用した。

Ningama • 忍鎌

Ningama entwines the enemy's weapon with a chain and cuts it off with a sickle.

鎖で敵の武器をからめ、鎌でかき切る。

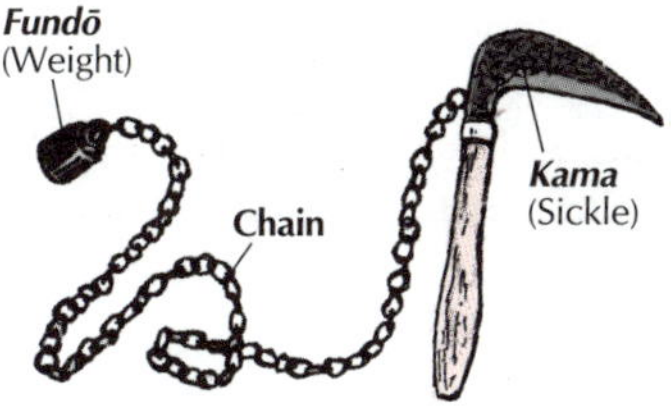

Shuriken • 手裏剣

Shuriken are sharp-ended devices for throwing, end-over-end, at the enemy.

相手に投げつけて攻撃する。

SHRINES
神社

Shrines are buildings dedicated to the deities of Shinto, the unique religion of Japan. There are more than 80,000 shrines in Japan. People visit shrines on occasions such as New Year's day, the birth of a child, and during the celebration of *shichigosan*.

神社は日本独自の宗教である神道の神を祭る建物で、全国に8万以上も存在する。人々は正月の初詣や、お宮参り、七五三のお参りなどで神社を訪れる。

SHRINE COMPOUND
神社境内

THOSE WHO SERVE AT A SHRINE
奉仕者

Kannushi • 神主

The chief Shinto priest who performs the rituals at a shrine.

神社で神事に仕える神職の長。

Miko • 巫女

Unmarried woman in the service of deities.

神に奉仕する未婚の女性。

SMALL ARTICLES IN A SHRINE
神社で見る小物

Ema • 絵馬

A votive offering board with a horse drawing, dedicated to the deities. Used for expressing prayers or acknowledging when a wish has been fulfilled.

祈願したり願いがかなった時に、社寺に奉納する板絵。馬の絵が描かれている。

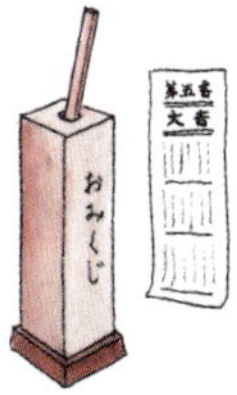

Omikuji • おみくじ

An oracle drawn to determine one's fortune. When the person chooses a stick, he/she is given a paper on which the corresponding fortune is written.

吉凶を占うためにひくくじ。棒を1本ひき、運勢が書かれた紙をもらう。

Omamori • お守り

A paper charm of a god or Buddha used for protection or making a wish.

災いから身を守ったり、祈願のための神や仏の守り札。

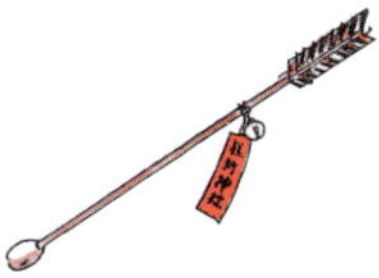

Hamaya • 破魔矢

Arrows given by shrines to visitors on New Year's day, wishing them good luck.

初詣の際に縁起を祈って神社から授けられる矢。

TEMPLES

寺院

Temples house Buddhist statues, which believers pray to, especially during *bon* holidays or equinox week when people visit their ancestors' graves. People also visit temples on New Year's day to wish for happiness and health in the new year. Temples have facilities for training monks as well as for housing and feeding them.

寺院は、仏像を祭り、仏教信者が参詣するための施設をもつ。盆や彼岸に、境内にある先祖の墓参りをしたり、正月に初詣に出かける人も多い。また、僧職者の修行をしたり、居住の場所にもなっている。

TEMPLE COMPOUND

寺院境内

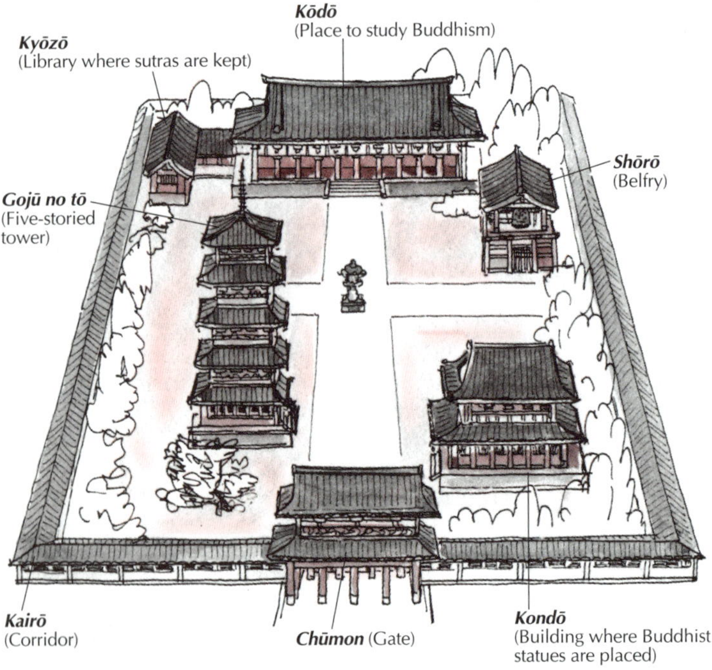

BUDDHIST STATUES
仏像

Besides *nyorai* and *bosatsu*, there are also the *myōō* or *tembu* styles of Buddhist statues. Statues are usually made from wood or metal.

如来形、菩薩(ぼさつ)形以外に、明王形や天部(てんぶ)形などもある。主に木、金属で造られている。

Nyorai • 如来

Depicts Buddha after retiring into religion, so it is not adorned with personal ornaments.

仏陀の出家の姿で、装身具はない。

Bosatsu • 菩薩

Depicts Buddha before retiring into religion, so it is adorned with many personal ornaments.

装身具を多くつけ、釈迦の出家以前の姿を表す。

●THE WORLD OF NOTHINGNESS THROUGH ZEN

The Zen sect made *zazen* the core of its creed to reach spiritual awakening. *Zazen* is the ascetic practice of concentrating mind and body, and meditating.

禅宗では、悟りにいたるために座禅を教義の中心とした。座禅は身心を統一し、瞑想(めいそう)する修行法である。

HOW TO DO ZAZEN • 座禅の仕方

- Put your left foot on your right thigh, placing the right foot on the left thigh.
  左足を右ももの上に置き、その左足を押さえるようにして右足を重ねて組む。
- Put your right palm on your left palm.
  左手のてのひらの上に右手のてのひらを重ねる。
- Breathe from the abdomen.
  腹式呼吸する。

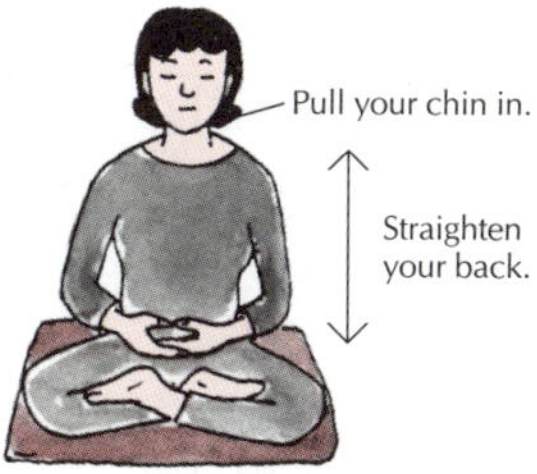

CASTLES

城

Guns were introduced to Japan in 1543, which led to an abrupt change in warfare style: lords built modern castles to defend themselves from the enemy. The Azuchi castle, built by Oda Nobunaga in 1576, was the first of its kind to have a tower, a characteristic of modern castles. Castles were the residences of lords, as well as centers of political and economic activities.

鉄砲の伝来（1543年）で、戦闘様式が急激に変化し、外敵を防ぐために、近世的な城が出現した。近世城郭の天守閣をもつ最初の城は織田信長の築いた安土城（1576年）である。城は大名の館であり、領国の政治、経済の中心であった。

TENSHU (MAIN TOWER)

天守

The main tower, or *tenshu*, was located in the main castle enclosure (*hommaru*). The outside of the building was of white plaster. Strategic points were equipped with gunports and stone-dropping ports.

天守は、本丸に建てられた中心となる櫓（やぐら）である。外部を白しっくいで塗りこめ、要所に銃眼や石落としを設けてある。

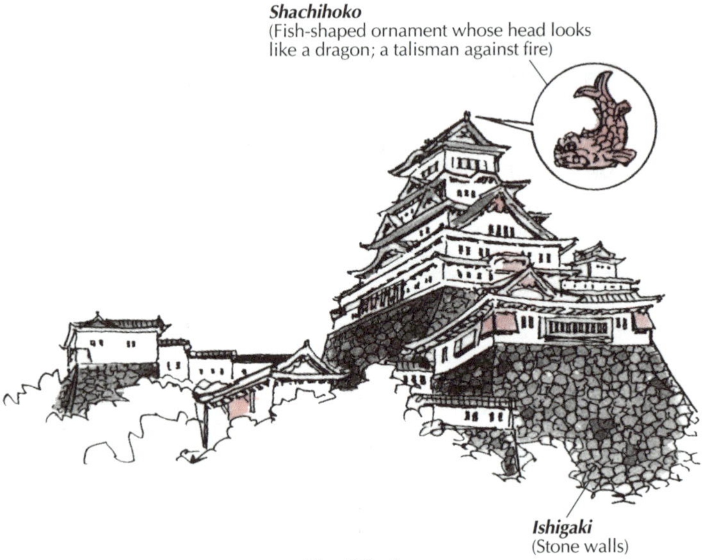

Himeji Castle

INTERIOR DEVICES
内部の工夫

Stone-dropping Ports • 石落とし

A corner of the building protruded such that stones could be dropped on enemies attempting to climb the castle walls.

隅の床の端部をせり出し、そこをあけて石を落とせるようにして、よじ登ってくる敵を防いだ。

Gunports • 銃眼

"Peepholes" in the tower allowded for guns to be used. To facilitate sighting the enemy more easily, the hole was bigger inside than on the outside.

天守ややぐらから鉄砲を発射する穴。内側から外の敵をのぞきやすいように内側を大きく、外側を小さくしてある。

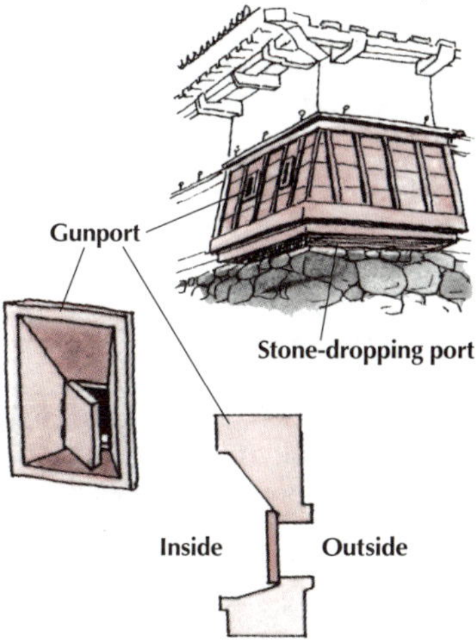

CASTLE FLOOR PLAN
縄張り図（城の構成・平面図）

The layout of a castle was carefully planned to withstand enemy attack.

城全体の配置計画にも工夫をこらし、敵が天守へ簡単には攻めこめないようにしてある。

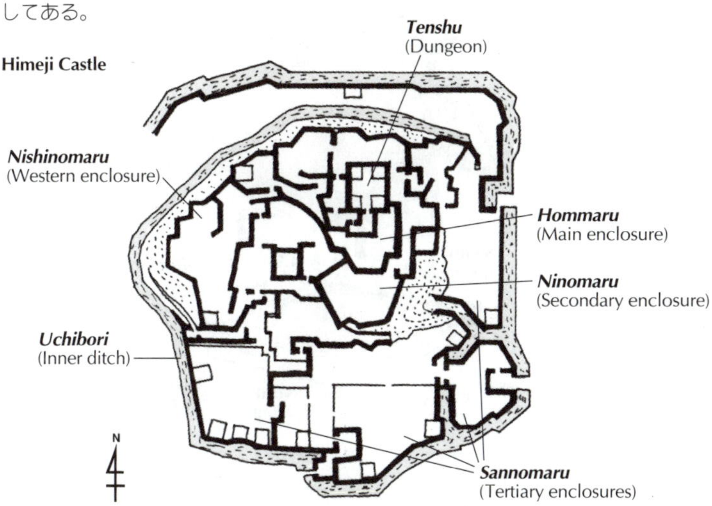

SUMŌ

相撲

Sumō is the national sport of Japan. It is a match of two *sumō* wrestlers who wear only belly belts in the ring. Originally, *sumō* was used to measure the wrestlers' strength or for dueling, but it is now a professional spectator sport.

日本の国技で、腰にまわしを締めただけの姿の力士2人が土俵で取り組む競技。もとは力くらべや決闘として行われたものであるが、今ではスポーツとしてみて楽しむものとなった。

ŌZUMŌ

大相撲

Nihon Sumō Kyōkai (the Japan Sumō Association) holds six tournaments a year: in Tōkyō (Jan., May, Sept.), Ōsaka (Mar.), Nagoya (July) and Fukuoka (Nov.). The competition is conducted in accordance with traditional rituals such as a ring-entrance ceremonies by wrestlers in the *makuuchi* and *yokozuna* (grand champion) divisions, and a bow-twirling rite.

日本相撲協会による年6回の本場所が、東京(1月、5月、9月)、大阪(3月)、名古屋(7月)、福岡(11月)で行われる。幕内力士の土俵入り、横綱の土俵入り、取組(対戦)、弓取り式まで、伝統のある儀式にのっとって進行する。

DOHYŌ (SUMŌ WRESTLING RING)

土俵

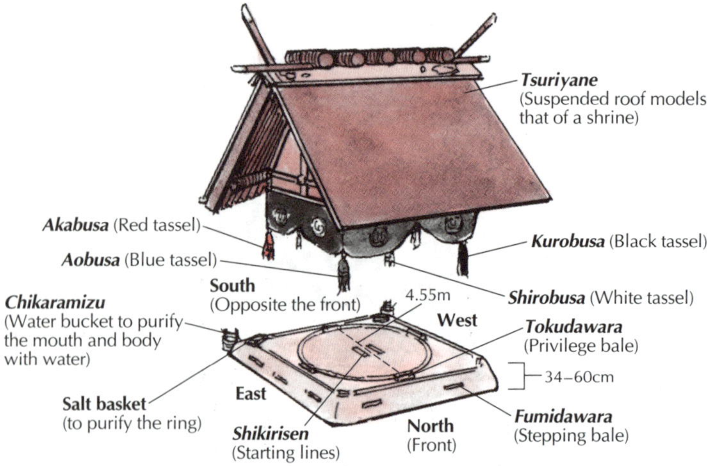

Good luck talismans such as chestnuts, rice, kelp, dried squid and salt have been buried in the center of the ring.
土俵の中央に、勝栗、米、昆布、するめ、塩など縁起物が埋められている。

RIKISHI (SUMŌ WRESTLER)
力士

Height: Over 173cm
身長：173cm以上

Weight: Over 75kg
体重：75kg以上

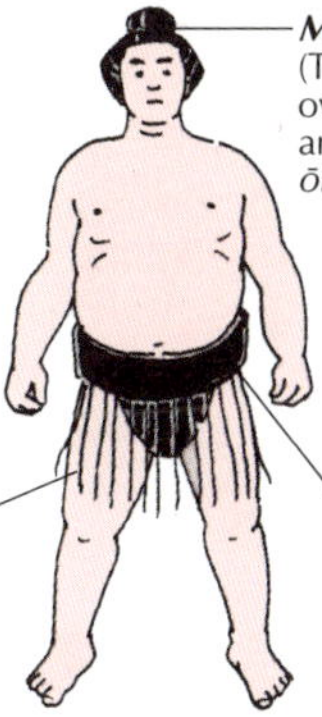

MATCH
取組

① When called by the ring steward, the wrestler will go up into the ring, and lift his legs and stamp his feet (*shiko*).

呼出しに名前を告げられた力士は、土俵へ上がって四股(しこ)を踏む。

② The wrestler is given *chikaramizu*, sprinkles salt over the ring, and performs *shiko* in the middle of the ring, facing his opponent.

力水をつけてもらい、清めの塩を土俵にまき、向かい合って四股を踏む。

③ The wrestler takes his place and sprinkles salt over and over, until the time limit is reached.

仕切りをする。制限時間まで塩まきと仕切りを繰り返す。

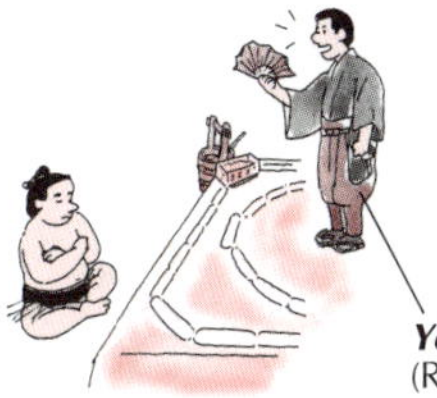

④ After the 4-minute limit, the match starts.

4分過ぎると勝負。

⑤ The referee judges the match and the winner is declared.

勝負は行司が裁き、勝者は勝ち名乗りを受ける。

VARIOUS TECHNIQUES
技いろいろ

The winner is decided when the opponent is forced out of the ring or when any part of his body including the topknot touches the ground. It is said that there are 48 winning techniques, but *Nihon Sumō Kyōkai* has classified up to 70.

一方が土俵から出るか、足の裏以外の体の一部が地面につくと負けである。決まり手四十八手といわれるが、相撲協会では七十手に分類している。

The wrestler in the black belt is the winner.

Yorikiri
(Forcing out)

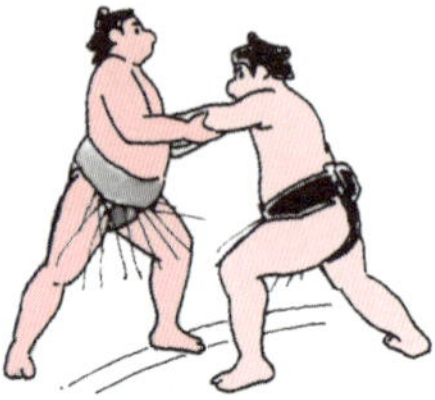

Oshidashi
(Pushing out)

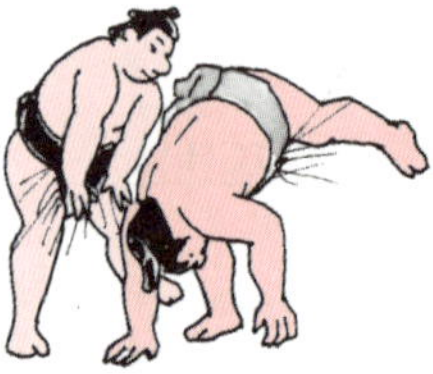

Hatakikomi
(Slapping down)

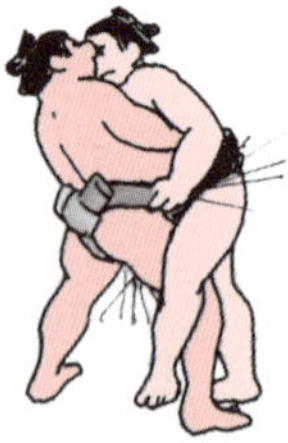

Sotogake
(Tripping with an outside leg)

Uwatenage
(Arm throw with an outside grip)

Shitatenage
(Arm throw with an inside grip)

Tsuridashi
(Lifting out)

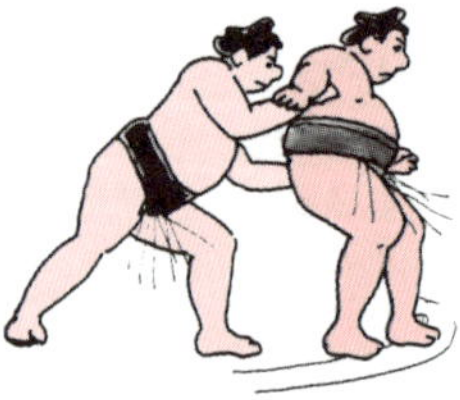

Okuridashi
(Pushing out from behind)

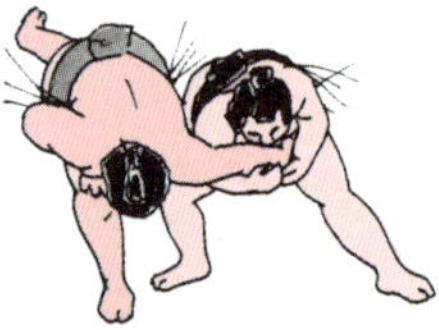

Tottari
(Arm-twist throw)

BANZUKE (RANKING LIST)
番付

The eight wins of each tournament are called *kachikoshi* and the eight losses are *makekoshi*, both of which affect ranking.

15日の取組中、8勝以上すると「勝ち越し」、8敗以上すると「負け越し」といい、次の番付での地位にかかわる。

Makuuchi • 幕内

The wrestlers line up from right to left in the order of highest to lowest ranking: *yokozuna, ōzeki, sekiwake, komusubi, maegashira.*

横綱、大関、関脇、小結、前頭の順に上位から、右から左へ並ぶ。

Jūryō • 十両

The ranks above *jūryō* are called *sekitori*, who receive a monthly salary from *Nihon Sumō Kyōkai.*

十両以上を関取といい、相撲協会から給料がもらえる。

Banzukehyō

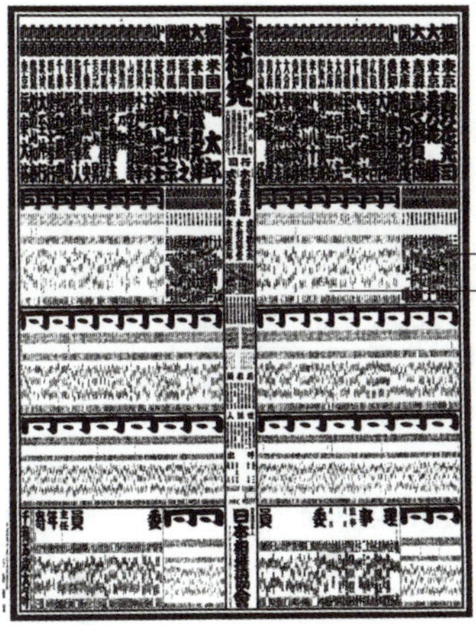

Yokozuna • 横綱

The highest ranked of all wrestlers, a *yokozuna* will not be demoted by the consequence of a tournament, but if the result turns out badly, he could be forced to retire.

力士最高位であり、成績の良し悪しで地位は動かないが、成績が悪ければ引退に追いこまれる。

Dohyōiri (Ring-entrance ritual)

JŪDŌ
柔道

Jūdō developed as a *samurai* art of self-defense in the Edo period (1600–1868). Using *jūdō*, one can defend oneself from attack, catch the opponent and defeat him without the use of weapons. In the early Meiji period (1868–1912), Kanō Jigorō not only established *jūdō* as a sport, but also founded *Kōdōkan jūdō* which aims for both physical and mental strength. *Jūdō* is now a world-class sport, and became an official Olympic sport at the 1964 Tōkyō Olympics.

江戸時代（1600～1868）の武士の護身術として発達した。素手で攻撃から身を守り、相手を倒し、抑えることができる。明治時代（1868～1912）初期に、嘉納治五郎が単にスポーツとして確立しただけでなく、精神修養を目標とした講道館柔道を創設した。柔道は国際的スポーツとしても注目され、第18回オリンピック東京大会（1964年）から正式競技種目となった。

JŪDŌ UNIFORM
柔道衣

Kanō Jigorō set up a system of ranks (*dan*) and classes (*kyū*) as an encouragement for his disciples.

段級制度は、嘉納治五郎が修業者の上達を奨励するために創案した。

Rank Shown by Belt (Obi) Color • 帯色による階級

- Red: higher than 9th rank (*dan*)
  紅：九段以上
- Red & white stripe: 6–8th rank (*dan*)
  紅白縞：六～八段
- Black: 1st–5th rank (*dan*)
  黒：初段～五段
- Brown: 1st–3rd class (*kyū*)
  茶：一～三級
- White: 4–5th class (*kyū*)
  白：四～五級

MATCHES
試合

- There are two divisions: open-weight and weight categories (7 divisions).
  無差別と体重別（7階級）がある。
- A match is fought within a 9.1m x 9.1m (50 *tatami*-mat) area.
  場内9.1m×9.1m（50畳）で試合を行う。
- The match period is 3–20 minutes.
  3～20分の試合時間。
- The player who defeats his or her opponent by *nagewaza* (throwing) so that he/she lands facing upward from the mat; or by *katamewaza* (grappling) submission, and holds him/her for more than 30 seconds, wins by ippon.
  一本（投げ技で仰向けに倒すか、固め技で30秒以上抑える）を先取すれば勝ち。

VARIOUS TECHNIQUES
技いろいろ

Throwing Techniques • 投げ技

These techniques may be used when the opponent is off-balanced to the front, or back.

前方や後方に崩れた時にかける技。

The man in gray uniform is exerting the technique.

Seoinage
(Shoulder throw)

Ōsotogari
(Major outer cut)

Hizaguruma
(Knee wheel)

Grappling Techniques • 固め技

A technique to make the opponent submit by controlling his movements.

相手の自由を制するための技。

Kesagatame (Diagonal hold)

Kami-shihōgatame (Upper four-corner hold)

KENDŌ
剣道

"Begin with a bow, end with a bow." This polite custom reflects the spirit of *kendō*. Using a bamboo sword instead of a steel one, *kendō* came from *kenjutsu* (old-style *kendō*), a kind of fencing only for *samurai*. Even now there are many *kendō* fans of the gallant *samurai* ideal.

「礼に始まり礼に終わる」この礼儀正しさが剣道の精神である。武士のものであった剣術が真剣を竹刀(しない)にかえたとはいえ、武士のいさぎよい理念のもと、今も愛好家は多い。

PROTECTORS
防具

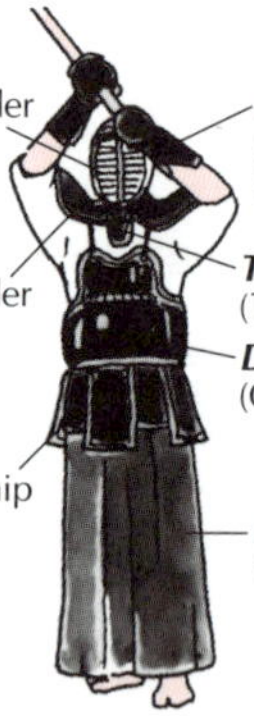

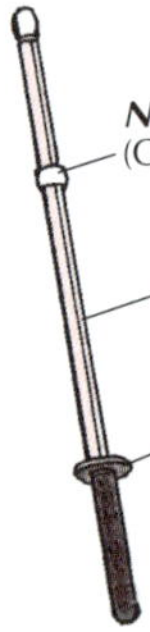

MATCHES
試合

- The *kendō* tournament is held in a 9–11 meter square area. A match may last for 5 minutes, and goes for 3 points. The winner is the person who gets 2 points first.

  9～11m四方の場内で、5分間、二本先取りの三本勝負で行われる。

- When the opponent's head, torso, or forearm is hit, or when a thrust to the opponent's throat is clearly achieved, one point can be gained.

  相手の面、胴、小手のいずれかを打ったり、のどを竹刀でついたりして決まれば一本となる。

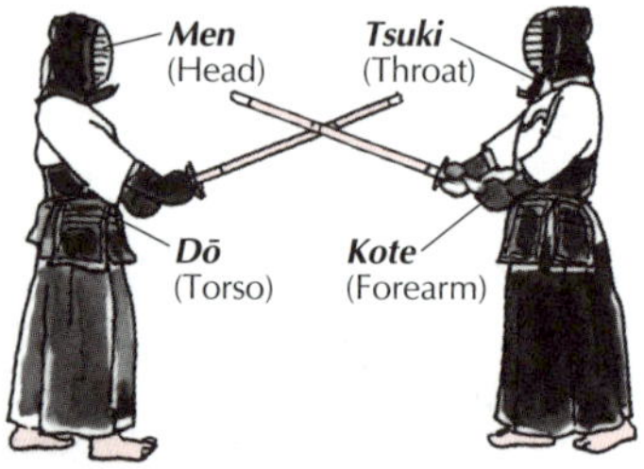

KYŪDŌ
弓道

Kyūdō, archery, has developed from prehistoric times in Japan. While people do join matches to hit a long-range target, its purpose of a *kyūdō* match is not only competition, but for training the mind and body through concentration in the realm of nothingness or *mushin* ("no-mind").

日本に古くから伝わる弓と矢で遠く離れた標的を射る競技である。スポーツ競技としてだけでなく、無我無心で競技するという、心身両方の鍛練を目的としている。

The stance is half the archer's height.

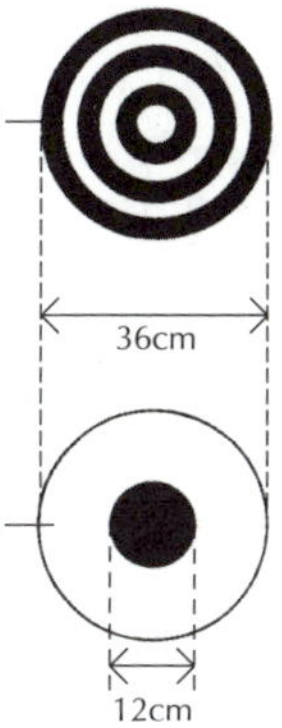

MATCHES
競技

A match winner is determined by the accumulation of total points scored from both shooting arrows and form.

勝敗は、当たり矢・フォームなどの総合で得点を競う。

Short-range Match • 近的競技

The range is 28m. The target's diameter is 36cm. Mainly held indoors.

射距離28m、的は径36cm。主として屋内で行う。

Long-range Match • 遠的競技

The range is 60m. The target's diameter is 100cm. Mainly held outdoors.

射距離60m、的は径100cm。主として屋外で行う。

KARATEDŌ

空手道

The native martial art of the *Ryūkyū* kingdom (now Okinawa), *karate* took its original influence from Kung-fu, which later changed into *tōde* (Chinese hands) and developed into *karate*.

琉球(現在の沖縄)土着の武術が、中国拳法の影響を受け、唐手(とうで)が生まれ空手となった。

VARIOUS TECHNIQUES
技いろいろ

MATCHES
競技

Sparring Match • 組手試合

When a quick, strong punch, strike or kick (these must stop just short of the opponent) is executed correctly, one point is gained. The objective is to be the first to get 3 points within 3 minutes.

有効な、突き、打ち、当て、蹴り(攻撃目標の寸前で止める)が正確にきまったら1本となる。3分間で3本先取り方式である。

Form Competition • 型試合

Participants demonstrate a choreographed series of defensive and offensive skills, called *kata*.

攻防の技の組み合わせを披露して競い合う。

AIKIDŌ

合気道

Aikidō came from *jūjutsu* in which one can cause the enemy to submit simply by using empty hands as weapons. The feature of this martial art is the throw that uses submission and control. Also, one can raise spiritual awareness and develop body flexibility through *aikidō* training.

素手で相手を制圧する柔術で、関節技を利用した、投げと抑えに特徴がある。練習による精神の高揚、身体の柔軟性を養うこともできる。

VARIOUS TECHNIQUES

技いろいろ

Kamae (Posture)

Throwing Techniques • 投げ技

Throw the opponent by twisting his wrist or elbow.

手首や肘（ひじ）関節をひねり返すことにより、投げる。

Shihōnage
(Four-direction throw)

Controlling Techniques • 固め技

By locking the opponent's wrist or elbow, you can easily bring him facedown and "pin" him to the mat.

関節をきめて、うつ伏せに抑えるために、少しの力で反抗できなくさせる。

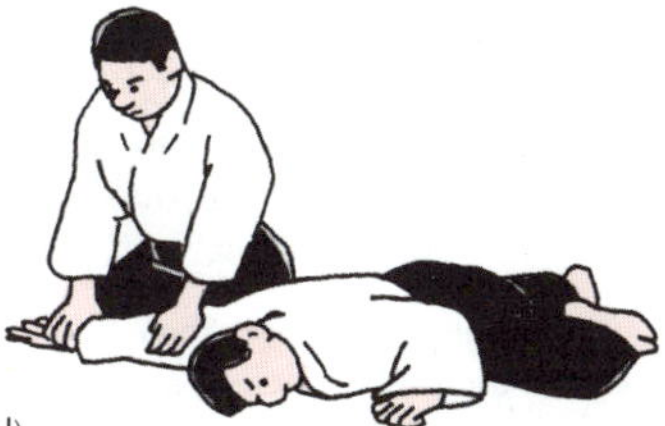

Ikkajō-osae (First control)

SHŌGI
将棋

An indoors game in which two persons sit across from each other at a board and move each of their pieces strategically. This game was created in ancient India at a river's basin, and later became the European game of chess. It came via China to Japan where it changed into *shōgi*.

将棋盤をはさんで向かい合った2人が、互いの駒を動かしながら勝敗を競い合う室内ゲーム。古代インダス川流域に生まれたゲームがヨーロッパに渡ってチェスとなり、また中国を経て日本に伝えられて将棋となった。

Shōgiban (Square wooden board)

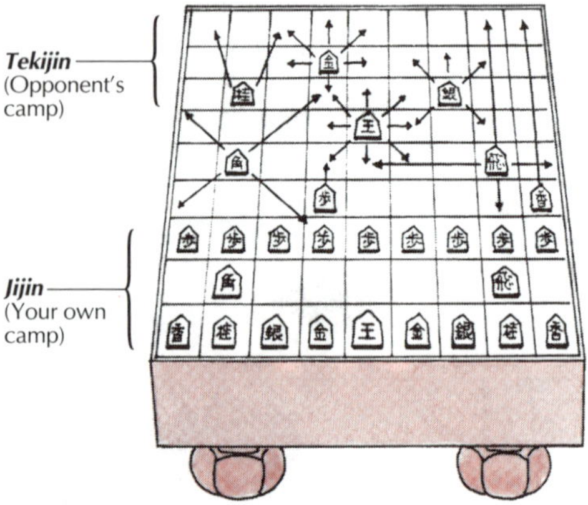

Koma (*Shōgi* pieces)
(Name of *koma*: the number of *koma*)

Total of 8 kinds, 20 pieces.

RULES OF THE GAME
競技のきまり

- Move your pieces alternately with your opponent's pieces. The person who "checkmates" first is the winner.
  盤上の駒を交互に動かし、相手の王将を先に詰めたほうが勝ち。
- When your piece moves into an opponent's position, you can take the opponent's piece and use it as yours.
  動いた方向にある敵駒を取り、自駒として使える。
- When your piece enters the opponent's camp, it will be flipped over and will take on the same function as the piece known as the Gold.
  敵陣に入ったら駒を裏返し「金」と同じ機能をもつ。

IGO

囲碁

An indoors game in which two persons alternately place black (one opponent) and white (the other opponent) stones on a board as they try to take each other's stones or occupy their field on the board. This game came to Japan from China via Korea in the 5th–6th centuries. It is very popular; the current playing population is reportedly ten million.

黒、白の石を交互に盤上に置き、相手の石と空間を取り合う室内ゲーム。5、6世紀頃、中国から朝鮮半島を経由して日本に伝わった。人気があり、囲碁人口は1,000万ともいわれている。

RULES OF THE GAME
競技のきまり

- The person who makes the first move or who is a lower-grade player uses the black stones. The two people alternately place the black and white stones one by one on the board. (Total: black stones=181, white stones=180)

  先番の人、もしくは下級者が黒石をもち、黒白交互に1個ずつ打つ。（合計：黒181個、白180個）

- You can put a stone anywhere on the board except at the point where a stone already is, or where placement is prohibited.

  石の置かれた所と、着手禁止点以外、盤上どこに打ってもよい。

- The game is decided by the area your stones cover and the number of stones you captured from the opponent.

  自石で囲んだ領地と取石の数で勝敗が決まる。

Capturing • 石のとり方

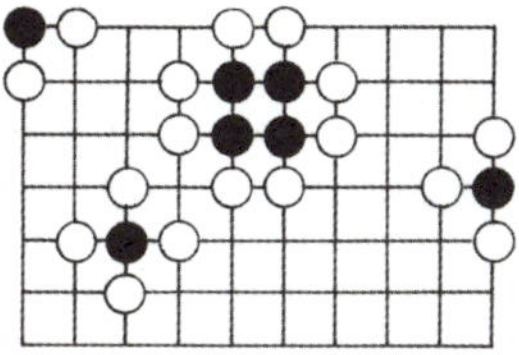

When black stones are surrounded by white stones, the black ones are considered to be "captured."

白石で四方をふさがれると、黒石は死ぬ。

Chakushu kinshiten • 着手禁止点

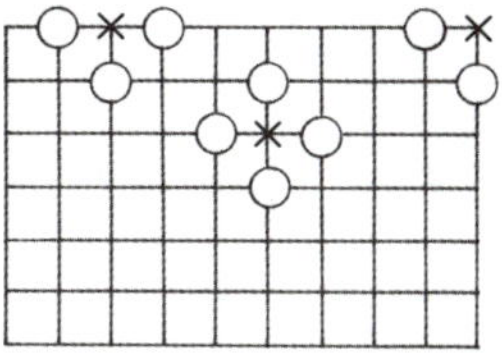

Don't put stones in an unviable position where they can be captured.

自分の石が取られる価値のない場所には石を置くことができない。

HANAFUDA

花札

Japanese playing cards. The playing cards that the Portuguese brought to Japan in the 16th century developed into *hanafuda*. The pictures on the cards represent the natural scenes from the four seasons. Thus, it can be said that this game reflects Japanese people's love of nature.

日本の代表的なカルタで、16世紀にポルトガル人が伝えた西洋カルタを改良してつくられた。それぞれ四季の花鳥風月があしらわれており、まさに自然を愛する、日本人的感覚から生みだされたものといえる。

CARDS' COMPOSITION

札の構成

From January to December, each month has four cards with the total set being 48.

1月から12月まで各4枚ずつで1組48枚である。

Jan.
(Pine)

Feb.
(Plum)

Mar.
(Flowering cherry blossoms)

Apr.
(Wisteria)

May
(Iris)

Jun.
(Tree peony)

July
(Bush clover)

Aug.
(Eulalia)

Sept.
(Chrysanthemum)

Oct.
(Maple)

Nov.
(Rain)

Dec.
(Paulownia)

HOW TO PLAY

遊び方

Hanafuda games include "*hachi-hachi,*" "*hana-awase,*" "*oichokabu,*" "*koi-koi,*" and so on.

「八八(はちはち)」、「花合わせ」、「おいちょかぶ」、「こいこい」などがある。

PACHINKO & KARAOKE
パチンコ／カラオケ

PACHINKO
パチンコ

The game requires releasing 11mm-diameter steel balls that drop them into the holes of the game board which is encased in a box. When the steel balls drop into the holes, you receive a few times more balls than you dropped into the holes.

ばねじかけで直径11mmの鋼球をはじき、当たり穴に入れるとさらに何倍かの球を得ることができる遊戯。

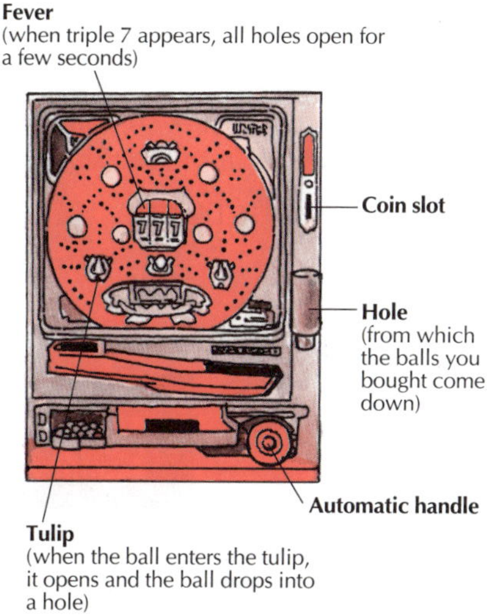

Depending on the number of balls you win, you can trade them for small goods or sundries.

玉の数に応じてたばこや日用品などの景品がもらえる。

KARAOKE
カラオケ

There are many places called "*karaoke*-boxes." Here, people sing songs whose lyrics appear on a TV screen from which only the melody of the song comes.

伴奏だけを録音したカラオケをかけて、TV画面の歌詞を見ながら歌って楽しむ「カラオケボックス」という店も多い。

PROFESSIONAL SPORTS
プロスポーツ

Many kinds of players and sports groups take part in the Pro Sport Association, which includes baseball, soccer, golf, *sumō*, boxing, etc.

野球、サッカー、ゴルフ、相撲、ボクシングなど様々な分野の選手、団体がプロスポーツ協会に加盟している。

BASEBALL
野球

Influenced by American major league baseball, professional baseball leagues started in Japan in 1930. Teams in the Central and Pacific leagues play the game in a pennant race from April to October. The winners of each league play in the Japan Series for the Japanese top team.

アメリカ大リーグの影響を受け、1930年、日本にもプロリーグが発足した。セントラル・リーグとパシフィック・リーグの各チームで4～10月のペナントレースを戦い、各リーグの優勝チームが日本シリーズで日本一をかけて戦う。

CENTRAL LEAGUE
セントラル・リーグ

Yomiuri Giants
読売ジャイアンツ（巨人）

Chunichi Dragons
中日ドラゴンズ

Hiroshima Toyo Carp
広島東洋カープ

Yakult Swallows
ヤクルトスワローズ

Yokohama Bay Stars
横浜ベイスターズ

Hanshin Tigers
阪神タイガース

PACIFIC LEAGUE
パシフィック・リーグ

Orix Blue Wave
オリックス・ブルーウェーブ

Nippon Ham Fighters
日本ハムファイターズ

Seibu Lions
西武ライオンズ

Kintetsu Buffaloes
近鉄バファローズ

Chiba Lotte Marines
千葉ロッテマリーンズ

Fukuoka Daiei Hawks
福岡ダイエーホークス

SOCCER (J. LEAGUE)
サッカー（Jリーグ）

The J. League began in 1993 as a professional soccer league and was eagerly welcomed by fans. 7 teams have been added since its inception; now there are 17 teams.

1993年、プロスポーツとして、ファンの熱い期待のなか、Jリーグが開幕した。現在、発足当時から7チーム増え、17チームとなっている。

Kashima Antlers
鹿島アントラーズ

JEF United Ichihara
ジェフユナイテッド市原

Kashiwa Reysol
柏レイソル

Urawa Red Diamonds
浦和レッドダイヤモンズ

Verdy Kawasaki
ヴェルディ川崎

Yokohama Marinos
横浜マリノス

Yokohama Flügels
横浜フリューゲルス

Bellmare Hiratsuka
ベルマーレ平塚

Shimizu S-Pulse
清水エスパルス

Júbilo Iwata
ジュビロ磐田

Nagoya Grampus Eight
名古屋グランパスエイト

Kyoto Purple Sanga
京都パープルサンガ

Gamba Osaka
ガンバ大阪

Cerezo Osaka
セレッソ大阪

Vissel Kobe
ヴィッセル神戸

Sanfrecce Hiroshima
サンフレッチェ広島

Avispa Fukuoka
アビスパ福岡

GOLF
ゴルフ

Once the sport of those from the monied or so-called upper classes, and often used as the "working recreation" of businessmen and their clients, golf has now spread to the general public. The golf-playing population has recently increased, such that in 1996 the number of professional golfers is 3,046 males and 484 females.

ビジネスマンの接待や高級志向のスポーツであったものが大衆化した。ゴルフ人口も増え、1996年にはプロゴルファーは、男性3,046人、女性は484人になった。

TRADITIONAL GAMES
伝承遊び

Even now, there are many regions where the traditional games harking back to olden days have been retained. In some areas, old-style games are adopted in kindergarten or pre-school classes in order to ensure that they are handed down to future generations.

昔から受け継がれている「伝承遊び」が、今なお残る地方が多い。また、それらを伝えるために、教育や保育の場で実践しているところもある。

AYATORI (CAT'S CRADLE)
あやとり

You can make many figures by inserting the wrist or fingers into a piece of string that encircles the hand. Usually, the game is played by yourself or two people who pass the string back and forth between themselves.

輪にした糸を両手首や指にかけて、いろいろな形を作りだしていく遊び。1人で遊んだり、2人で受け渡しをして遊ぶ。

Broom • ほうき

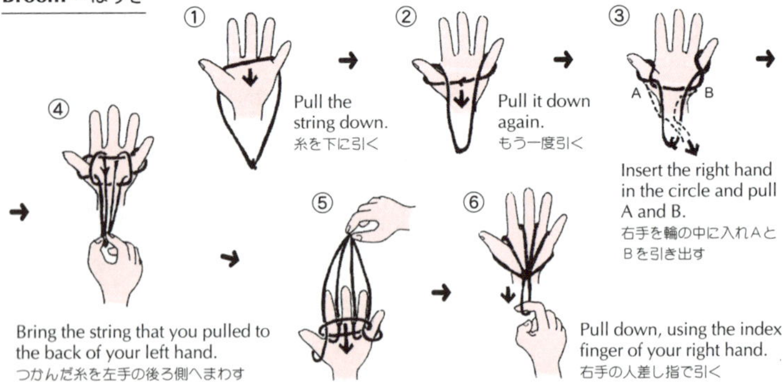

OTEDAMA (JUGGLING)
お手玉

Toss up the "mother" bean bag, while picking up one of the bean bags on the floor, then catch the "mother" bean bag in the same hand. Continue this action until you can pick up two, three or all five bean bags simultaneously with the "mother."

親玉を投げている間に、床においたお手玉を1つ取り、その手でさらに落ちてきた親玉も取る。それを2個、3個と、5個全部取れるまで続ける。

Otedama
(Bags made of cloth filled with red beans or rice)

DARUMA-OTOSHI
だるまおとし

Pile up the cylindrical wooden pieces and put the Bodhidharma doll on top of the pile. Hit each piece with the wooden hammer so as not to make the doll fall down.

数個の円筒形の木片を重ね、その上にだるまの人形をおいて、人形を落とさないように木づちで木片をはずす。

KENDAMA
けん玉

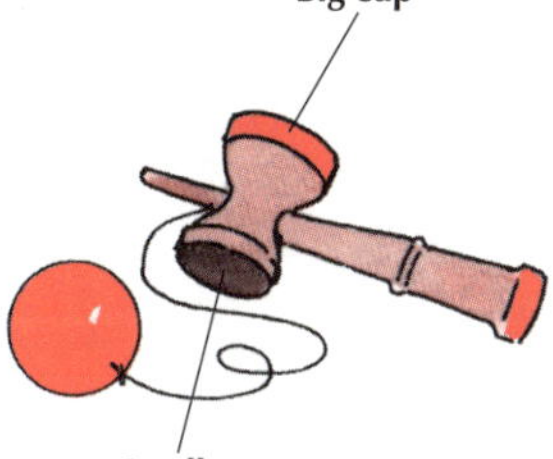

Toss the ball up and try to catch it in the big or small cup.
玉を振り上げ大皿や小皿にのせる。

Trip around the World • 世界一周

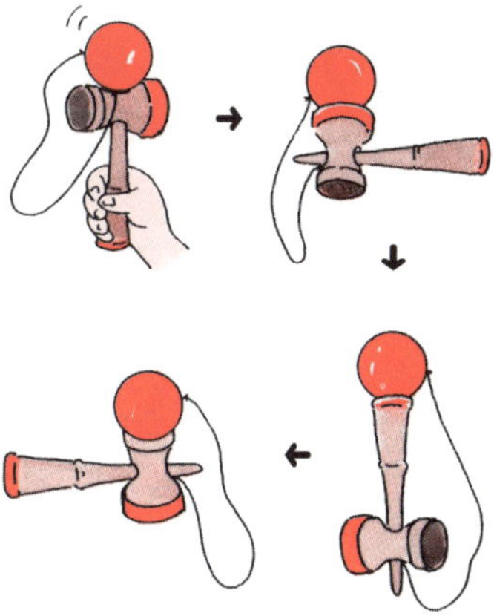

Furiken • ふりけん

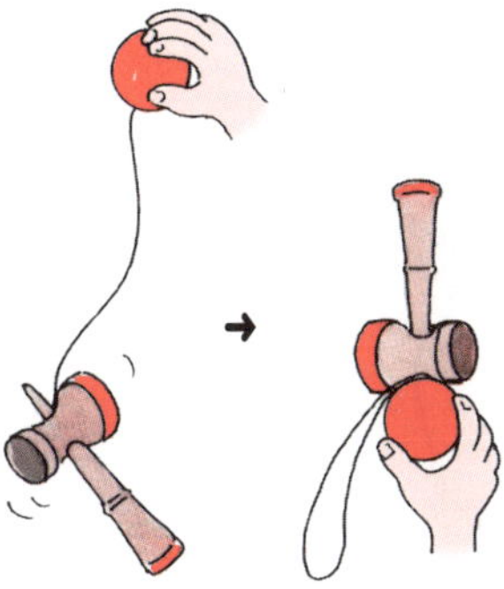

Lighthouse • 灯台

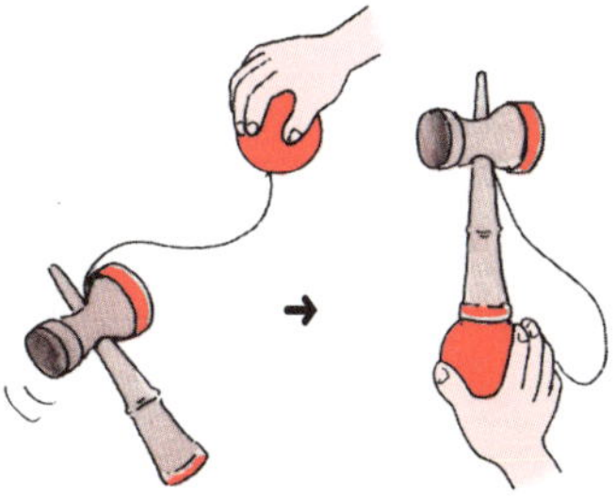

PAPER DOLL SUMŌ
紙相撲

Paper doll *sumō* is a simple game which has been much beloved by children since days gone by.

手作りの紙相撲は手軽な遊びとして昔から親しまれてきた。

Let's Make Strong Wrestlers
強い力士を育てよう！

① Copy the *sumō* wrestler's picture from this page. Make it the same size (or 1.5 times bigger). Paste the copy onto thick paper and trim the edges. Fold the picture along the dotted line.

下の力士を原寸大または1.5倍にコピーし、裏に厚紙を貼ってまわりを切り取る。中心線で2つに折る。

② Draw a circle on a good size box for use as the *sumō* wrestling ring.

適当な大きさの空き箱に円を描いて土俵を作る。

③ Put your and your friend's wrestlers in the center of the circle and fold their arms over each other's. Then, tap the edge of the box lightly with your fingers. The person whose *sumō* wrestler makes the other fall down or get pushed out of the ring wins.

土俵に力士を立たせ、組ませる。2人が土俵をたたいて、相手の力士を倒すか、土俵の外に押し出したほうが勝ちとなる。

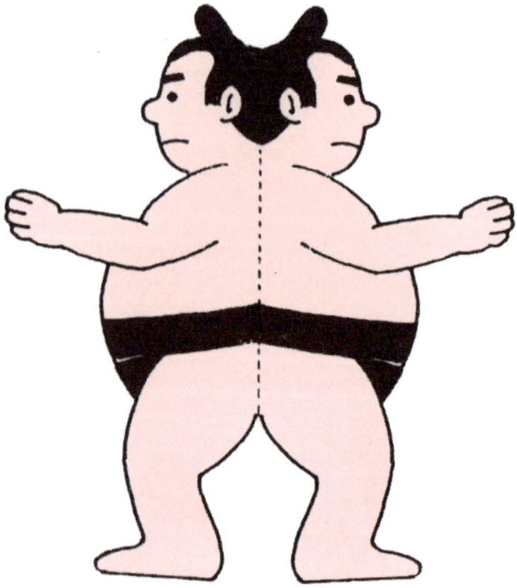

JANKEN
じゃんけん

Saying "*Jankempon*," each person makes a one-handed gesture representing paper (*pā*), scissors (*choki*) or stone (*gū*). Stone wins against scissors, scissors win against paper, and paper wins against stone. *Janken* is used to decide who goes first or who will be "it" in a game of tag, for example.

「じゃんけんぽん」と言いながら、紙(パー)、はさみ(チョキ)、石(グー)のどれかを片手で示して見せる。石ははさみに、はさみは紙に、紙は石に勝つ。子供の遊びの中で、順番を決めたり、鬼を決めたりする時にじゃんけんをする。

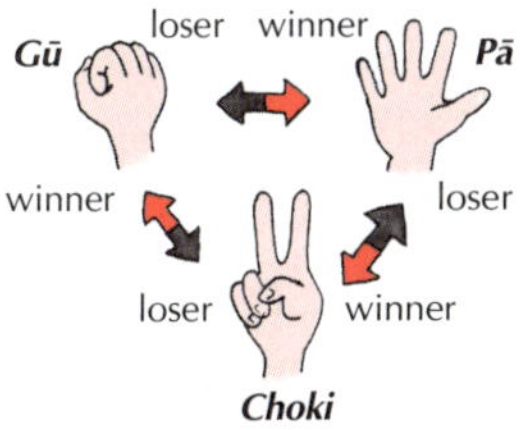

Let's Make Friends by Playing Janken Game
じゃんけん遊びで友達をつくろう！

●Atchi Muite Hoi! • あっちむいてホイ！

One against one
1人対1人

① Do *janken*.

じゃんけんをする。

② Point your forefinger in each direction—left, right, up, down—while saying, "*Atchi muite hoi!*" (Turn that way, hey!).

勝者は「あっち向いてホイ!」と言いながら、人差し指で、上下左右いずれかを指す。

③ At the same time as "*Hoi!*" is said, the *janken* loser should be facing a different direction than where the *janken* winner is pointing.

敗者は、ホイと同時に、指とは異なる方向に顔を向ける。

④ If the *janken* loser faces the same way as the winner directs, he/she loses again. The faster the action is, the more exciting this game becomes.

指された方向に顔を向けたら負けになる。速くするとおもしろい。

●Jumbo Janken • ジャンボじゃんけん

One against many
1対多

① Everybody stands up and does *janken* against the leader, who stands in front of them.

全員立って、前に出たリーダーとじゃんけんをする。

② Any person defeated by the leader must sit down.

リーダーに負けた人は座っていく。

③ The last person still standing does a final *janken* game with the leader.

最後に残った人とリーダーとで決勝戦。

ORIGAMI
折り紙

Origami is one of Japan's traditional paper-craft arts. You can make many shapes simply by folding a small square of paper. Children are taught how to make *origami* by their parents or grandparents. Sometimes they learn in kindergarten or preschool.

折り紙は日本の伝統的芸術の一つで、正方形の小さな紙を折るだけで、いろいろな形を作りだしていく。子供達は親や祖父母から折り方を教わったり、時には幼稚園や保育所で習うこともある。

STEP 1 DOG AND CAT
犬と猫

------------ **Valley fold** (Fold over)

Turn over

①

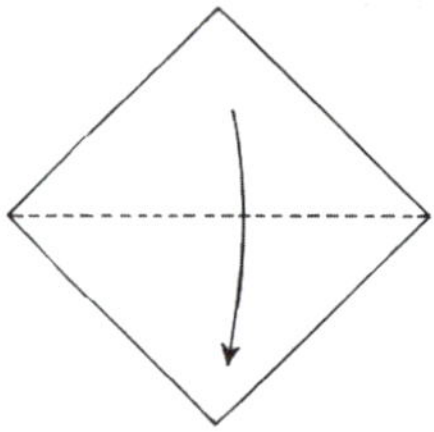

Fold the paper in half.

半分に折る

②

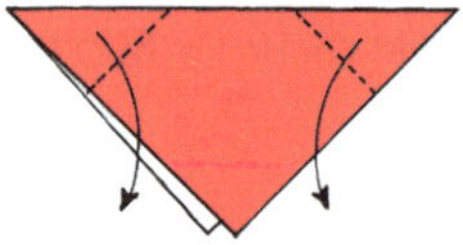

Fold the two pointed ends down.

両角を下に折る

③

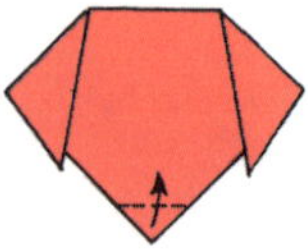

Fold the tips of the bottom up.

下の部分を折り上げる

④

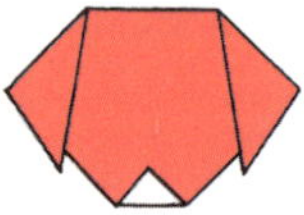

⑤

Draw eyes and a nose.

目と鼻を描く

⑤

Turn over.

裏返す

STEP 2 SAMURAI HELMET
かぶと

①

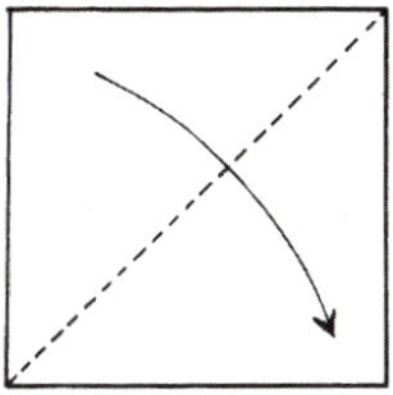

Prepare a piece of square paper.
Newspaper is suitable.

新聞紙を正方形にして使う

②

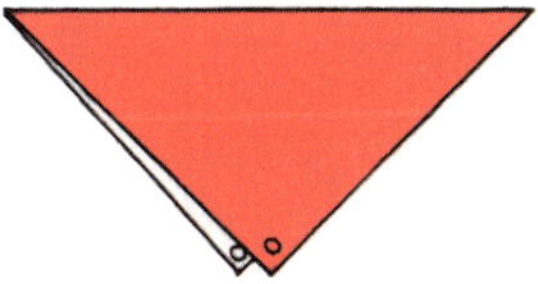

Fold to make a triangle.

角を合わせて三角に折る

③

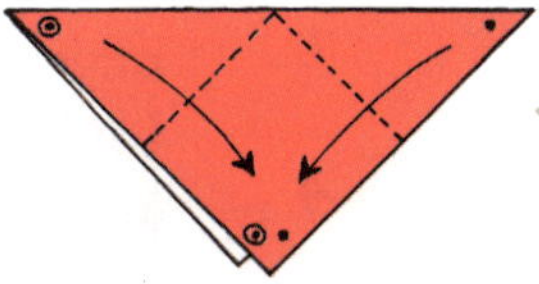

Fold on the dotted lines.

折り目に沿って折る

④

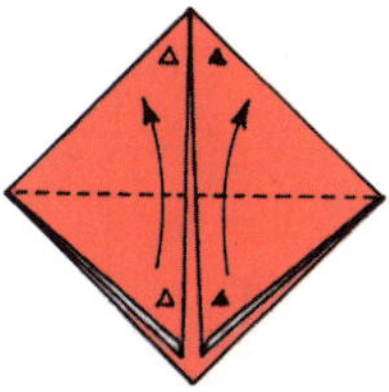

Fold up so as to connect each symbol.

印どうしを合わせて折り上げる

⑤

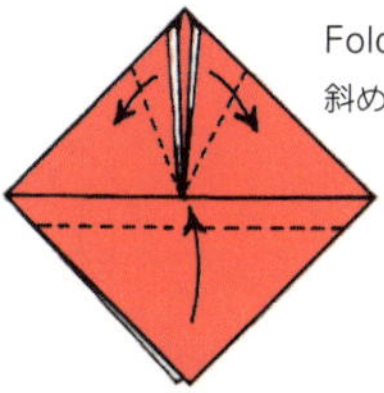

Fold back.

斜めに折り返す

Fold up the facing bottom flap.

上の1枚を折り上げる

⑥

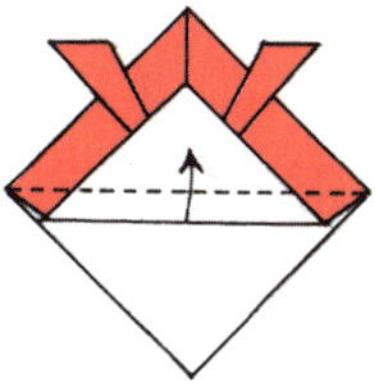

Fold up again.

もう1回折り上げる

⑦

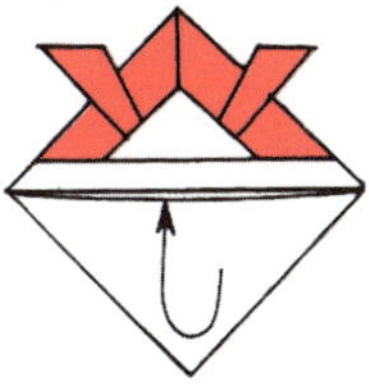

Fold the other bottom flap inside.

中に折り込む

STEP 3 TRICK BOAT
だまし舟

Valley fold (Fold over)
Mountain fold (Fold under)
Turn over

①

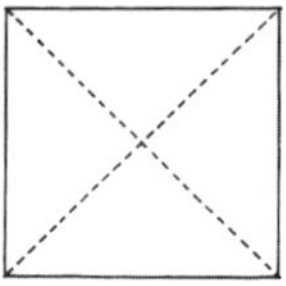

Make creases.
三角に折り、折り目をつける

②

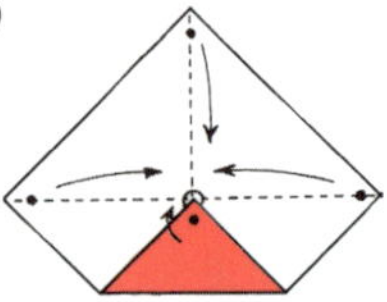

Bring the corners to the center point.
中央に折り合わせる

③

Bring the corners to the center point again, then unfold.
もう一度中央に折り合わせ、広げる

④

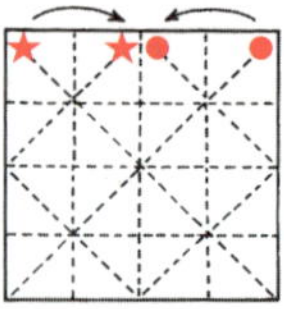

Bring each symbol to match the same one.
折り目まで合わせて折る

⑤

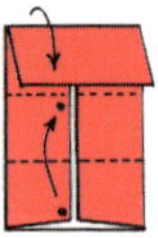

Bring the top and bottom sides to the center line.
中央に折り合わせる

⑥

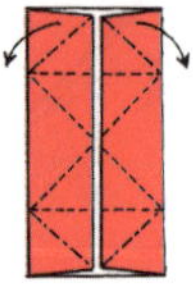

Open.
引き出す

⑦

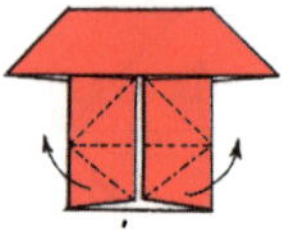

Open.
引き出してつぶす

⑧

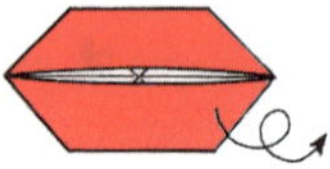

Turn over.
裏返す

⑨

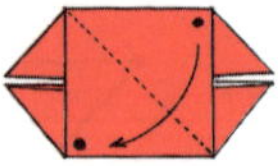

Fold so the two points match.
斜めに折り上げる

⑩

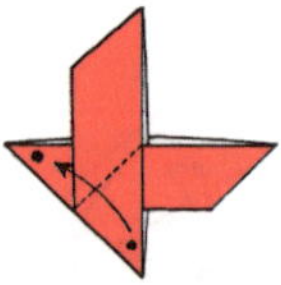

Fold so the two points match.
斜めに折り上げる

⑪

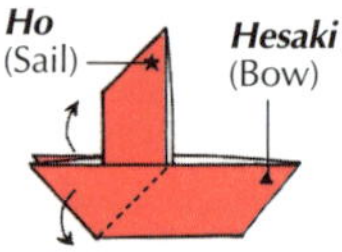

By folding down the stern part, the sail changes into the bow.
折り下げると帆がへさきに変わる

STEP 4 CANDY BOX 菓子入れ

① Fold twice to make a triangle, then open the top layer and flatten into a square.
三角折りを2回し、上の1枚を開いて四角につぶす

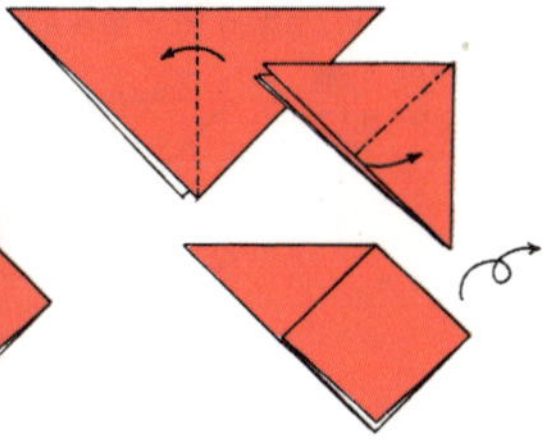

②

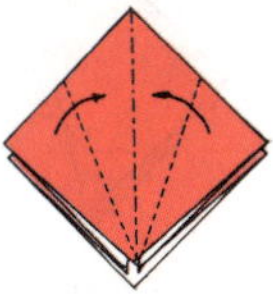

Fold to the center.
中央に折り合わせる

③

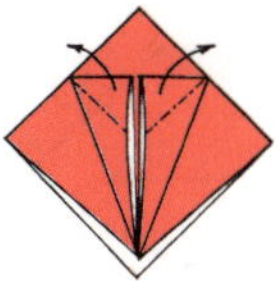

Flatten to a triangle.
開いてつぶす

④

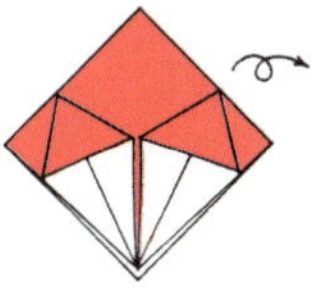

Turn over. Do the same on the other side.
裏返して同じように折る

⑤

Do the same as ②, ③, ④.
②③④を繰り返す

⑥

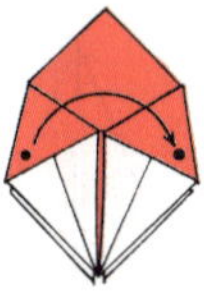

Fold so the two points match.
折り合わせる

⑦

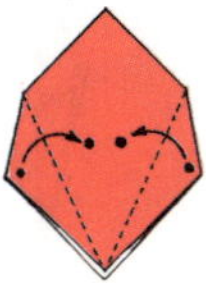

Fold so the two points match.
中央に折り合わせる

⑧

Turn over, then do the same on this side.
裏返して同じように折る

⑨

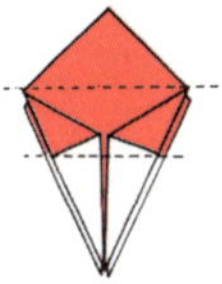

Fold up the flap.
上の1枚を折り上げる

⑩

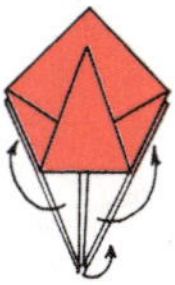

Fold the other flaps in the same way.
残りも折り上げる

⑪

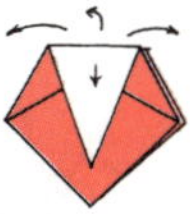

Open and give final shape.
開いて箱にする

⑫

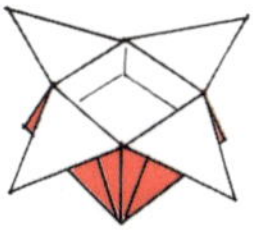

STEP 5 CRANE 鶴

① Fold twice to make a triangle, then open the top layer and flatten to make a square.

三角折りを2回し、上の1枚を開いて四角につぶす

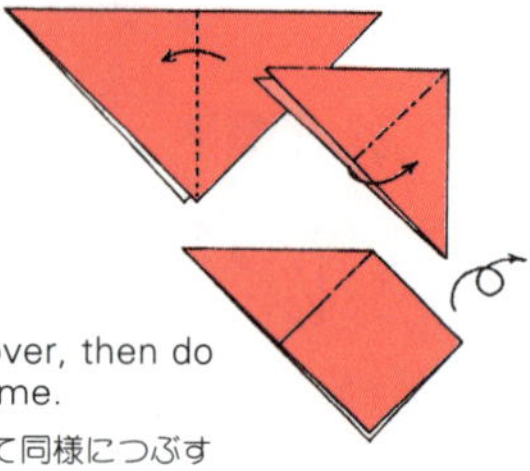

Turn over, then do the same.

裏返して同様につぶす

② Make creases.

三角形の折り目をつける

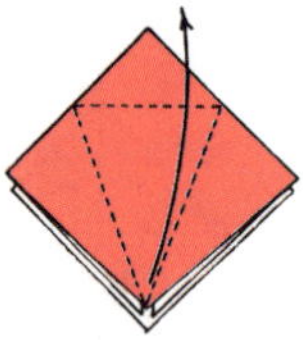

Open top layer and flatten as in ③.

上の1枚を開き、折り線に沿って折り、ひし形につぶす

③

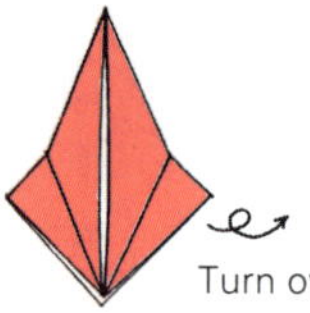

Turn over.

裏返す

④

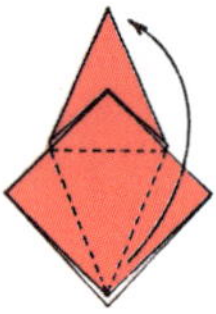

Make creases again. Do the same thing.

同じように折り目をつけて開き、ひし形につぶす

⑤

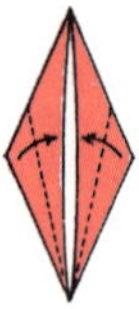

Fold the top layer edges to the center.

上の1枚を中央に折り合わせる

⑥

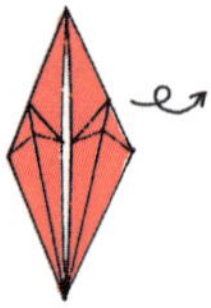

Turn over.

裏返す

⑦

Do the same thing on the other side.

裏側も同じように折り合わせる

⑧

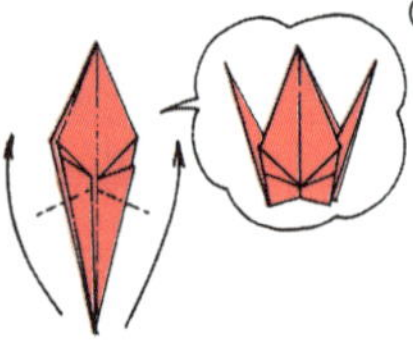

Fold up right and left bottom tips.

左と右を中わり折りし、首と尾を作る

⑨

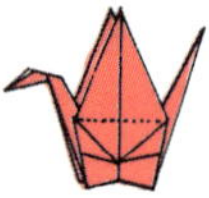

Fold down head.

中わり折りして頭を作る

⑩

Spread wings and blow into the hole in the underside.

羽を広げ、穴から息を吹きこむ

STEP 6 BOOKMARK しおり

● Prepare：準備

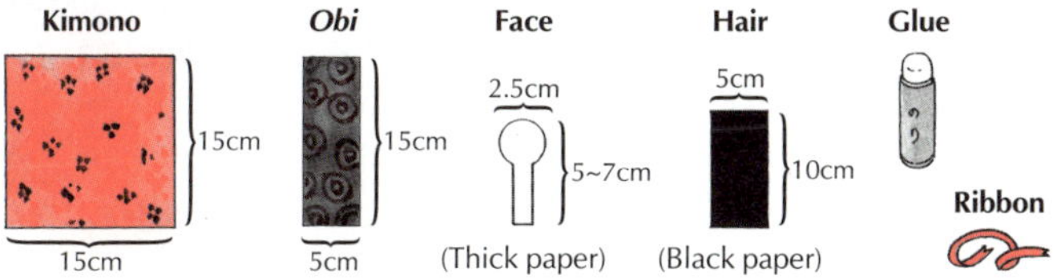

① Make a head：頭部を作る

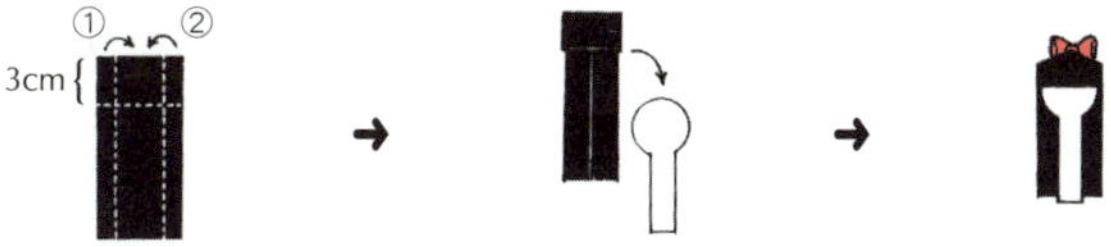

Fold along the lines.
折り目にそって折る

Glue rolled cylinders of paper (for hair) on forehead and to hang on shoulders.
筒状の髪を顔にかぶせる

Decorate with ribbon.
リボンをしばる

② Make a kimono and doll：着物を作って着せる

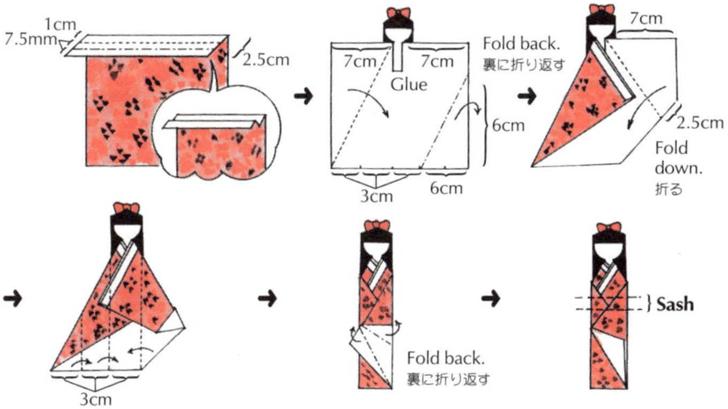

③ Make an obi：帯を作る

JAPANESE SONGS

日本の歌

The song the Japanese most like to sing during the transition of the seasons is “Sakura” (cherry blossoms), which has been popular over the ages.

四季の移り変わりのなかで、古くから日本人に最も愛され歌い続けられている歌の一つが、「さくら」である。

Sakura

1 *Sakura, sakura,* all over the fields, mountains and villages, as far as I can see. Is it mist or clouds? Shining in the rising sun, *sakura, sakura* in full bloom.

2 *Sakura, sakura.* The spring sky, as far as I can see. Is it mist or clouds? It is awash in color. Let us go, let us go see the blossoms.

"Furusato" (hometown) is a song with a tender expression, for which the Japanese have a strong emotional attachment.

日本人の心のよりどころである「ふるさと」も、また日本的な情緒のある美しい歌である。

Furusato

Words: Takano Tatsuyuki
Music: Okano Teiichi

1 I chased rabbits on the hill and fished carp from the river. I dream of that day, even now. How can I forget my hometown?

2 How are my parents doing? Are my friends doing well? Whether it rains or the wind blows, my hometown is what I remember.

3 When I reach my goals some day, I will go home to those green mountains and that river where clear water flows.

OLD JAPANESE FOLKTALES
むかし話

Old Japanese folktales are legends beginning "once upon a time," which have been handed down from generation to generation.

昔から、母から子へ、子から孫へと語り継がれてきた空想的な内容の説話で、冒頭は「昔、昔」で語り始められる。

MOMOTARŌ (THE PEACH BOY)
桃太郎

Once upon a time, there lived an old man and an old woman. One day when the old woman was doing the wash by the river, a big peach floated by.

昔、昔、あるところに、おじいさんとおばあさんが住んでいました。ある日、おばあさんが川で洗濯をしていると、大きな桃が流れてきました。

She brought the big peach home, and when she tried to cut it, it opened up. Out came a lively baby boy, whom they named Momotarō.

家に持って帰り、包丁で切ろうとすると、桃は割れて中から元気な赤ん坊が出てきました。この赤ん坊を桃太郎と名づけました。

Momotarō grew up to be a strong boy. One day, fiends attacked the village, going on a wild rampage, disturbing the villagers.

桃太郎は心やさしい力持ちに育ちました。その頃、鬼たちが村にやってきては大暴れして帰っていくので、村人達はたいへん困っていました。

Momotarō decided to set out for the fiend's island. The old woman made millet dumplings (*kibidango*) for Momotarō to take with him.

桃太郎は鬼が島へ鬼たいじに行こうと決めました。おばあさんは日本一のきびだんごを作り、桃太郎に持たせました。

On the way, Momotarō met a dog. He gave the dog a *kibidango* and the dog became his companion. Momotarō then met a monkey and a pheasant, both of which became his companions after he gave them *kibidango* too.

途中で犬にあいました。きびだんごをあげると、犬は家来になりました。次に猿に、そしてきじにあいました。猿もきじも、きびだんごをもらって鬼たいじのお供をすることになりました。

Once on the island, Momotarō and his followers attacked the fiends: the dog bit, the monkey clawed, and the pheasant pecked their eyes out. Momotarō defeated the fiends' leader.

鬼が島に着いた桃太郎たちは鬼たちに襲いかかりました。犬はかみつき、猿はひっかき、きじは目を突っつきました。桃太郎は鬼の親分をやっつけました。

The fiends surrendered and apologized to Momotarō, who brought back treasures. He returned to the village where all lived happily ever after.

鬼たちは桃太郎の強さに降参し謝りました。桃太郎は取り返した宝物を持って村へ帰り、みんなで幸せに暮らしましたとさ。

KAGUYAHIME (THE MOON PRINCESS)
かぐや姫

Once upon a time, there lived a man called the Old Bamboo Cutter. One day he found a stalk of shining bamboo. He cut the bamboo and found a pretty baby girl inside of it.

昔、昔、あるところに、竹取りの翁というおじいさんがいました。ある日、おじいさんが光る竹を見つけたので切ってみると、中にはかわいい女の子がいました。

The baby girl, named Kaguyahime, grew up to become a beautiful maiden who was talked about far and wide.

「かぐや姫」と名づけられた女の子は、村で評判の美しい娘に成長し、そのうわさは都中に広まりました。

Five young noblemen came from the city to propose to Kaguyahime. She made difficult requests of them, saying that she would marry the man who could do what she asked.

5人の公家たちが都からやってきて、かぐや姫に結婚を申し込みました。かぐや姫は5人に難しい注文をだし、その望みをかなえた人と結婚すると誓いました。

Her requests were quite difficult to fulfill, such as obtaining the five-colored jeweled necklace hanging around the dragon's neck. None of the five noblemen succeeded.

しかし、かぐや姫が注文した竜の首についた五色の玉も他のものも手に入れ難く、5人の誰一人として望みをかなえることができませんでした。

In the meantime, Kaguyahime began to shed tears in the moonlit night, since it was on such a night that People of the Moon would come to fetch her and she would have to go back to the moon.

やがて、かぐや姫は月夜になると涙をこぼすようになりました。満月の夜になると月からお迎えがきて、月の世界に戻らなくてはならないからでした。

Hearing that she would have to return to the moon, the old man and woman asked the emperor to have his men keep guard over their house. On the full moon night when the messengers came, it was so bright that no one could keep their eyes open.

おじいさんとおばあさんは帝(みかど)にお願いをし、家来達に屋敷の周りを守ってもらいましたが、月から使者がやってくると、まぶしさに誰も身動きができなくなりました。

Kaguyahime was reluctant to leave the old man and woman, but returned to the moon with People of the Moon.

おじいさんとおばあさんの見守るなか、かぐや姫は別れを惜しみながら、天女達と月に帰っていきましたとさ。

JAPANESE FESTIVALS
日本の祭り

Festivals were originally religious events to worship the gods, send requests to the Buddha for a good harvest, or to welcome the souls of the departed who come back to this world to visit us. Recently, some festivals have become tourist attractions.

祭りは、元来宗教的行事の一つで、神や仏を祭りあげ、豊作を願ったり、亡くなった人の霊魂を人間の世界に迎えてもてなす意味がある。今日では、観光名物になっているものもある。

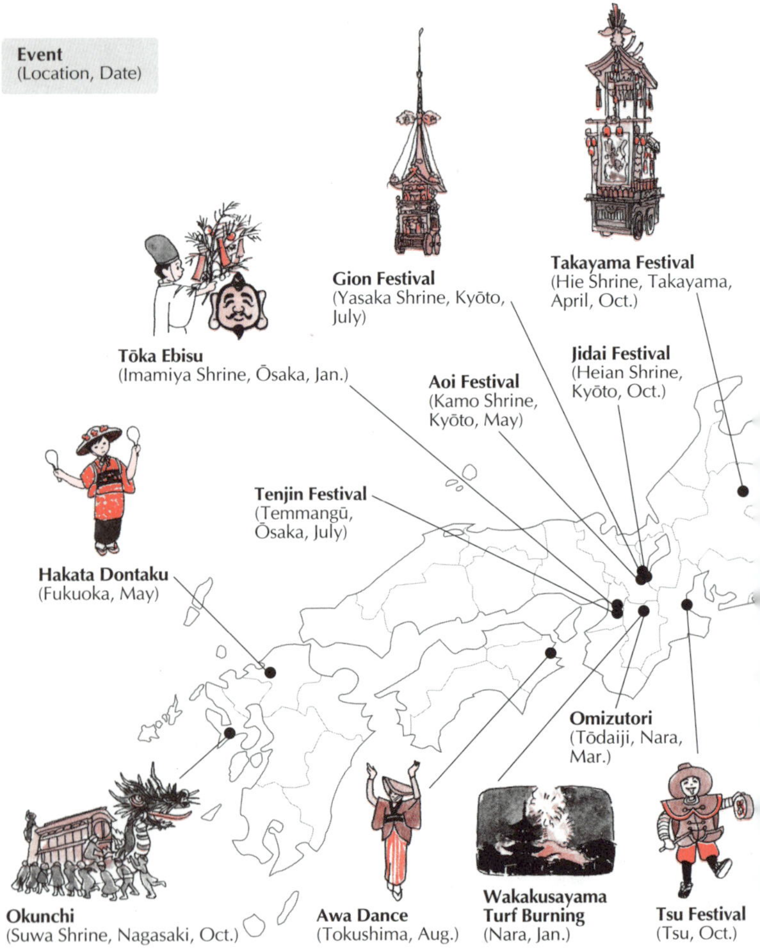

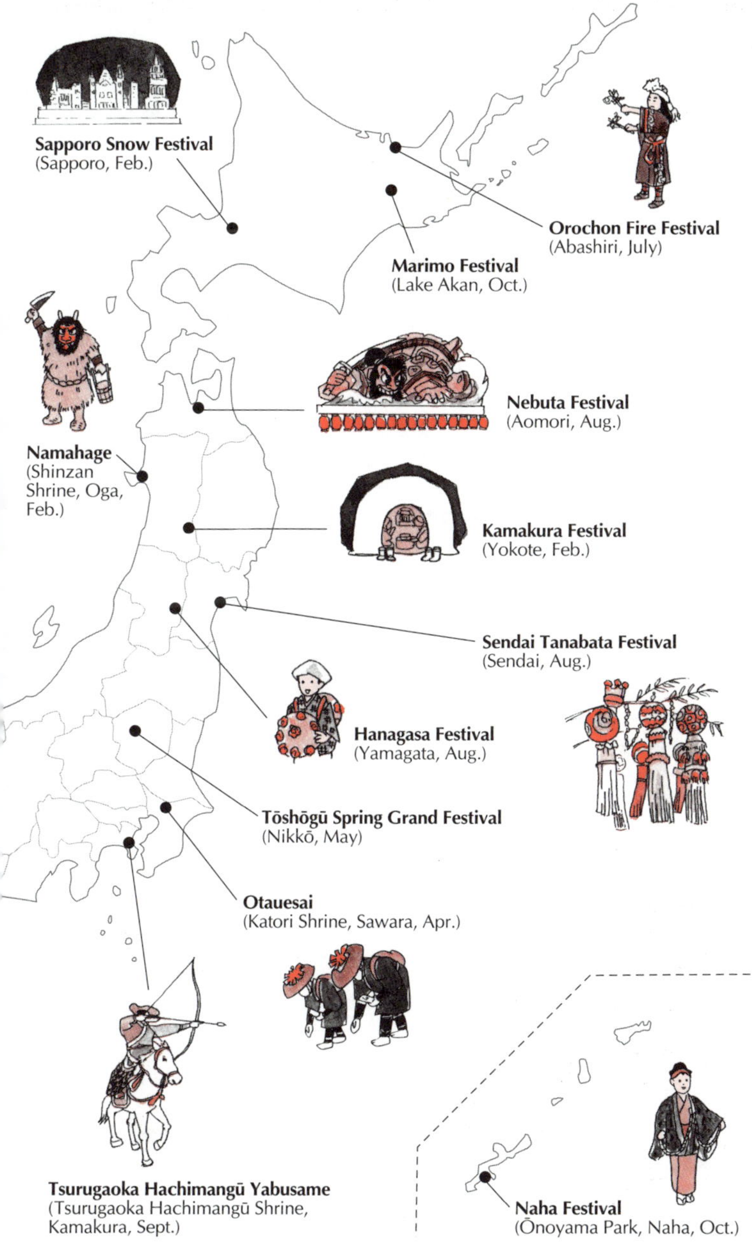
Sapporo Snow Festival
(Sapporo, Feb.)
Orochon Fire Festival
(Abashiri, July)
Marimo Festival
(Lake Akan, Oct.)
Nebuta Festival
(Aomori, Aug.)
Namahage
(Shinzan Shrine, Oga, Feb.)
Kamakura Festival
(Yokote, Feb.)
Sendai Tanabata Festival
(Sendai, Aug.)
Hanagasa Festival
(Yamagata, Aug.)
Tōshōgū Spring Grand Festival
(Nikkō, May)
Otauesai
(Katori Shrine, Sawara, Apr.)
Tsurugaoka Hachimangū Yabusame
(Tsurugaoka Hachimangū Shrine, Kamakura, Sept.)
Naha Festival
(Ōnoyama Park, Naha, Oct.)

SIGHT-SEEING
観光

Taking a trip for sight-seeing or recreation is becoming part of today's lifestyle.

遊覧や保養のための旅行など、余暇を楽しむための旅が定着しつつある。

KINDS OF ACCOMMODATIONS
宿の種類

There are Japanese-style inns, lodgings like tourist homes, government-run lodgings, Western-style hotels, *pension* (Western-style *minshuku*) and youth hostels. *Minshuku* and Japanese-style inns usually serve breakfast and dinner.

和室中心の旅館、民宿、国民宿舎、洋室中心のホテル、ペンション、ユースホステルなどがある。民宿、旅館などは1泊2食（朝、夕）付きのことが多い。

Ryokan (Japanese-style Inn) • 旅館にて

Arrival • 到着

State your name, and register your name and address in the guest book. Take off your shoes and change into slippers.

名前を告げ、宿帳に記帳する。くつを脱ぎ、スリッパにはきかえる。

Guest Rooms • 客室にて

You will be guided to your room which has tatami mat floors and Japanese bedding (*futon*). Therefore take off your slippers at the entrance to the room.

部屋に案内される。客室は畳敷きの和室で、夜は布団を敷く。入り口でスリッパを脱ぐ。

Guest Rooms • 客室にて

Japanese tea and sweets will be served in the room.

部屋で日本茶と菓子のサービスを受ける。

Meals • 食事

Meals may be served in your room or in the dining room.

部屋に運ばれる場合と、食堂へ食べにいく場合がある。

Breakfast **Dinner**

Large Communal Bath • 大浴場

Many people wear *yukata,* cotton kimono, to go to the large communal bath or hot spring. While you are taking a bath, the room-maid will prepare your *futon.*

温泉や大浴場に行く時も浴衣のまま行く人が多い。部屋を空けている間に布団を敷いておいてくれる。

Paying the Bill • 精算

Pay the bill at the front desk before leaving.

出発前に帳場にて精算する。

SIGHT-SEEING SPOTS
観光名所

There are many interesting spots where ancient, traditional culture has been preserved in magnificent natural settings, whose beauty can be admired from season to season. Japanese like to visit those places where people live in close contact with nature.

移り変わる四季折々の雄大な自然のなかで、古くからの文化を守り続けてきた名所が、日本各地にある。自然と人とのつながりが今も息づく、そんな名所を訪れてみたい。

Three Famous Spots of Scenic Beauty • 三景

- Amanohashidate (Kyōto)
  天橋立（京都）
- Itsukushima Shrine (Hiroshima)
  厳島神社（広島）
- Matsushima (Miyagi)
  松島（宮城）

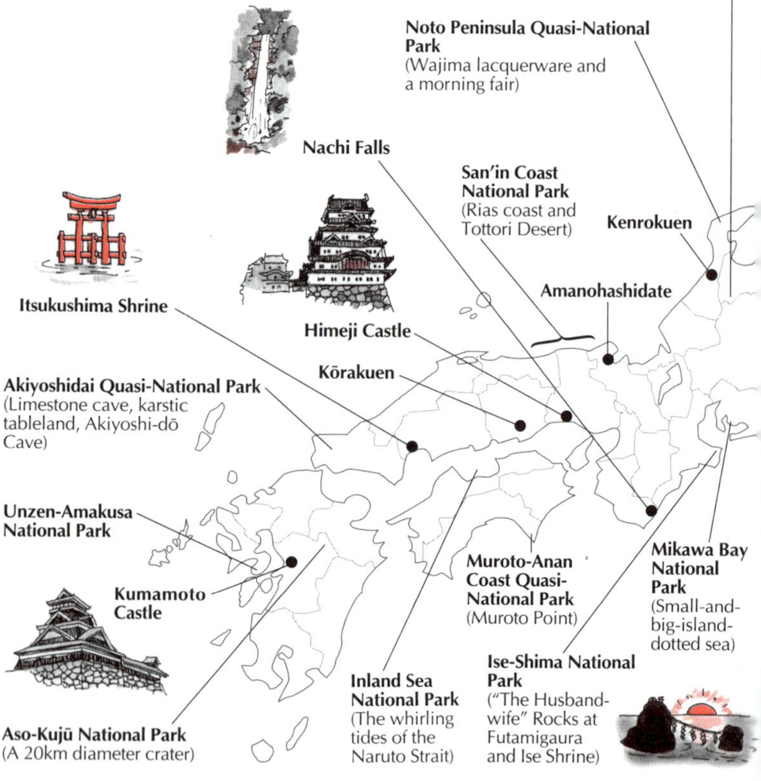

Three Famous Gardens • 三名園

- Kairakuen (Ibaraki)
  偕楽園（茨城）
- Kenrokuen (Ishikawa)
  兼六園（石川）
- Kōrakuen (Okayama)
  後楽園（岡山）

Three Famous Castles • 三名城

- Himeji Castle (Hyōgo)
  姫路城（兵庫）
- Matsumoto Castle (Nagano)
  松本城（長野）
- Kumamoto Castle (Kumamoto)
  熊本城（熊本）

Three Famous Waterfalls • 三名瀑

- Nachi Falls (Wakayama)
  那智の滝（和歌山）
- Kegon Falls (Tochigi)
  華厳の滝（栃木）
- Fukuroda Falls (Ibaraki)
  袋田の滝（茨城）

Tōkyō—10 Recommended Trips
東京のおすすめコース・ベスト10

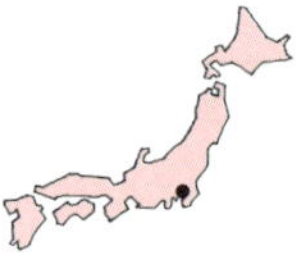

Tōkyō, one of the biggest cities in the world, is the main center of politics, economy, culture, transportation and other activities in Japan. The highest state bodies such as the Diet and the Supreme Court are located there, as are the headquarters of major companies and financial organizations, and fine & applied arts museums that are well worth seeing.

東京は世界でも有数の巨大都市に数えられ、日本の政治、経済、文化、交通などあらゆる活動の中心となっている。国会議事堂や最高裁判所などの最高機関だけでなく、大手会社や金融の本社、美術館、博物館なども集中しており、観光地としての見ごたえも十分にある。

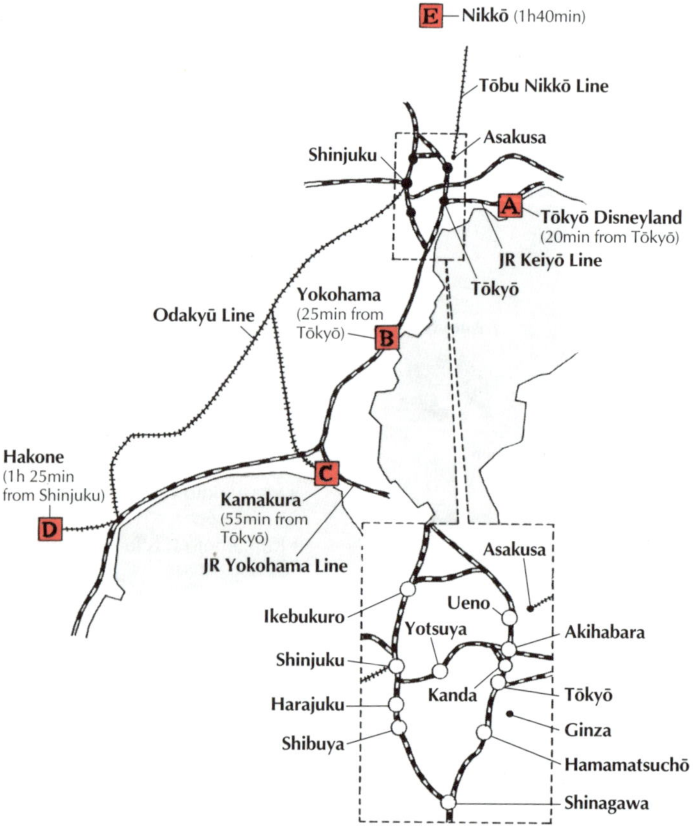

Tōkyō Metropolitan Area • 東京都内

1 The Imperial Palace & Akasaka • 皇居／赤坂

JR Tōkyō Station—The Palace Garden—Nijūbashi Bridge—Imperial Palace East Garden (the Edo Castle ruins)—The Japanese Diet Building—National Theater (the theater for traditional performing arts)—Akasaka Palatial Reception Hall—JR Yotsuya Station

JR東京駅……皇居外苑……二重橋……皇居東御苑（江戸城天守閣跡）……国会議事堂……国立劇場（伝統芸能が上演される）……迎賓館、赤坂離宮……JR四ツ谷駅

2 Ginza & Shiba • 銀座／芝

Subway Ginza Station—Chūōdōri Street (department stores, specialty shops, movie theaters)—Kabukiza Theater—JR Hamamatsuchō Station—Hamarikyū Detached Palace Garden (a villa belonging to a counsel of the Shōgun Tokugawa)—Tōkyō Tower (sightseers can view Mt. Fuji and Izu Peninsula from the 333m-high tower)

地下鉄銀座駅……銀座中央通り（デパートや高級専門店、映画館など）……歌舞伎座……JR浜松町駅……浜離宮恩賜庭園（徳川家の大名庭園）……東京タワー（333m、伊豆、富士山の展望も可能）

3 Shinjuku • 新宿

Subway Nishi-shinjuku Station—Tōkyō Metropolitan Building (the 45th floor is open to the public as an observantory from which all of Tōkyō can be viewed)—Kabukichō (an amusement center)—Shinjuku Gyoen National Garden (French-, English- and Japanese-style gardens)—Subway Shinjuku-Gyoen-mae Station

地下鉄西新宿駅……東京都庁舎（45階の展望台に昇り、東京を全望することができる）……歌舞伎町（歓楽街）……新宿御苑（フランス庭園、イギリス庭園、日本庭園もある）……地下鉄新宿御苑前駅

4 Harajuku & Aoyama • 原宿／青山

JR Harajuku Station—NHK Broadcasting Center (Japan's latest broadcasting technical equipment is used in TV and radio studios, which are partially open to the public)—Meiji Shrine (dedicated to Meiji Emperor who was a significant force in modernizing the country, famous 12m-high *torii*)—Takeshitadōri, Omotesandō, Aoyamadōri (shopping streets)—Nezu Museum (Oriental classic arts, tea ceremony utensils)—Jingū Gaien (Jingū Baseball Stadium, National Stadium)—Subway Gaienmae Station

JR原宿駅……NHK放送センター（日本最新の放送機器を使ったTV、ラジオスタジオが一部公開されている）……明治神宮（日本の近代化に尽力した明治天皇が祭ってある。高さ12mの鳥居が有名）……竹下通り、表参道、青山通り（ショッピング）……根津美術館（東洋の古美術、茶器など）……神宮外苑（神宮球場、国立競技場）……地下鉄外苑前駅

5 Asakusa & Ueno • 浅草／上野

Subway Asakusa Station—Kaminarimon (gods of Wind and Thunder stand on both sides of Thunder Gate), Sensōji, Nakamise (a covered shopping street lined with souvenir shops which gives poetic charm to Asakusa)—JR Ueno Station—Ueno Park (the famous place for cherry blossom viewing, Tōshōgū Shrine, Kan'eiji)—Tōkyō National Museum (Japanese fine and applied arts; historical and artistic objects of Asian countries; Hōryūji temple treasures)—Ameya-Yokochō (between Ueno and Okachimachi Stations, a narrow pedestrian mall lined with many discount stores)—Akihabara (an electronic shopping mall)—JR Akihabara Station

地下鉄浅草駅……雷門（風神が門の両脇に立つ）、浅草寺、仲見世（土産物店が並ぶ、浅草の風物詩）……JR上野駅……上野恩賜公園（花見の名所、東照宮、寛永寺）……東京国立博物館（日本の工芸・美術品、アジア諸国の美術品、法隆寺の宝物）……アメ屋横丁（上野、御徒町駅間のディスカウントショッピング通り）……JR秋葉原駅（秋葉原電気店街）

Tōkyō Suburbs • 東京近郊

A Tōkyō Disneyland • 東京ディズニーランド

JR Maihama Station：JR舞浜駅

- 6 theme lands: World Bazar, Adventureland, Westerland, Critter Country, Fantasyland and Tomorrowland
  6つのテーマランド：古き良きアメリカの街並、冒険とロマンの世界、西部開拓時代のアメリカ、小動物のくに、夢と童話の世界、宇宙と未来の世界を楽しめる。

B Yokohama • 横浜

JR Ishikawachō Station：JR石川町駅

- China Town (Kantei Shrine to the spirit of Kan'u, more than 200 restaurants)
  中華街（関羽（かんう）を祭った関帝廟や200店もの料理店）
- Landmark Tower (70 floors, the tallest building in Japan)
  ランドマークタワー（地上70階、日本一の高さの建物）

C Kamakura • 鎌倉

JR Kamakura Station：JR鎌倉駅

- Kōtokuin (Kamakura Great Buddha)
  高徳院（鎌倉大仏）
- Engakuji, Kenchōji (Zen temples)
  円覚寺、建長寺（禅宗寺院）

D Hakone • 箱根

Hakone-Yumoto Station/Odakyū Line (Hakone railway and cable cars are available as local transportation)：小田急線箱根湯本駅（箱根では登山鉄道とケーブルカーを利用する。）

- Lake Ashinoko (a lake caused by volcanic eruptions)
  芦ノ湖（箱根火山の爆発でできた湖）
- Hakone Yumoto Hot Springs (old hot springs, many Japanese-style inns)
  箱根湯本温泉（昔からの温泉で、日本旅館も多い）

E Nikkō • 日光

Nikkō Station/Tōbu Nikkō Line：東武日光線東武日光駅

- Tōshōgū Shrine (gaudiness on which the Tokugawa family spent their wealth)
  東照宮（徳川家の財力を注ぎこんだきらびやかさ）
- Kegon Falls (a dynamic 99m waterfall that runs from Lake Chūzenji.)
  華厳の滝（落差99mで迫力満点、水源は中禅寺湖）

Kyōto—10 Recommended Trips
京都のおすすめコース・ベスト10

Having been the capital of Japan for more than a thousand years after 794, Kyōto has many cultural sight-seeing spots which the Japanese take pride in. Over 250 shrines, as many as 1,600 temples and other cultural properties of the long history of the city impress visitors. Kyōto also boasts several excellent museums, including the Kyōto National Museum.

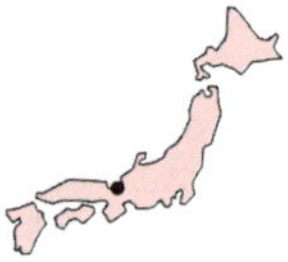

794年以来千余年にわたって日本の都として栄えた京都は、世界に誇る日本の文化観光都市である。250を超す神社や1,600余におよぶ寺院、数々の文化財が長い歴史を感じさせてくれる。京都にはまた、京都国立博物館などのすばらしい博物館がある。

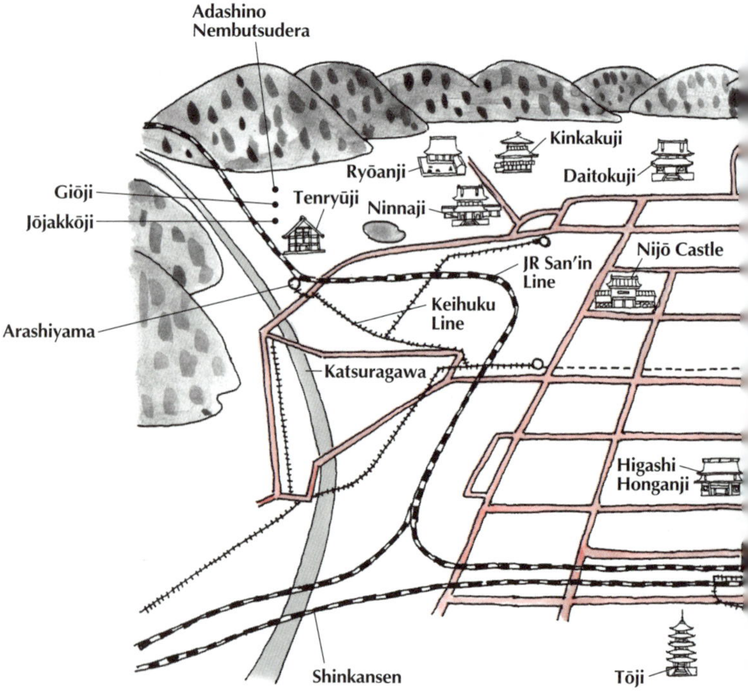

1 Kurama Station/Eizan Line—Kuramadera (the young warrior Minamoto no Yoshitsune is said to have led an ascetic life in Mt. Kurama)—Kibune Shrine (the path to Kibune shrine is heavily wooded, a deity of marriage is enshrined there)

叡山電鉄鞍馬駅……鞍馬寺（牛若丸が修行したといわれる鞍馬山）……貴船神社（貴船神社への道はうっそうと樹木の茂る道、良縁の神様）

2 Ōhara Bus Stop—Sanzen'in (famous for radiant autumn foliage)—Jakkōin (an isolated nunnery in Ōhara village)

バス停大原……三千院（紅葉の名所）……寂光院（大原の里にたたずむ静かな尼寺）

Oharame
(Woman peddler from Ōhara who peddles brushwood or firewood)

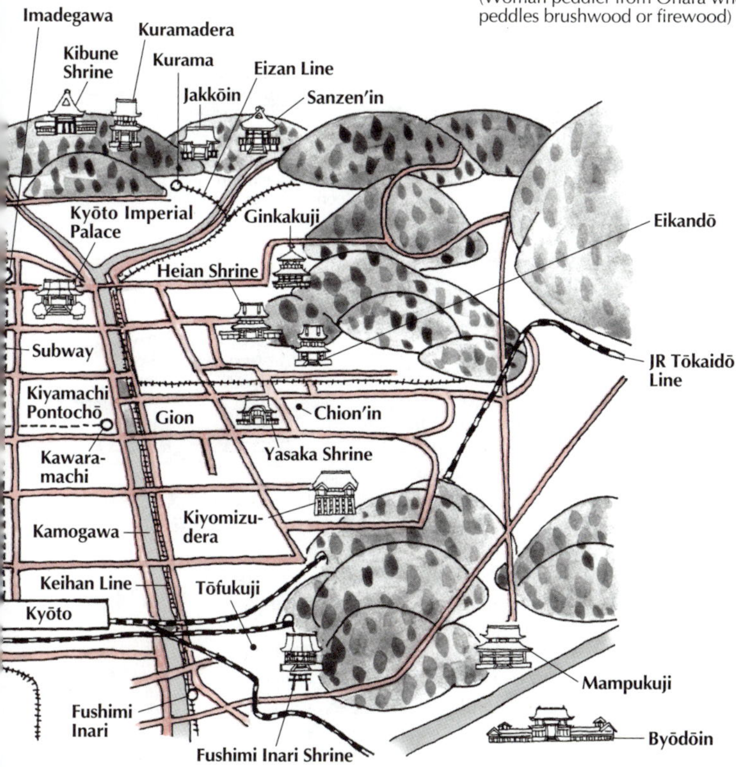

Rakusei (Western Part of Kyōto) • 洛西

3 Stroll through Sagano—Arashiyama Station/Keifuku Line—Tenryūji (the temple has a beautiful garden with Arashiyama forming a scenic backdrop)—Jōjakkōji (known as the temple where the *Ogura hyakunin isshu* was compiled)—Giōji (the temple related to *The Tales of the Heike*)—Adashino Nembutsuji (8,000 stone Buddhist images and tombstones for people who die leaving no one to tend to their graves)

嵯峨野散策……京福嵐山駅……天竜寺（嵐山を借景とした名園がある）……常寂光寺（ここで小倉百人一首が編さんされた）……祇王寺（平家物語ゆかりの寺院）……化野念仏寺（無縁仏の8,000体の石仏や石塔がある）

4 Daitokujimae Bus Stop—Daitokuji (the temple where Sen no Rikyū created the tea ceremony)—Kinkakuji (the gorgeous Golden Pavilion)—Ryōanji (a famous Japanese rock garden)—Ninnaji (the main hall is famous as originally being part of the imperial palace)

バス停大徳寺前……大徳寺（千利休が茶道を完成させた寺）……金閣寺（金箔が施された楼閣は豪華）……竜安寺（石庭で有名な枯山水庭園がある）……仁和寺（京都御所から移した金堂が有名）

Ryōanji rock garden
(Fifteen rocks are placed at a ratio of 7:5:3)

Rakuchū (Central Kyōto) • 洛中

5 Subway Imadegawa Station—Kyōto Imperial Palace (Emperor's residence up until the Meiji Restoration)—Nijō Castle (the shogun Tokugawa Ieyasu's lodging when he visited Kyōto)—Higashi Honganji (this huge wooden temple is famous for Goeidō)—Tōji (the tallest five-tiered pagoda in Japan)

地下鉄今出川駅……京都御所（明治維新までの天皇の住居）……二条城（家康の上洛の際の宿舎）……東本願寺（大木造建築、御影堂が有名）……東寺（我が国最大の五重塔がある）

6 Shijōkawaramachi Bus Stop—Kiyamachi (many bars and restaurants are lined up from north to south along the Takase River)—Pontochō (the area extending between the Kamo and Takase Rivers where there are many upscale Japanese restaurants and you can sometimes see *maiko*)

バス停四条河原町……木屋町（高瀬川に沿って南北に続く飲み屋街）……先斗町（鴨川と高瀬川に沿って続く料理処、多くの舞妓さんが行き交う）

Rakutō/Higashiyama (Eastern Part of Kyōto) • 洛東（東山）

7 Canalside Walk for Meditating—Ginkakuji-michi Bus Stop—Ginkakuji (representative architecture in Higashiyama culture)—Eikandō (renowned for its crimson foliage)—Nanzenji (a famous main gate)—Heian Shrine (beautiful vermilion painted pillars and gardens)

哲学の道（疏水べりを思索しながら散策）……バス停銀閣寺道……銀閣寺（東山文化の象徴）……永観寺（紅葉の名所）……南禅寺（三門が有名）……平安神宮（朱塗りの柱と庭園が美しい）

8 Gion Bus Stop—Gion (guests enjoy drinks and Japanese dishes while being entertained by *maiko* dancers)—Yasaka Shrine (people pray here for success in business)—Chion'in (famous as the largest two-story Sammon Gate in Japan, at a height of 24m)—Kiyomizudera (a marvelous view from the main hall, built on a towering scaffold)

バス停祇園……祇園（舞妓の踊りを楽しみながら、食事をする）……八坂神社（商売繁盛の神社）……知恩院（高さ24mの三門は我国最大の楼門）……清水寺（清水の舞台で名高い本堂からの眺めは最高）

Rakunan (Southern Part of Kyōto) • 洛南

9 JR Ōbaku Station—Mampukuji (an unusual Chinese Ming-style Zen temple)—JR Uji Station—Byōdōin (an elegant Phoenix Hall)

JR黄檗駅……万福寺（異国情緒がただよう中国明様式の禅寺）……JR宇治駅……平等院（優美な姿の鳳凰堂）

10 Fushimi Inari Station/Keihan Line—Fushimi Inari Shrine (the headqurters of Inari shrines all over Japan; the fox deity, a form of animism, guards the shrine; people pray for abundant crops and prosperous business)—Tōfukuji (one of the five most important Zen temple in Kyōto, a famous Japanese rock garden called Hōjō)

京阪伏見稲荷駅……伏見稲荷大社（日本全国の稲荷神社の総本山、きつねは稲荷神社の守護神、五穀豊穣・商売繁盛を願う神社）……東福寺（京都五山のひとつ、方丈庭園は枯山水式庭園）

Nara—5 Recommended Trips
奈良のおすすめコース・ベスト5

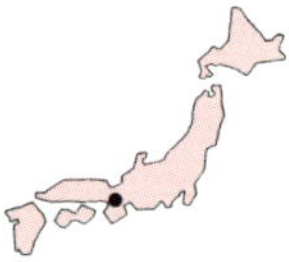

As described in ancient poetry, Nara is a wonderful place blessed with abundant nature. Its cultural property, temples, and historical spots attract many people. Nara has been the theme of many beloved Japanese poems, and is known and favored as the home of literature.

「大和(奈良)は国のまほろば(すぐれてよい所)」と昔からいわれるように、豊かな自然に恵まれ、文化財や社寺、史跡などが人々の心を引きつける。また奈良を題材にしたすぐれた歌も多く、文学の故郷としての魅力も大いにある。

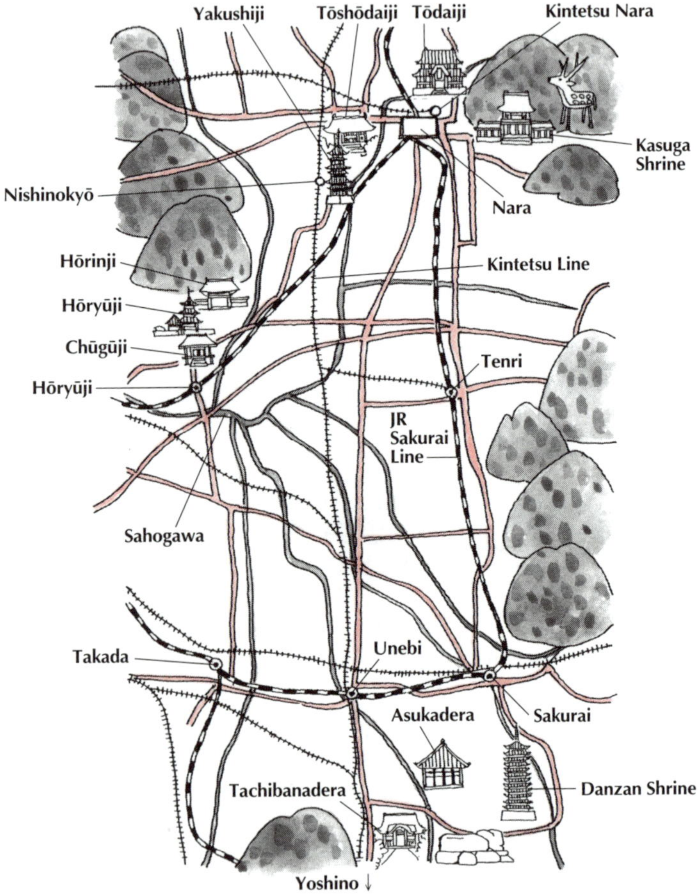

1 Nara City Walk • 奈良市街地散策

Nara Station/Kintetsu Line—Nara Park (a huge park including famous spots such as Tōdaiji, Shōsōin, Kasuga Shrine, Wakakusayama, etc.)

近鉄奈良駅……奈良公園（東大寺、正倉院、春日大社、若草山などの名所が含まれる広大な公園）

2 Around Nishinokyō • 西ノ京めぐり

Nishinokyō Station/Kintetsu Line—Yakushiji (unique architecture featuring three-tiered pagodas at the east and west sides)—Tōshōdaiji (founded by the Chinese priest Ganjin, the largest existing example of Tempyō architecture, with beautiful entasis pillars)

近鉄西ノ京駅……薬師寺（東西に三重の塔がそれぞれ配される独特の構成）……唐招提寺（唐の高僧鑑真による創建。エンタシスの柱が美しい現存する最大の天平建築）

3 Ikaruga no sato • 斑鳩の里

JR Hōryūji Station—Hōryūji (a vast treasure house of the Asuka art including the world's oldest wooden building, Buddhist statues and objects of art preserved as national treasures)—Hōrinji, Chūgūji, Hokkiji (old temples related to Shōtoku Taishi, the father of Japanese Buddhism)

JR法隆寺駅……法隆寺（世界最古の木造建築物や国宝の仏像や美術品も多く飛鳥美術の宝庫）……法輪寺、中宮寺、法起寺など、聖徳太子ゆかりの古寺が多い。

4 Hiking in Asuka • 飛鳥路ハイキング

JR Sakurai Station—Danzan Shrine (the sacred place dedicated to the memory of Fujiwara Kamatari)—Tōnomine—Ishibutai (the largest tomb made of rocks: horizontal cave style)—Tachibanadera (Shōtōku Taishi's birthplace)—Asukadera (the oldest temple founded by Soga no Umako)

JR桜井駅……多武峰……談山神社（藤原鎌足を祭る）……石舞台（日本で最大級の横穴式石室）……橘寺（聖徳太子誕生の地）……飛鳥寺（蘇我馬子が創建した日本最古の本格的寺院）

5 Yoshino Cherry-blossom Viewing • 吉野の花見

Yoshino Station/Kintetsu Yoshino Line—Yoshinoyama Station (by ropeway from Sembonguchi Station)—Kimpusenji (the center of Shugendō sect)—Chikurin'in (a founder of archery)

近鉄吉野駅……吉野山駅（千本口駅よりロープウエーを利用）……金峯山寺（修験道の修行道場）……竹林院（弓道の開祖）

ONSEN (HOT SPRING)
温泉

Japan is a volcanic land with more than 2,000 hot spring resorts all over the country. Generally, the temperature of the hot spring water is higher than 25°C (77°F). Hot spring water is said to be good for the treatment of chronic disease (rheumatism, neuralgia, gastroenteric disorders, respiratory disorders, etc.) and the promotion of health. Japanese people enjoy spas, particularly open-air baths set in natural surroundings.

火山国である日本には、全国に2,000以上の温泉地がある。一般に温泉のわき出口の温度は25℃以上である。温泉は慢性疾患（リューマチ、神経痛、呼吸障害、胃腸疾患など）の治癒や健康増進などに効能がある。日本人は温泉を好み、自然と触れ合う露天風呂を楽しむ人も多い。

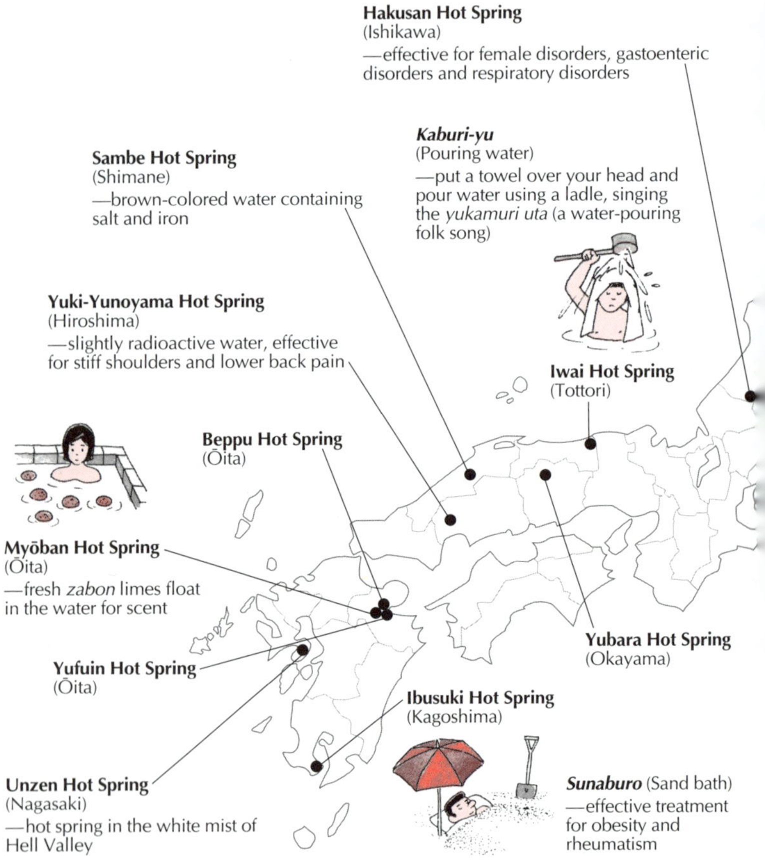

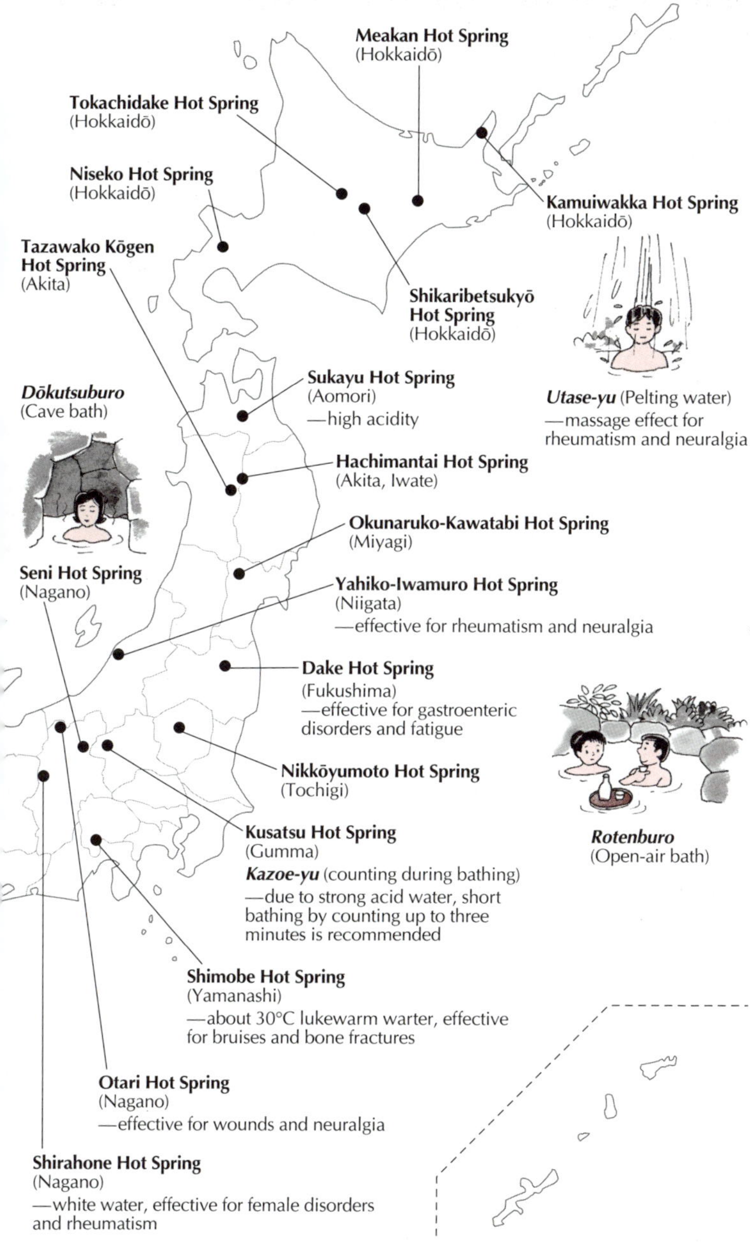
Meakan Hot Spring
(Hokkaidō)
Tokachidake Hot Spring
(Hokkaidō)
Niseko Hot Spring
(Hokkaidō)
Kamuiwakka Hot Spring
(Hokkaidō)
Tazawako Kōgen
Hot Spring
(Akita)
Shikaribetsukyō
Hot Spring
(Hokkaidō)
Sukayu Hot Spring
(Aomori)
—high acidity
Dōkutsuburo
(Cave bath)
Utase-yu (Pelting water)
—massage effect for
rheumatism and neuralgia
Hachimantai Hot Spring
(Akita, Iwate)
Okunaruko-Kawatabi Hot Spring
(Miyagi)
Seni Hot Spring
(Nagano)
Yahiko-Iwamuro Hot Spring
(Niigata)
—effective for rheumatism and neuralgia
Dake Hot Spring
(Fukushima)
—effective for gastroenteric
disorders and fatigue
Nikkōyumoto Hot Spring
(Tochigi)
Kusatsu Hot Spring
(Gumma)
Kazoe-yu (counting during bathing)
—due to strong acid water, short
bathing by counting up to three
minutes is recommended
Rotenburo
(Open-air bath)
Shimobe Hot Spring
(Yamanashi)
—about 30°C lukewarm warter, effective
for bruises and bone fractures
Otari Hot Spring
(Nagano)
—effective for wounds and neuralgia
Shirahone Hot Spring
(Nagano)
—white water, effective for female disorders
and rheumatism

TRADITIONAL JAPANESE ARTICLES
日本的小物

Chōchin (Paper Lantern) • ちょうちん

Made of thin bamboo sticks and paper, these foldable lanterns were portable lights before, but nowadays are used in festivals or as ornaments.

竹ひごと紙でできていて、折りたたむことができる。携行用の照明器具だが、今では祭りや装飾用に使われる。

Uchiwa • うちわ

A kind of fan that is made from paper or silk pasted over a thin bamboo bone structure. Fan with *uchiwa* to make breeze.

細い竹を骨として、紙や絹を張って柄を付けたもので、あおいで風を起こす。

Sensu • 扇子

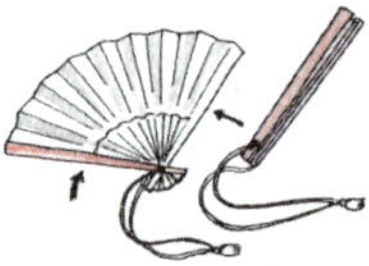

The *uchiwa* was imported from China and developed into *sensu* (a folding style fan) in Japan. The *suehirogari* (skirt) shape of *sensu* is said to be a lucky symbol.

中国から伝わった「うちわ」を日本人が折りたたみ式にした。末広がりが幸運の象徴といわれる。

Hanten • はんてん

A kimono-style short coat with quilting regularly worn by those living in cold areas.

中に綿の入った着物式の上着、寒い地域の人々はよく着る。

Kappōgi • かっぽう着

Japanese-style apron mostly worn for cooking. The sleeves prevent the inner sleeves from getting wet or dirty.

炊事の時に着る日本独特のエプロン。袖がついているので、着物や服の袖がぬれたり汚れたりしない。

Soroban (Japanese Abacus) • そろばん

An old-style manual calculator. The ball on the top line indicates "five" while the lower balls indicate "one" each. Calculations are made based on the decimal system.

計算をするための道具。上の玉が5、下の玉がそれぞれ1を示し、10進法で計算する。

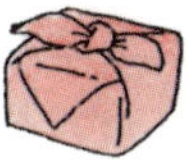

Furoshiki Magic
ふろしきマジック

A piece of *furoshiki* wraps almost anything. Let's learn Japanese-style wrapping!
1枚の布でなんでも包んでしまうふろしき。日本独特のラッピングをマスターしよう。

●How to wrap a box • 箱の包み方

①

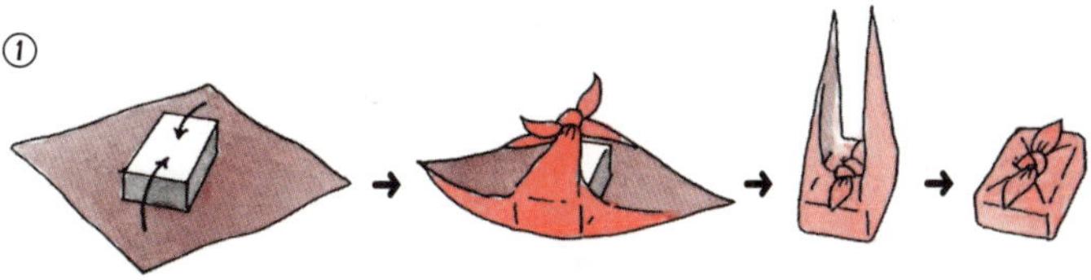

②

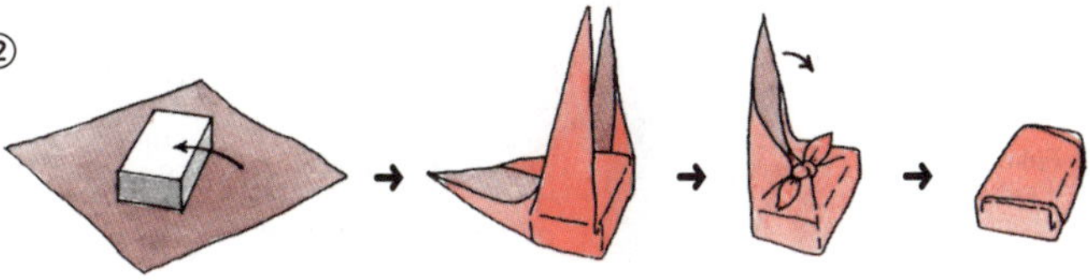

●How to wrap a round thing • 丸いものの包み方

●How to wrap bottles • びんの包み方

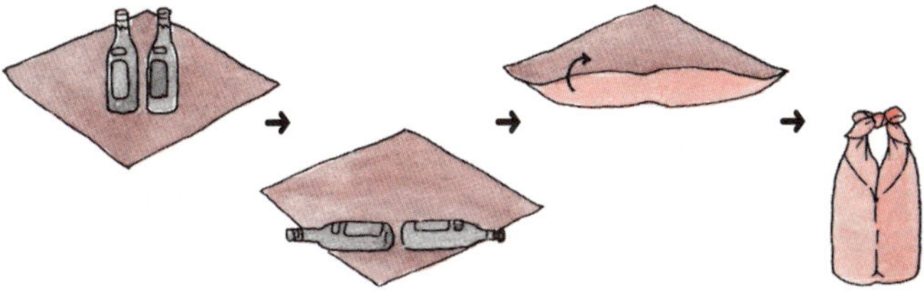

LUCKY TALISMANS
縁起物

To wish for good health, safety or prosperity in business, people buy the following small lucky talismans and display them at home.

健康、安全、商売繁盛など幸運が訪れるように、神社などでこれらの小物を買い求めて飾る。

Shichifukujin (The Seven Deities of Good Fortune) • 七福神

Shichifukujin are the seven deities that bring good fortune.

七福神は福をもたらす7人の神である。

Manekineko • 招き猫

Manekineko are displayed in restaurants and shops in windows or on shelves, to invite customers and money in.

客やお金を招くように、食堂や店先の棚などに飾られている。

Daruma • だるま

One eye is painted on while making a wish, and the other eye is drawn after the wish has come true.

願をかけて片目を書き入れ、願い事がかなった時、もう片方の目玉を書き足す。

JIKKAN JŪNISHI

十干十二支

Eto is a combination of *jikkan* or ten calendar signs and *jūnishi* or twelve zodiac signs (60 signs) which were composed in China more than 1,000 years ago to indicate the day, month, year, time and direction. These days it is common for New Year's cards to have a picture of the animal of the new year.

十干（幹）と十二支（枝）を組み合わせたもの（60組）を干支（えと）と呼び、紀元前1,000年以上も前に中国でつくられ、日、月、年、時刻、方位を示すために用いる。今日では、年に当てられた動物の絵を年賀状に描く習慣がある。

After a cycle, one sign lags. In 60 years, it comes back to the original position.
一周回ると、一つずつずれ、60年でもとにもどる。

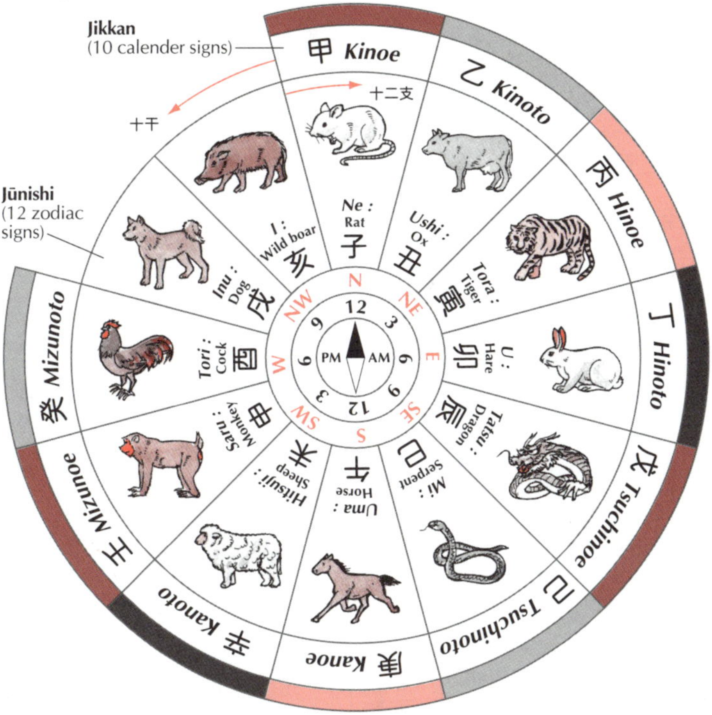

"Man of the Year" & "Woman of the Year" • 年男／年女

People are called this when the sign of the year they were born in cycles back.
自分の生まれた年の十二支が12年に1度回ってきた時に、このように呼ばれる。

JAPANESE-ENGLISH

和製英語

In the process of westernization, some foreign words in Japan were modified and adopted into a hybrid language called Japanese-English. Some Japanese assume these words are real English.

日本人の生活が欧米化する中で、独自につくりだした横文字文化がある。それが和製英語であり、これを英語だと勘違いしている人もいる。

Konsento • コンセント

Handoru • ハンドル

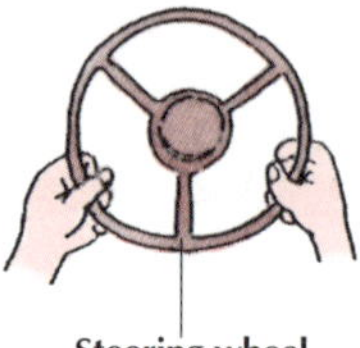

Hotchikisu • ホッチキス

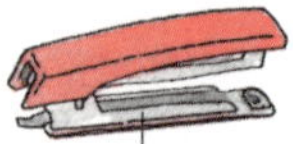

Mōningu-sābisu • モーニング・サービス

Herusu-mētā • ヘルスメーター

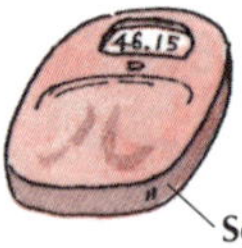

Kafusubotan • カフスボタン

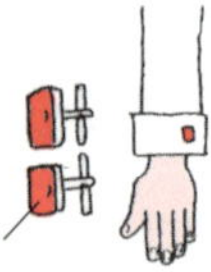

Pantī-sutokkingu • パンティーストッキング

Waishatsu • ワイシャツ

Pasokon • パソコン

PART 4

The Shape of Japan Today

今日の日本の姿

POPULATION
人口

The population of Japan is 125,568,504, the sixth largest in the world. Nearly half is concentrated around the Tōkyō, Nagoya and Ōsaka metropolitan areas. (Management and Coordination Agency, 1995)

日本の人口は125,568,504人で世界6位である。首都圏、名古屋圏、大阪圏の3大都市に日本の人口の半分近くが集中している。(総務庁、1995)

6th – Japan

1st – China

2nd – India

3rd – U.S.A.

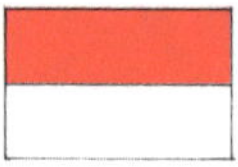

4th – Indonesia

5th – Brazil

POPULATION DENSITY
人口密度

(Unit: person 人/km²)

Japan – 331

China – 124

India – 279

U.S.A. – 28

Indonesia – 101

Brazil – 18

(United Nations 国連 1994)

POPULATION TRENDS
人口動態

The average life span and the number of the elderly (14% over 65) is increasing accordingly. The population as a whole is aging.

平均寿命がのび、全人口に占める65歳以上の老人の割合が14%としだいに高くなり、人口全体が高齢化している。

(Rate per 1,000 persons 1,000人当たりの率)

Birthrate 出生率	Mortality rate 死亡率	Natural growth 自然増加率	Average life span 平均寿命	
			Males 男	Females 女
9.5	7.4	2.1	76.36	82.84

(Ministry of Health and Welfare 厚生省 1995)

RELIGION
宗教

Only 30% of the Japanese populace actually believe in a religious creed. However, religious observances, such as visiting shrines on New Year's Day and visiting ancestors' graves during *bon* holidays, have been incorporated into the ordinary customs and practices of their lives.

特定の信仰をもっている人は3割強であるが、正月に神社に初詣に出かけたり、盆には先祖の供養のために墓参りをしたりと、宗教的行事が日常の生活の中に習俗として浸透している。

BUDDHISM
仏教

The doctrines of Buddha was introduced to Japan via China and Korea. People pray at the foot of statues of the Buddha and Buddhist saints. Funerals are often Buddhist, and other Buddhist rituals have become a part of Japanese life.

中国、朝鮮を通じて移入された仏陀の教え。仏像や菩薩（ぼさつ）像を礼拝する。葬祭など日本人の生活に溶けこんでいる。

SHINTOISM
神道

Both nature deities (forest or mountain) and human deities (legendary figures, or outstanding people) are worshipped at shrines. People have *kamidana*, personal altars in their homes as well.

自然神（森や山の神）や人間神（偉人など）を神社に祭る。家庭では神棚のある家も多い。

CHRISTIANITY
キリスト教

This doctrine was first introduced by Francis Xavier. It exerted considerable influence during Japan's modernization and westernization, and over ways of thinking in the Meiji era.

ザビエルによって伝えられ、明治期には日本の近代化、西洋化、ものの考え方に大きな影響を与えた。

Number of Believers • 信者教

(Unit: person 人)

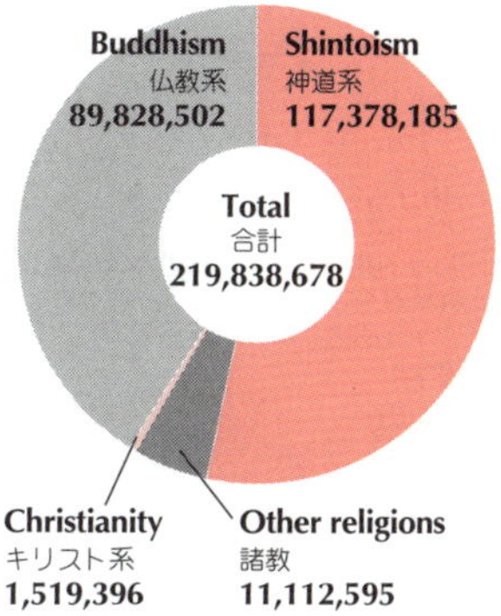

(Agency of Cultural Affairs 文化庁 1994)

JAPANESE MENTALITY
日本人の意識

KEY JAPANESE CONCEPTS FROM FOLKLORE AND PROVERBS
故事ことわざにみる日本人の心

Ishin-denshin • 以心伝心

Shared communication that needs no words.

言葉や文字はなくとも心で思っていることが相手に伝わる。

Onko-chishin • 温故知新

Preserving and respecting doctrines and manners handed down from old times helps one understand the new.

昔からのしきたりを十分に習熟したうえで、新しい知識や道理を知っていく。

Ishi no ue nimo sannen • 石の上にも三年

A cold stone becomes warm if one sits on it for three years. Difficult work or problematic matters will eventually be settled if one perseveres.

冷たい石でも三年座っていれば温かくなる。つらい仕事やいやなことも我慢すればうまくいくという忍耐の大切さ。

SOURCES OF JAPANESE PRIDE
日本人の誇り

(Multiple response 複数回答)

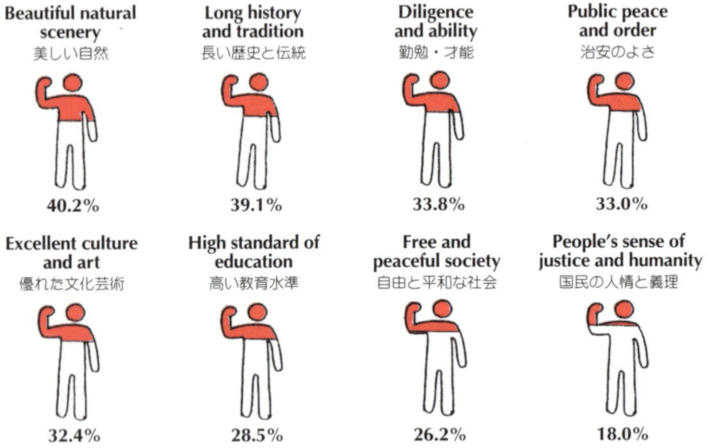

(Prime Minister's Office 総理府 1995)

NOBEL PRIZE WINNERS
ノーベル賞受賞者

Physics • 物理学賞

- **YUKAWA HIDEKI 湯川秀樹** (1907–1981) ❖ Awarded in 1949.
  For research in the meason theory and the theory of nonlocal fields.
  「中間子理論」と「非局所場理論」の研究。

- **TOMONAGA SHIN'ICHIRŌ 朝永振一郎** (1906–1979) ❖ Awarded in 1965.
  For research in the theory of quantum electrodynamics and the super-many-time theory.
  量子電気力学の「繰り込み理論」と「超多時間理論」の研究。

- **ESAKI REONA 江崎玲於奈** (1925–) ❖ Awarded in 1973.
  For research into "tunneling effects" of semi- and superconductors. Invention of what was later called the "Esaki diode."
  半導体、超電導体のトンネル効果の研究。エサキダイオードの発明。

Literature • 文学賞

- **KAWABATA YASUNARI 川端康成** (1899–1972) ❖ Awarded in 1968.
  For *Snow Country, The Izu Dancer* and other works.
  「雪国」「伊豆の踊子」などの作品に対して。

- **ŌE KENZABURŌ 大江健三郎** (1935–) ❖ Awarded in 1994.
  For *The Catch, The Silent Cry* and other works.
  「飼育」「万延元年のフットボール」などの作品に対して。

Peace • 平和賞

- **SATŌ EISAKU 佐藤栄作** (1901–1975) ❖ Awarded in 1974.
  For strategic promotion of Three Principles of Denuclearization.
  非核三原則政策の推進に対して。

Chemistry • 化学賞

- **FUKUI KEN'ICHI 福井謙一** (1918–) ❖ Awarded in 1981.
  For theoretical solution of chemical reaction. Research in frontier orbital theory.
  化学反応の理論的解明。「フロンティア電子理論」の研究。

Medicine and Physiology • 医学生理学賞

- **TONEGAWA SUSUMU 利根川進** (1939–) ❖ Awarded in 1987.
  For research in gene rearragement mechanism.
  抗体遺伝子の組み換え理論の研究。

EDUCATION

教育

The Japanese education system, which includes 9 years of compulsory education in elementary school and junior high school, is shown in the chart below. The school year begins in April and ends the following March of the next year. Some schools are run on the new 5-day schedule, while others are still on the 5 1/2-day plan.

小学校、中学校の計9年間の義務教育を含む学校体系は下の図のとおりである。1学年は4月に始まり、翌年の3月に終わる。現在週休2日制も取り入れられ、完全定着までの過渡期といえる。

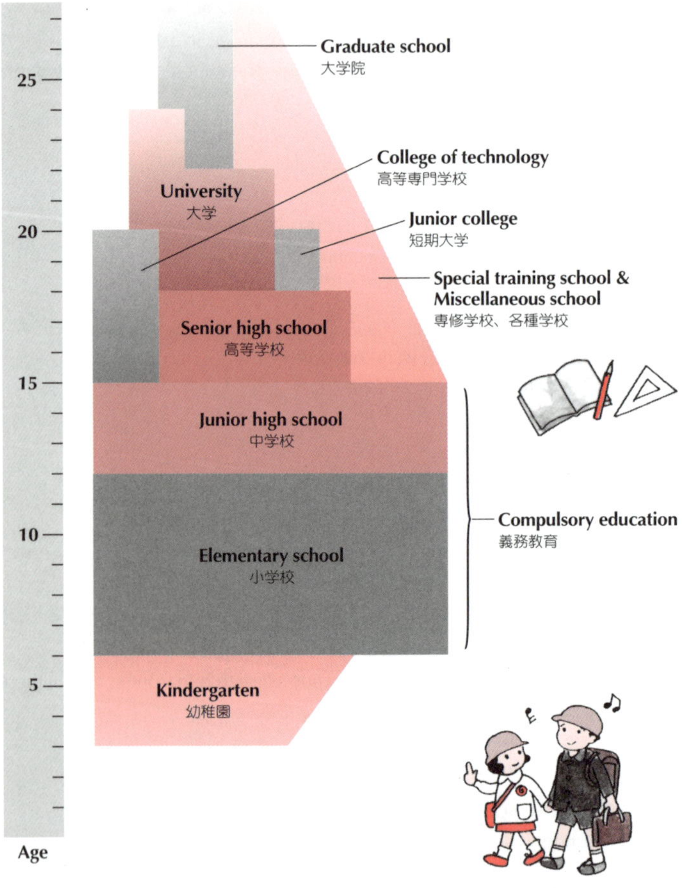

PRESCHOOL
保育所

A facility for child care under the jurisdiction of the Board of Health and Welfare. Trained staff take care of infants and small children in lieu of their busy parents.

厚生行政に基づく児童福祉施設の一つ。保護者がその乳幼児を保育できない場合、保護者に代わって保母が保育する。

KINDERGARTEN
幼稚園

One of the schools designated by the Education Law and under the jurisdiction of the Board of Education. Children receive a kind of preliminary education, experience group life, and learn basic social skills.

文部行政に基づく学校教育法の学校の一種。教諭によって保育がなされ、集団生活の体験や社会性がつちかわれる。

Age 対象年齢	**0–6 years old** 0〜6歳	**3–6 years old** 3歳から6歳
Care hours/day 保育時間／日	**In principle, 8-hour care (with evening care as well)** 原則として8時間保育（夜間保育もある）	**4 hours, on average** 標準は4時間保育
Content of care 保育内容	**Basic courtesies** 基本的な生活習慣 **Nap time** 昼寝 **Tea time** おやつ	**Monthly birthday party** お誕生会 **Coloring, *origami*** 絵・折り紙 **Singing** 歌
	Outdoor play 外遊び **Rhythmic dance and play** リズム遊戯	
Transportation to and from preschool 送迎	**Picked up by parents on foot or by bicycle** 父母（徒歩、自転車）	**Picked up by parents or school bus** 父母、スクールバス

ELEMENTARY SCHOOL
小学校

Children from 6 to 12 years of age (1st to 6th grade) have a compulsory elementary education. They usually walk to local elementary schools, where children of the same-age pupils study together in classrooms. One teacher takes charge of a class of about 40 pupils and, in principle, teaches all subjects.

6～12歳（1～6年生）の児童は6年間の初等教育を受けることが義務づけられており、通常、居住地域の小学校に徒歩で通う。同じ年齢の児童が1教室で学習する。1学級約40人の生徒を1人の教師が担任し、原則として全教科指導する。

The Elementary School Year • 小学校の1年間

- **Spring vacation (2 weeks)** 春休み
- ★**Graduation ceremony** 卒業式
- ★**School-ending ceremony** 終業式
- ★**The third term starts** 3学期開始
- **Winter vacation (2 weeks)** 冬休み
- **Art exhibition** 美術展
- **Concert** 音楽会
- **Field trip** 遠足
- **Sports day** 運動会

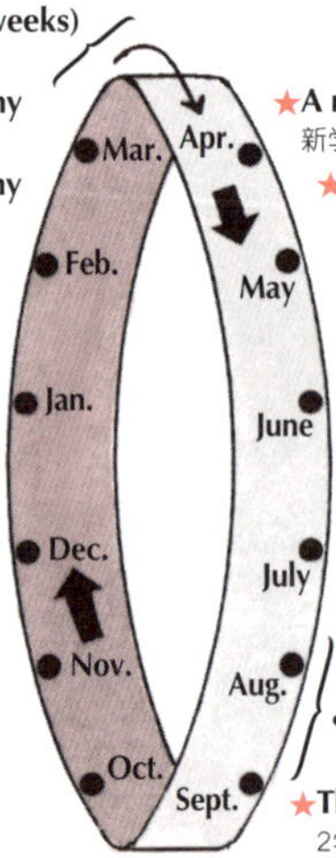

- ★**A new school year starts** 新学年開始
- ★**Enrollment ceremony** 入学式
- **Excursion** 遠足
- **Teachers visit children's homes** 家庭訪問
- **Parents' observation day and meetings with teachers** 参観日・懇談会
- **Summer vacation (6 weeks)** 夏休み
- **Swimming classes** 水泳教室
- ★**The second term starts** 2学期開始

Curriculum • 教科

Japanese, Arithmetic, Science, Social Studies, Music, Arts and Crafts, Gymnastics, Ethics and Home Economics (5th and 6th grades)

国語、算数、理科、社会、音楽、図画工作、体育、道徳、家庭科（5、6年生のみ）

School Schedule • 時間割

	Go to school：登校
8:30–8:45	**Morning assembly (all students attend)**：朝の会（全校朝礼）
8:45–9:30	**1st class**：第1校時
9:40–10:25	**2nd class**：第2校時
10:45–11:30	**3rd class**：第3校時
11:40–12:25	**4th class**：第4校時
12:25–13:05	**Lunch**：給食
13:05–13:25	**Recess**：遊び
13:25–13:45	**Cleaning duty**：全校清掃
13:45–14:20	**5th class**：第5校時
14:35–15:20	**6th class**：第6校時
15:20–15:30	**Home-class assembly**：終わりの会
15:30–17:00	**After school**：放課後
	Go home：下校

Lunch • 給食

Children take turns serving food prepared by cooks.

調理士によって作られた食事を、当番の児童が配る。

After-school Schedule • 下校後

50% of children in the 5th and 6th grades go to private "cram-schools" (*juku*) after regular school and 80% of children to piano or swimming lessons, etc. They also enjoy playing computer games, watching TV and reading comic books.

5年生、6年生の約5割が塾に行き、全体の8割がピアノや水泳などの習い事をしている。その他、コンピューターゲームをしたり、テレビを見たり、漫画を読んだりして過ごす。

Cleaning (Whole School) • 全校清掃

Every child cleans his/her assigned areas simultaneously.

全校生徒が、担当場所を一斉に掃除する。

JUNIOR HIGH SCHOOL
中学校

The remaining 3 years of the 9-year compulsory education consist of junior high school education. Most children in the 13–15 age group attend public junior high schools within their district, but some go to private schools.

9年間の義務教育の残りの3年間は中学校で受ける。対象者（13～15歳）の大部分は居住地域の公立中学へ行くが、私立中学へ通う者もいる。

Uniforms • 制服

Girls wear sailor-collar dresses or blazers; boys wear stiff-collar jackets. These days some schools have more modern uniforms. Summer uniforms are worn from June to September.

制服として、女子はセーラー服やブレザースーツ、男子は詰めえりの学生服を着る。近年、よりモダンなスタイルに変わりつつある中学校もある。6～9月は夏用制服を着用する。

School Life • 学校生活

In junior high school, teachers specialize in a particular area. English classes are also introduced. Students put much effort into studying for five regular tests a year and for high school entrance examinations, as well as participating in sports or club activities. To learn social-interaction skills, they take part in special events: the cultural festival (*bunkasai*), sports festival (*taiikusai*) and the school trip (*shūgaku ryokō*).

中学になると教科担任制となり、英語学習が始まる。年5回の定期テストが行われ、高校入試に向けての勉強と、運動部や文化部のクラブ活動に力を注ぐ。特別行事として、文化祭、体育祭、修学旅行があり、生徒はこれを通して共同生活を学ぶ。

SENIOR HIGH SCHOOL
高等学校

There are full-time, part-time, and correspondence high schools. In addition to regular courses, some schools offer more specialized studies such as industrial and agricultural sciences. Some 96.7% of junior high school graduates go on to senior high school. (Ministry of Education, 1995)

高校には全日制と定時制及び通信制があり、普通科のほかに、工業科や農業科など専門分野をより深く学習する課程もある。中学卒業者の96.7%が高校進学者である。(文部省、1995)

Curriculum • 教科

The curriculum consists of modern Japanese, Japanese classics, Chinese classics, mathematics, English, history, geography, politics, economics, chemistry, physics, biology, physical geography, health and physical education, technical arts, home economics, and art (music, fine arts, calligraphy). Students choose subjects with a view to university entrance examinations.

教科は、現代国語、古文、漢文、数学、英語、地理、歴史、公民、化学、物理、生物、地学、保健体育、技術家庭、芸術(音楽、美術、書道)で、大学への進路によって選択する科目が異なる。

School Trips • 修学旅行

Students make school excursions and overnight trips to places of cultural significance in Kyōto and Nara, Kyūshū, Hokkaidō, or even overseas.

学校生活の思い出に宿泊を伴う旅行をする。京都や奈良の文化財見学や、北海道、九州への旅、近年では海外へ旅行する学校もある。

Club Activities • クラブ活動

Sports clubs may build strong ties between seniors and juniors, a traditional but still-retained custom.

運動クラブのなかには、先輩、後輩の関係の残るクラブもある。

Cultural Festival • 文化祭

The cultural festival is a time when the students, as a club or a class team, display their accomplishments for all to see.

文化祭は生徒がクラブやクラスごとに成果を発表する場である。

UNIVERSITY
大学

45.2% of senior high school graduates go on to university or junior college. (Ministry of Education, 1995)

高等学校卒業者の45.2%（文部省、1995）が、大学もしくは短期大学に進学している。

Entrance Examination • 入学試験

Entrance Examinations are very competitive and difficult to pass. If a student fails, he/she attends a special school to prepare for next year's exam.

入学試験は競争率が高く、大変難しい。失敗すると、予備校で1年間勉強して次の年の試験に備える。

Cost of Enrollment • 入学時の必要経費

Private University • 私立大学

Enrollment, study and equipment fees in private schools average 4.6 million yen in Medicine and Dentistry, 1.04 million yen in Liberal Arts. Students may be asked to contribute to various endowment funds.

私立大学医歯系の入学金、授業料、施設費は、平均460万円で、文化系は104万円である。このほかに寄付金や学校債の費用が必要なところもある。

National University • 国立大学

Students pay but 710,000 yen to enroll and study.

入学金、授業料はあわせて71万円である。

Medicine and dentistry 医歯系　**Liberal arts** 文化系

(Ministry of Education 文部省 1994)

University Life • 大学生活

Graduating from university is not as difficult as entering, so once they pass the stressful entrance examinations many students prefer to enjoy student life rather than study hard.

卒業することが入学試験のように難しくないこともあり、厳しい受験戦争を勝ち抜いたあとは、のびのびと大学生活を楽しむ若者が多い。

Motivation for Part-time Jobs • アルバイトをする動機

- To make money for leisure-time activities.
  レジャー資金づくりのため。
- To make living more enjoyable.
  生活をゆとりあるものにするため。
- To buy luxury items.
  金額のはる商品を買うため。

Job Hunting • 就職活動

Groups of senior students wearing formal suits visit companies with a view to getting a job.

4年生になると就職に向けて、スーツ姿で会社訪問を始める。

Volunteer Work • ボランティア

Increasing numbers of students do volunteer work in their free time.

余暇を利用して、ボランティアなど社会的な活動をする学生が増えてきた。

Kompa (Social Gatherings) • コンパ

Parties are held with fellow club members, or to get to know students in other departments in or from other universities.

クラブ相互や他学部や他の大学との交流を兼ねたパーティーが開かれる。

THE COMPANY
会社

Lifetime employment and seniority systems once characterized Japanese companies, but in recent years the situation has been changing. Companies take on new staff (recent graduates) regularly each April.

年功序列、終身雇用の制度が日本の会社の大きな特徴であったが、近年変わりつつある。新入社員は、4月に定期採用される。

SALARYMEN
サラリーマン

Under the lifetime employment system, there is a give-and-take relationship between labor and management. Labor enjoy a steady salary (hence, "salarymen") and certain status, and in turn are loyal to the company.

終身雇用制度のもと、社員の安定した所得や、身分保障と会社への忠誠心で労使関係が成り立っている。

●A DAY IN THE LIFE OF A SALARYMAN

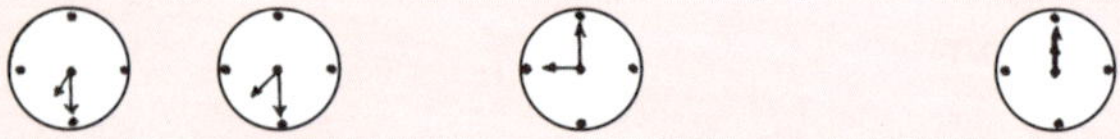

6:30	7:30	9:00	12:00
Get up 起床	**Commute** 通勤	**Morning work** 午前の仕事	**Lunch** 昼食

Lunch 昼食
- Pack lunch (from home)
  弁当
- Company dining room
  社員食堂
- Restaurant
  レストラン

Retirement System • 定年制

Most companies set 55–60 as the retirement age.

ほとんどの会社で55～60歳を定年退職の年齢と決めている。

Ringi System • 稟議制（りんぎせい）

In order to get consensus, the person in charge of a matter prepares a draft of a proposal and circulates it. The final decision is made by management.

担当者は起案書を関係者に順次、回し、承認を得て、最後に幹部の決裁を得る。

Labor Unions • 労働組合

Most unions in Japan are company unions, and labor disputes are rare. A "labor offensive"—asking for higher pay—is carried out every spring.

労働組合は、企業別に組織されることが多いが、労働争議は少ない。春闘は毎年行われる。

OFFICE LADIES
オフィス・レディ

The Equal Employment Opportunity Law was passed in 1986 to ensure that women have equal opportunities and working conditions to men. However, quite a few "office ladies" resign after marriage and/or childbirth.

男女雇用機会均等法が1986年に施行され、男女平等に働くことが可能になったが、結婚や出産で退職する女性も多い。

13:00 17:00 20:30 22:00

Lunch break
昼休み

Afternoon work
午後の仕事

Overtime
残業

Socializing with colleagues
仕事仲間とのつきあい

Return home
帰宅

POLITICS
政治

The Japanese government is composed of a legislative branch, an administrative branch and a judiciary branch. Each branch is independent of the others, in order to avoid concentration of power in any particular one. (Separation of the Three Powers)

国の政治は、国会、内閣、裁判所の3つの機関がそれぞれ独立して仕事をすすめ、一つの機関に力が集中しないようになっている。（三権分立）

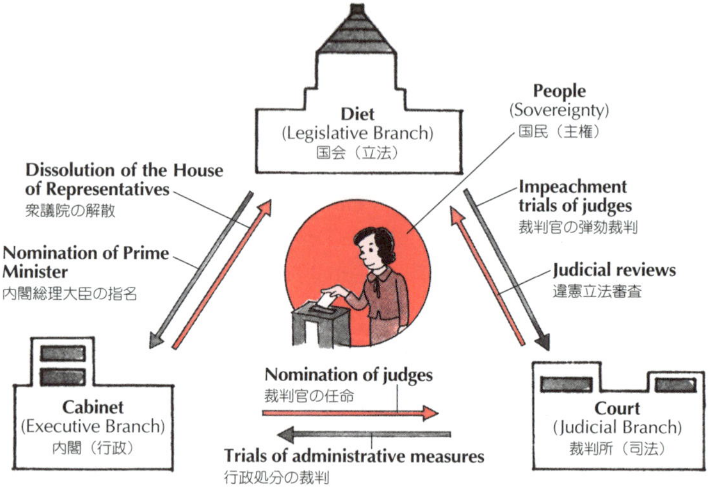

POLITICAL PARTIES
政党

After World War II, the Liberal Democratic Party (LDP) and the Social Democratic Party of Japan (SDPJ) became the two major parties, and for several decades the LDP was the ruling party. An LDP president always held the seat of Prime Minister. Lately, the public's distrust in politics has increased, which has led to the nomination of prime ministers from parties other than the LDP. The current parties consist of the LDP, the New Frontier Party, the Democratic Party of Japan, the Japanese Communist Party, the Social Democratic Party (the former SDPJ), the Taiyō Party, the New Party Sakigake, and the Kōmei.

戦後、自由民主党と日本社会党の2大政党のもと、自民党が政権をにぎり続け、総裁が首相の座についてきた。しかし、近年、国民の政治不信が高まり、最大政党自由民主党以外から首相を出すこともあった。現在、政党は自由民主党、新進党、民主党、日本共産党、社会民主党（旧日本社会党）、太陽党、新党さきがけ、公明党などがある。

DIET
国会

Diet members elected by the nation conduct the affairs of state. Based on the principles of democracy, the Diet, which consists of a two-chamber system, deliberates on and debates matters of national importance.

国民が選んだ国会議員が国の政治を行う。民主政治の考えのもと、慎重な審議が重ねられるよう二院制がとられている。

Diet System • 国会のしくみ

	House of Representatives 衆議院	House of Councillors 参議院
Number of Diet members 議員数	500	252
Term 任期	4 years 4年	6 years (half to be re-elected every 3 years) 6年（3年ごとに半数を改選）
Electoral eligibility 被選挙権	Age over 25 25歳以上	Age over 30 30歳以上
Dissolution 解散	Possible あり	Not possible なし

●DIET FUNCTIONS

① Makes laws.
法律をつくる。

② Decides government budget.
国の予算を決める。

③ Nominates Prime Minister from among Diet members.
内閣総理大臣を国会議員のなかから指名。

④ Conducts impeachment trials of judges.
裁判官の弾劾裁判。

Ordinary Diet Session : 通常国会

Yearly, for 150 days from January.
年1回、12月から150日間開会、法案の審議や国家予算の決定。

Extraordinary Diet Session : 臨時国会

After the elections or in time of national emergencies.
選挙後や緊急時。

Special Diet Session : 特別国会

To designate the Prime Minister.
内閣総理大臣を指名する。

CABINET
内閣

The Cabinet carries out the decisions of the Diet. The Chief executive office resides with the Prime Minister.

国会で決められたことを実際に行うのが内閣であり、その最高責任者が内閣総理大臣である。

Cabinet System • 内閣のしくみ

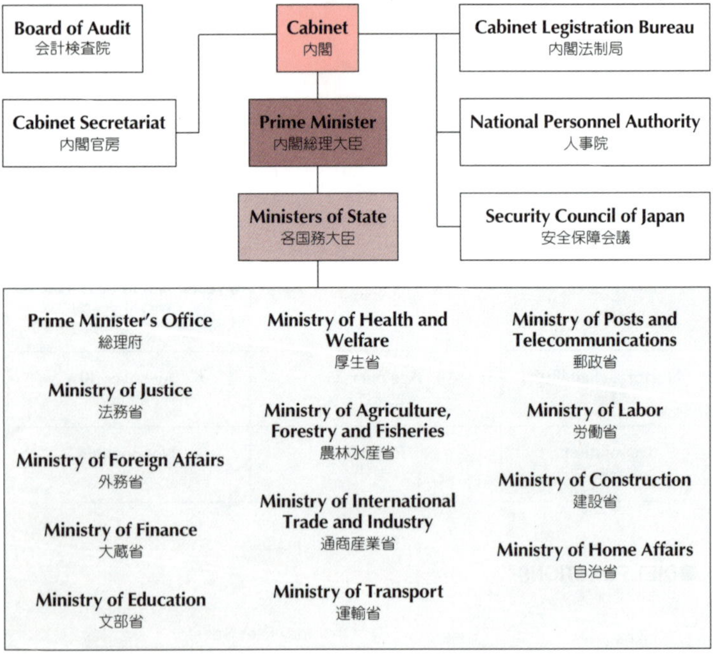

●CABINET FUNCTIONS

① Executes laws and attends state affairs.

法律を執行し、国務を行う。

② Prepares budget proposals and submits them to the Diet.

予算案を作成し、国会に提出する。

③ Nominates judges.

裁判官を任命する。

④ Handles diplomatic issues and agrees to treaties.

外交関係を処理したり、条約を締結する。

⑤ Establishes laws and institutions.

政令を制定する。

COURT
裁判所

The courts solve disputes based on the Constitution and laws that protect personal freedoms and rights.

裁判所は、憲法や法律に基づいて人々の争いごとを解決したり、国民の自由と権利を守る。

Court System • 裁判所のしくみ

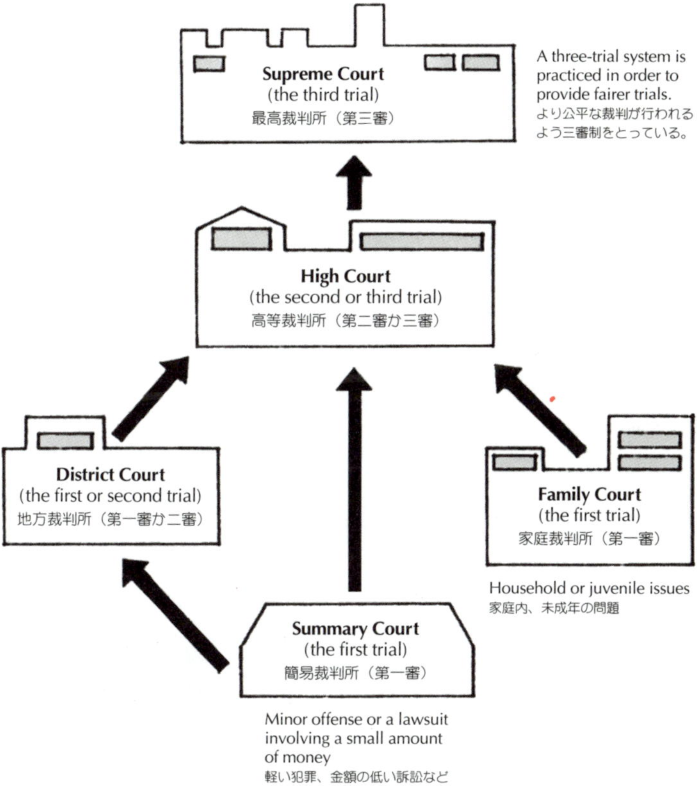

●COURT FUNCTIONS

① Presents fair judgment of disputes, based on to the law.

争いやもめごとを法にてらして公平に判断をくだす。

② Litigates in criminal, civil and administrative disputes.

刑事裁判、民事裁判、行政裁判をする。

ELECTION
選挙

Based on the principle that sovereignty resides in the people, every Japanese person over 20 years of age has the right to vote.

国民主権のもとに、20歳以上の国民は平等に選挙権をもつことができる。

House of Representatives • 衆議院

The election system consists of two voting methods: 300 seats are decided by single-seat constituency voting, and 200 by proportional representation in which seats are allocated to each party in proportion to the number of votes gained in the constituency balloting.

小選挙区・比例代表並立制：300議席は小選挙区制で、200議席は政党の得票率に応じ議席を配分する比例代表制で決定される。

House of Councillors • 参議院

A proportional representative system and an election based on electoral districts according to municipalities.

比例代表制と都道府県別選挙区制。

●ELECTION SYSTEM

① Public announcements are made：選挙の公示

② Candidates file their name：立候補の届出

- the House of Representatives: over 25 years old — 衆議院は25歳以上
- the House of Councillors: over 30 years old — 参議院は30歳以上

③ Election campaigns take place：選挙運動

Candidates can make speeches in public, in parks, in front of train stations, on street corners, etc., but they cannot visit voters' residences or proffer money or like incentives.

候補者は広場や駅前、街頭で演説ができる。戸別訪問や金品を贈ることはできない。

④ The people vote：投票

⑤ Ballots are counted and winners announced：開票と決定

THE CONSTITUTION
憲法

The Japanese Constitution, promulgated on November 3, 1946 and executed on May 3, 1947, is held together by three basic principles. It is comprised of a Preamble and 103 Articles.

1946（昭和21）年11月3日に公布され、翌年5月3日から施行された日本国憲法には、3つの基本原則がつらぬかれている。前文と103の条文から成りたっている。

THE THREE PRINCIPLES
基本三原則

Sovereignty of the People • 国民主権

People decide how the government should function.

国の政治のあり方を決めるのは、国民である。

Pacifism • 平和主義

The Japanese people forever renounce war in order to maintain peace.

世界の平和を永久に守るために戦争を放棄する。

Respect for Fundamental Human Rights • 基本的人権の尊重

Fundamental human rights are permanent and inalienable. They include the right to freedom, equality, life, suffrage, a fair trial.

基本的人権は侵すことのできない永久の権利である。自由権、平等権、社会権、参政権、請求権など。

THE EMPEROR IN THE CONSTITUTION
憲法と天皇

It is written in the Constitution that "The Emperor shall be the symbol of the State and of the unity of the people, deriving his position from the will of the people with whom resides sovereign power." The Emperor carries out the following official tasks: He officially appoints the Prime Minister as designated by the Diet. He officially appoints the Chief Judge of the Supreme Court as designated by the Cabinet. With advice and approval from the Cabinet, he performs the following acts in matters of state: promulgation of laws and treaties; convocation of the Diet; dissolution of the House of Representatives; proclamation of general elections; reception of foreign ambassadors and dignitaries; performance of ceremonial functions.

日本国憲法では、「天皇は、日本国の象徴であり日本国民統合の象徴であって、この地位は、主権の存する日本国民の総意に基づく。」と書かれ、天皇の仕事として、次のことをあげている。国会の指名に基づいて内閣総理大臣を任命する。内閣の指名に基づいて最高裁判所長官を任命する。内閣の助言と承認により告示に関する仕事をする。（法律、条約の公布、国会の召集、衆議院の解散、国会議員の選挙の公示、外国の大使や公使との会見、さまざまな儀式など。）

ECONOMY
経済

Having achieved high economic and industrial growth after World War II, Japan has become one of the wealthiest nations in the world.

第2次世界大戦後の工業の著しい発展に伴い、高度経済成長をとげた日本は、現在、世界でも最も豊かな国の一つとなっている。

Top Three Gross National Product (GNP) Nations • 国民総生産（GNP）上位3カ国

(Unit: US$1 million 100万ドル)

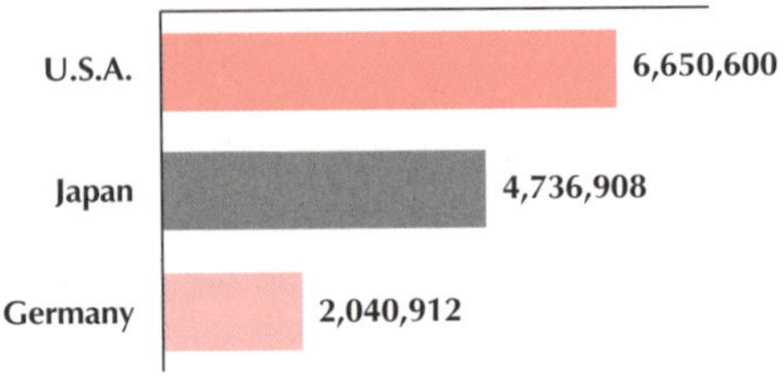

Top Three GNP per Capita Nations • 1人当たりGNP上位3カ国

(Unit: US$ USドル)

Top Three National Income per Capita Nations • 1人当たり国民所得上位3カ国

(Unit: US$ ドル)

(Economic Planning Agency 経済企画庁 1994)

The income per capita of Japan, an economic superpower, is on the increase annually. However, the key challenge is to achieve a high standard of living for each and every Japanese.

経済大国といわれる日本は、1人当たりの国民所得も世界のトップクラスで年々伸びている。しかし国民一人一人の豊かな生活が今後の大きな課題といえる。

LABOR
労働

Diligence is considered a virtue in Japan, as reflected in the motto "Catch up and Get Ahead." The Japanese have worked hard to build up the economy.

勤勉を美徳としてきた日本は、「追いつけ、追い越せ」の精神で懸命に働き、その労働力が日本の経済を支えてきた。

Employment Distribution in Industry • 産業別就業者数

(Over 15 years old 15歳以上) (Unit: 10,000 persons 万人)

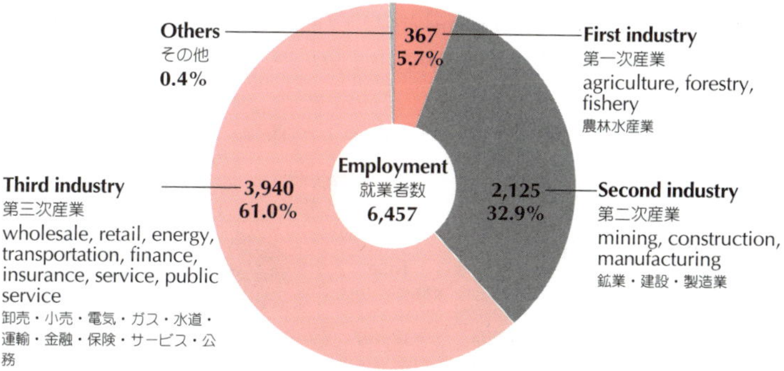

(Management and Coordination Agency 総務庁 1995)

ANNUAL WORKING HOURS AND HOLIDAYS
年間労働時間と休日日数

The five-day work week is not yet as widespread as in other industrially developed countries, and holidays are in general infrequent. After the collapse of the "bubble economy" many companies have put less emphasis on overtime and have tried, in fact, to reduce working hours.

日本では他国とくらべ週休2日制の普及が遅れ、全体として休日が少ない。また、バブル経済の崩壊後は、長時間労働を見直し、時短を促進する企業も多くなった。

(Workers in manufacturing industry 製造業労働者) (Unit: hours, days 時間、日)

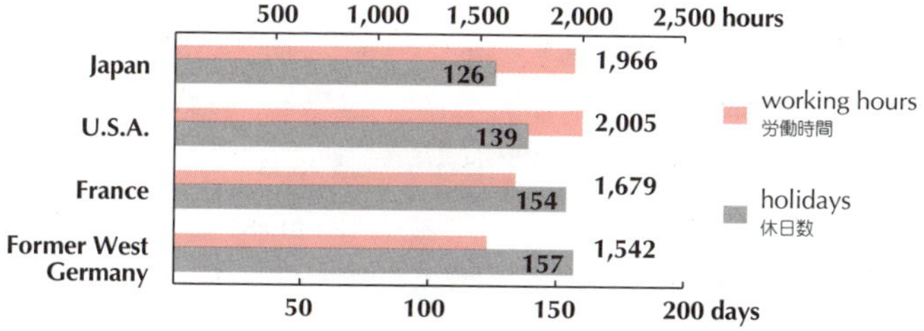

(Ministry of Labor 労働省 1994)

SOCIETY & WAY OF LIFE
社会／生活

The Japanese have become an affluent people, but there is dissatisfaction with the high property and commodity prices.

人々の暮らしは豊かになっているが、住宅問題、物価高など日常生活に対する満足度は低い。

HOUSEHOLD SPENDING
家計消費支出

Monthly Average per Worker's Household • 1勤労世帯1ヵ月平均

(Unit: Yen 円)

Average number of persons in household: 3.58
Average age of householders: 45.6
Net income: ¥570,818

平均世帯人数：3.58人
世帯主の平均年齢：45.6歳
実収入：570,818円

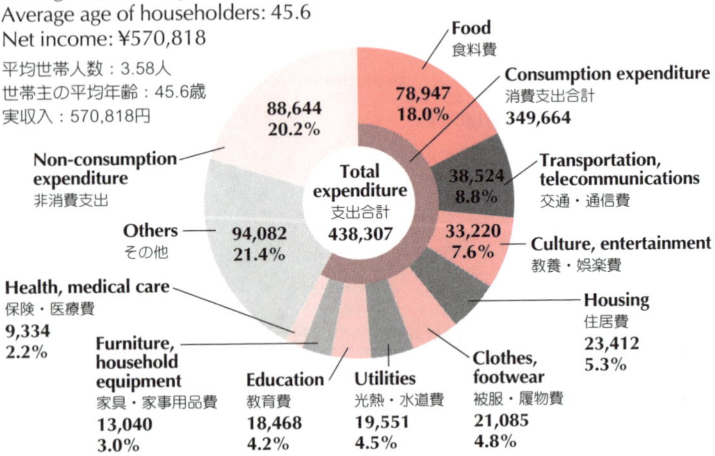

(Management and Coordination Agency 総務庁 1995)

HOUSING
住宅

Floor Space per Household (Newly Built Houses) • 1住宅当たり延べ面積（新築住宅）

(Unit: m²)

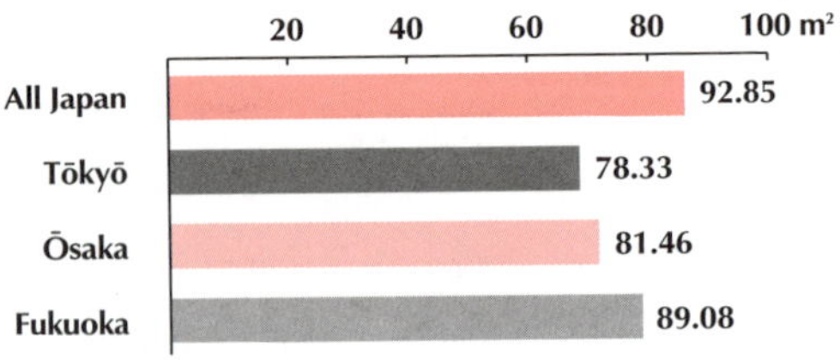

(Management and Coordination Agency 総務庁 1995)

SOCIAL SECURITY
社会保障

Japan has a social security system which tries to guarantee a decent life for each and every citizen. The system, however, still has some poorly developed aspects such as welfare for the elderly.

一人一人の国民が人間らしく暮らせるための社会保障制度があるが、老人福祉政策など、先進国のなかではまだまだ立ち遅れている面もある。

Social Security Expenditure • 社会保障給付費

(Unit: ¥1 million 100万円)

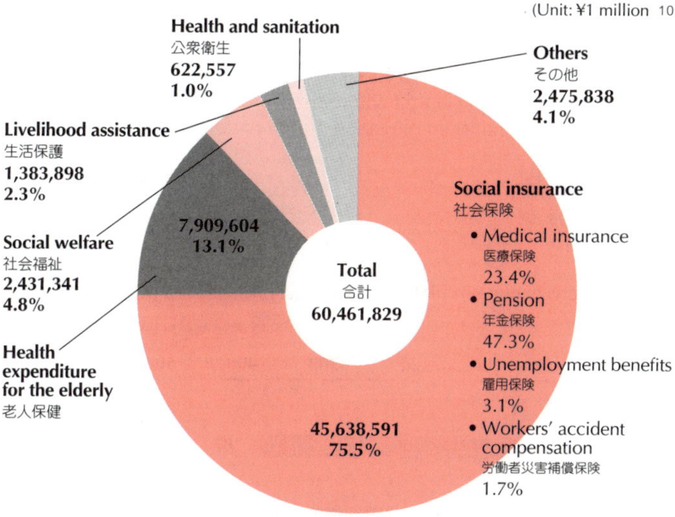

(Ministry of Health and Welfare 厚生省 Fiscal year 1994 1994年度)

Comparison of Social Security Expenditure • 社会保障給付費の対国民所得比

(Ratio of social security expenditure to national income 対国民所得比) (Unit: %)

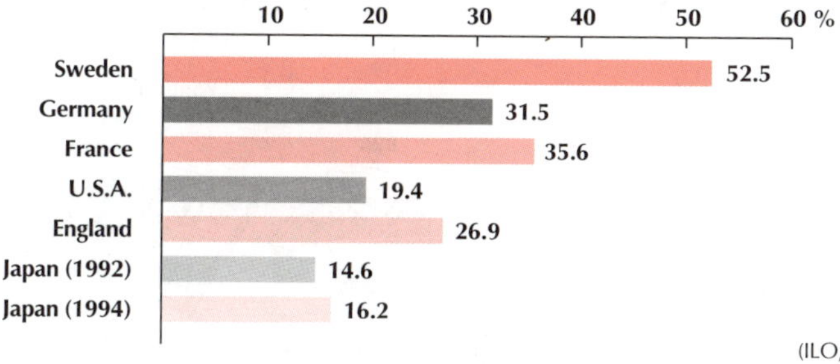

(ILO, 1992)

MASS COMMUNICATIONS
マスコミ

Newspapers, TV and radio in Japan convey useful information for daily life quickly and accurately. Also, they provide people with entertainment such as sports and music.

暮らしに役立つ新聞やテレビ、ラジオなどの放送は、速く正確な情報を伝えたり、スポーツや音楽などの娯楽を人々に与えている。

NEWSPAPERS
新聞

The Japanese have a reputation for being fond of reading newspapers. The first Japanese daily, "Yokohama Mainichi Shimbun," was published in 1870. Now there are national papers, regional papers, sports papers, specialty papers, etc.

日本人は世界でもよく新聞を読む国民といわれる。1870年、日本で初めての日刊新聞「横浜毎日新聞」が発行された。現在、全国紙、地方紙、スポーツ紙、専門紙などがある。

World Daily Newspaper Circulation • 世界の日刊新聞発行部数

(Unit: Copies per 1,000 capita 1,000人当たり部数)

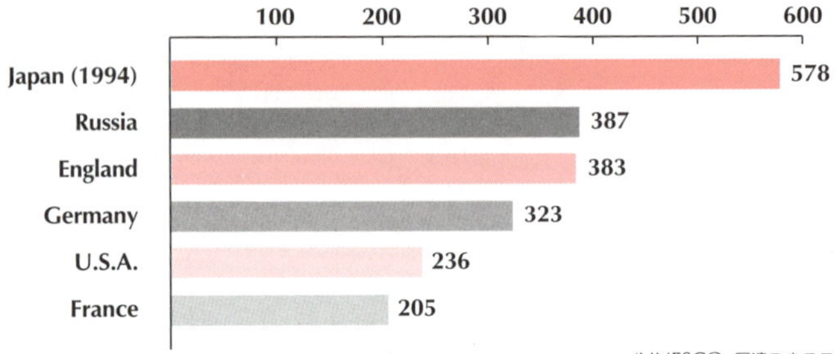

(UNESCO 国連ユネスコ 1992)

National Newspapers and Their Circulation • 全国紙と発行部数

(Unit: 10,000 copies 万部)

(The Japan Newspaper Publishers and Editors Association 日本新聞協会 1995)

BROADCASTING (TV)
放送（テレビ）

NHK TV broadcasting started in 1953. The first program was *kabuki*. Color broadcasting commenced in 1960. Most people get the bulk of their information from TV.

NHKのテレビ本放送が始まったのは1953年で（最初の番組は歌舞伎）、1960年にカラー放送が始まった。現在、人々が最も多くの情報を得ているのはテレビである。

TV Program Breakdown • テレビ番組の内訳

NHK (Nippon Hōsō Kyōkai), Japan Broadcasting Corporation, is operated on a viewer-reception fee basis. Commercial broadcaster, run on advertisement fees.

NHK（日本放送協会）は、国民からの受信料で運営され、民間放送はスポンサーからの広告料によつて運営されている。

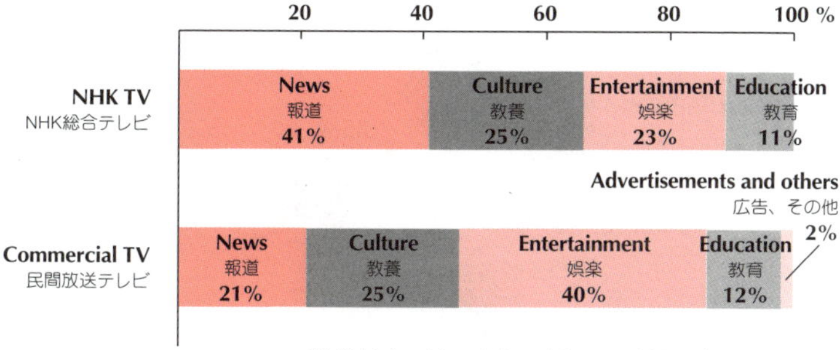

(NHK, National Association of Commercial Broadcasters in Japan
NHK、日本民間放送連盟 1994)

Satellite Broadcasting • 衛星放送

A broadcasting satellite transmits clear images and sounds anywhere in Japan. A communications satellite also transmits news and images from foreign countries, quickly and clearly.

放送衛星により、日本全国どんな所でも美しい画像や音が楽しめる。また外国からのニュースや映像も通信衛星によって正確に素早く伝えられる。

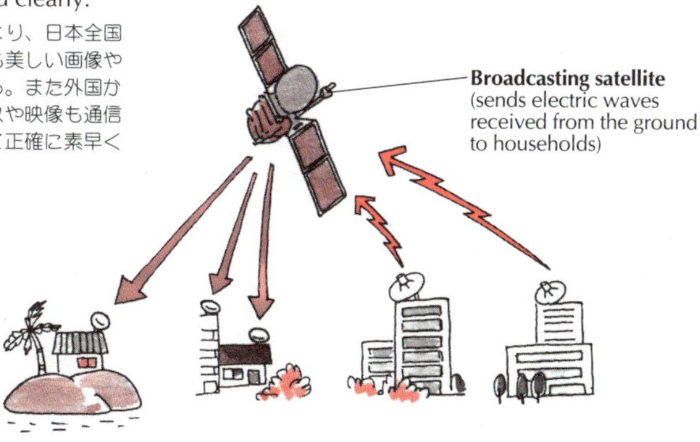

AGRICULTURE
農業

The number of farm workers in Japan has decreased to 1.4 persons per farm, while their average age has increased. Farmland is so limited that acreage under cultivation per farm can be as small as 1.2ha.

日本の農業は、農業就業人口が1農家当たり1.4人と労働力が減少し、高齢化している。また、狭い耕地のため、農家1戸当たりの耕地面積は約1.2haしかない。

PLANTED AREA PER PRODUCT
農作物作付け面積

Rice is the major agricultural product of Japan. Production in 1995 was 10,748,000 tons.

日本の農業は米作りが中心で、米の生産量は10,748（千t）である。（1995）

(Unit: 1,000ha)

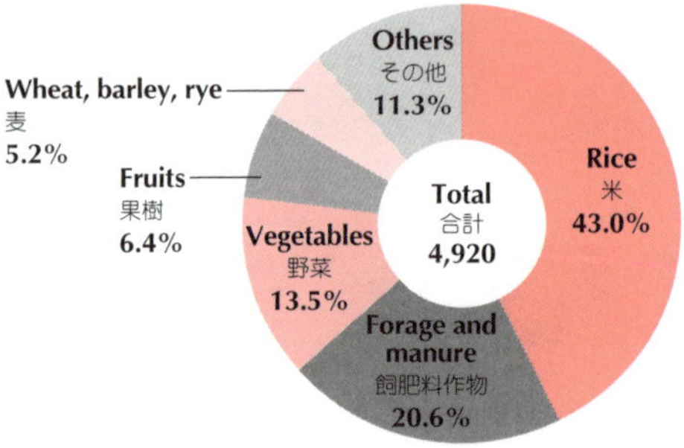

(Ministry of Agriculture, Forestry and Fisheries 農林水産省 1995)

SELF-SUFFICIENCY RATE OF MAJOR AGRICULTURAL PRODUCTS
主要農産物の自給率

The self-sufficiency rate is declining gradually, while the ratio of food in total imports is increasing.

日本の食糧自給率はだんだん低くなり、全輸入額に占める食糧の割合は大きくなってきている。

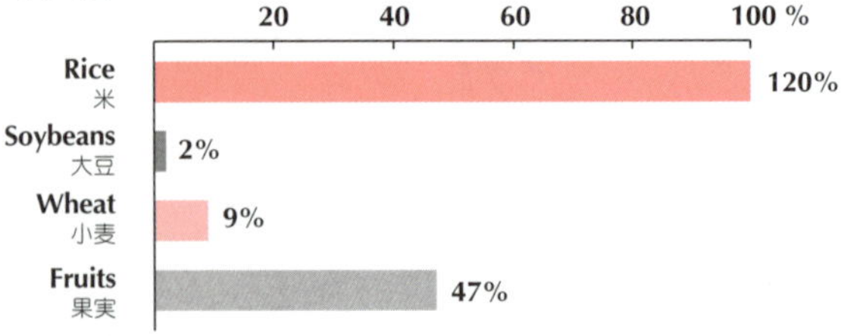

(Ministry of Agriculture, Forestry and Fisheries 農林水産省 Fiscal Year 1994 1994年度)

RICE
稲作

Hokkaidō, Niigata, Akita and Miyagi are the areas with the largest rice production.

米の生産量が多いのは、北海道、新潟県、秋田県、宮城県である。

●THE PROCESS OF PLANTING RICE

①

Plough the field.

田を耕す。

②

Cultivate rice seedlings in seedbeds.

苗床で苗を育てる。

③

Transplant the rice seedlings to the fields.

田植えをする。

④

Spray pesticides.

除草剤を散布する。

⑤

Reap rice with combine machine and thresher.

コンバインによる稲刈りと脱穀をする。

VEGETABLE AND FRUIT PRODUCTION
野菜・果物作り

Vegetables are produced in areas surrounding large cities; forced crops that take advantage of the climate are popular. Fruits typical of Japan are mandarin oranges (from Ehime) and apples (from Aomori).

大都市に近い地方で野菜生産が行われ、気候を利用した促成栽培が盛んである。また日本の代表的な果物は、みかん(愛媛県)とりんご(青森県)である。

LIVESTOCK
畜産

Dairy cattle are raised in Hokkaidō, beef cattle in Kyūshū respectively; and hogs in Kantō and Kyūshū. The demand for livestock feed far exceeds its production; more than half is therefore imported.

主に乳牛は北海道、肉牛は九州、豚は関東・九州地方で飼育されている。これらの飼料は生産が追いつかず、半分以上を輸入に頼っている。

FISHERY
漁業

Since Japanese eat all sorts of fish and seafood products, consumption is very high and the fish catch one of the largest in the world. Japan is surrounded by continental shelves with both cold and warm currents nearby, making the surrounding sea highly fertile fishing grounds.

日本人は様々な水産物・水産加工品を食べ、その消費量は世界でも特に多く、漁獲量も世界のトップクラスである。日本の周りには大陸棚が広がり、暖流や寒流も流れているため、よい漁場となっている。

FISHING GROUNDS AND MAJOR FISHERY PORTS
日本の漁場と主な漁港

VOLUME OF PRODUCTION BY TYPE OF FISHING
漁業部門別生産量

The amount of fish caught around Japan has levelled off recently, due to a decrease in fish resources caused by water pollution and intensified international restrictions on fishing. Consequently, cultivation of laver and oysters is practiced. Salmon and trout farming is also on the rise.

最近では海の汚れや200海里水域問題で、よい漁場が減少し、漁獲量は伸びなやんでいる。そこで人が育てる養殖(のり、かきなど)をしたり、栽培漁業(さけやますなどを稚魚になるまで育てたあと海に放流する)などにも目がむけられている。

(Unit: 10,000t)

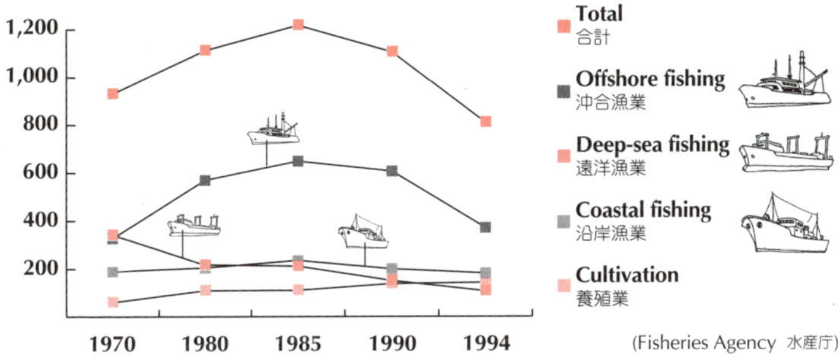

(Fisheries Agency 水産庁)

TYPES OF FISHING
漁法

Fixed Shore Net Fishing • 定置網漁

Several nets are installed in an area where salmon or trout pass.

さけ、ますの通り道に網で囲いをつくってとる方法。

Haul Net Fishing • 巻き網漁

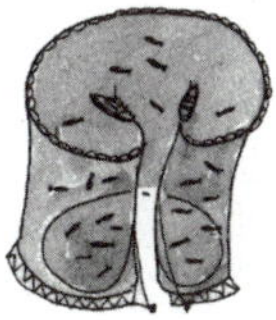

A net is thrown into the sea from a boat to surround the fish, and then hauled up. Effective for catching mackerel and sardines.

さばやいわしは、船で網をおろして群れごと取り囲み、網をしぼっていく方法。

Dragnet Fishing • 底引き網漁

A net is dropped to the bottom of the sea and pulled along by a boat. Effective for catching walleye pollacks, prawns, crabs, etc.

すけとうだら、えび、かには、船で網を底につけて引いて漁獲する。

INDUSTRY
工業

There are four main industrial areas in Japan: Keihin, Chūkyō, Hanshin and Kita-Kyūshū. Particular concentration is in the "Pacific Belt," which extends from southern Kantō to northern Kyūshū along the Pacific and Inland Sea coastline.

日本の工業が盛んな地域は4大工業地帯(京浜、中京、阪神、北九州工業地帯)を中心に太平洋ベルト(関東地方南部から九州の北部までの太平洋や瀬戸内海の沿岸地域)に集まっている。

INDUSTRIAL AREAS
工業地帯

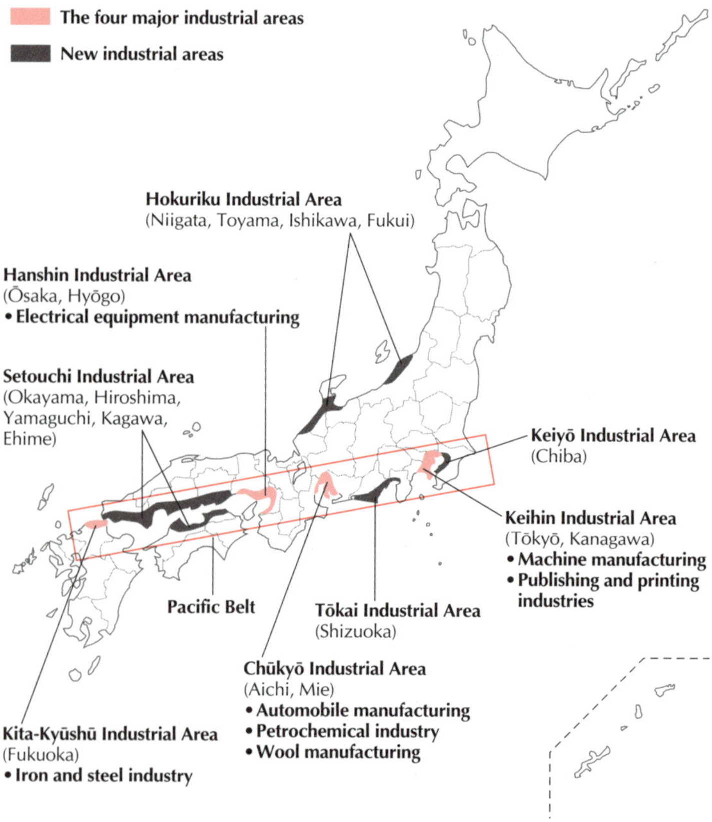

CHARACTERISTICS OF JAPANESE INDUSTRIES
日本の工業の特色

- Japan hosts mostly the chemical and heavy-machinery manufacturing industries. Machine manufacturing is particularly prominent.

  重化学工業が中心で、特に機械工業が盛んである。

- There are many small-to-medium-sized factories in Japan, but large facilities exceed them in production volume.

  工場の数は中小工場が多く、生産額は大工場が多い。

- Automated manufacture and product refinement are high priorities today. Production of ICs, computers and other high-tech electronic equipment continues to climb.

  今日、工業の合理化と製品の高品質化が追求され、IC（集積回路）を使ったエレクトロニクス製品（コンピューター、電気製品）の生産が増加している。

MANUFACTURING INDUSTRY BREAKDOWN
製造業の産業別構成

(Unit: ¥1 million 100万円)

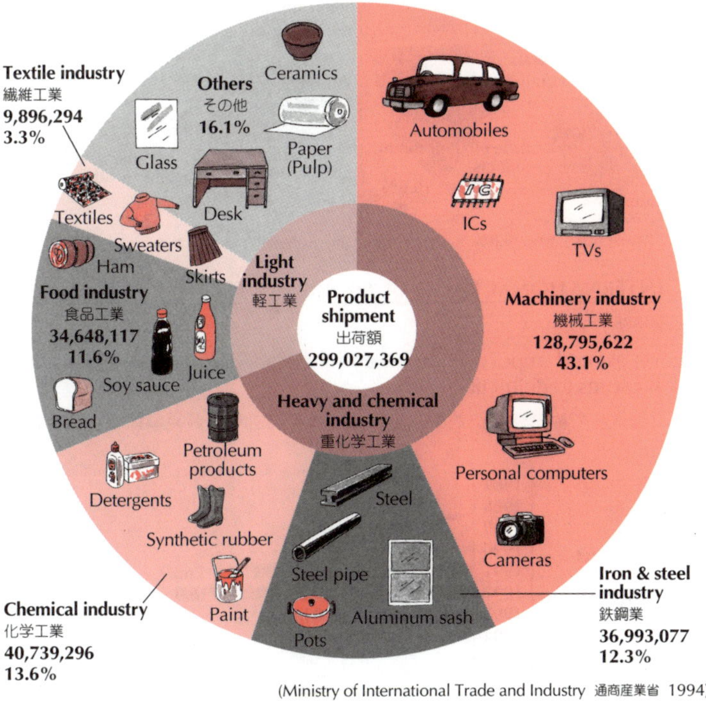

(Ministry of International Trade and Industry 通商産業省 1994)

TRADE
貿易

Japan relies mainly on raw materials and fuel imported from all over the world, particularly from Pacific Rim countries. It exports manufactured products from the so-called processing trade. Major export items are high-tech products such as automobiles, computers, etc.

太平洋をとりまく国々を中心に、世界各国から、主に工業原料や燃料を輸入し、製品を輸出する加工貿易を行っている。今日では、自動車やコンピューターなどの高度な技術の機械製品が輸出の主流となっている。

IMPORTS AND EXPORTS
輸入と輸出

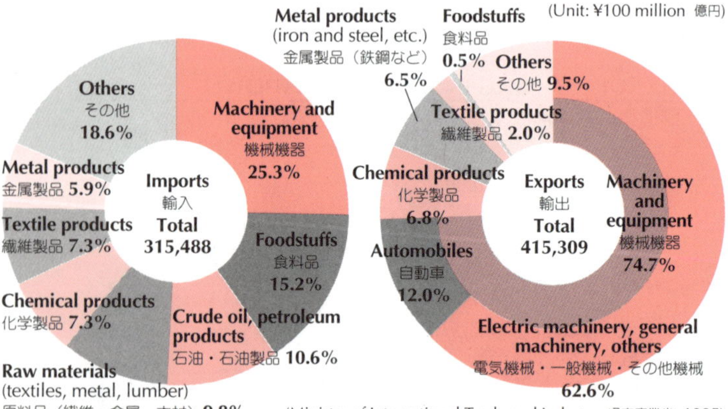

(Ministry of International Trade and Industry 通商産業省 1995)

INTERNATIONAL BALANCE OF PAYMENTS
国際収支

Exports exceed imports in Japan and the trade surplus keeps growing, which causes trade friction.

現在、輸入より輸出が多いため、黒字額が大きくなり、貿易摩擦の問題が起きている。

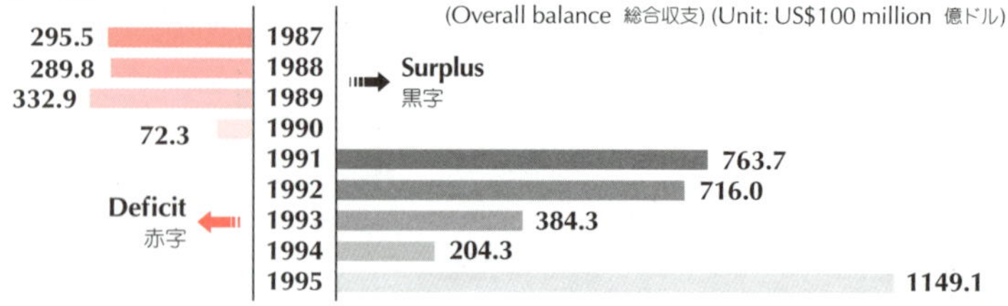

(Bank of Japan 日本銀行)

IMPORTED FOODSTUFFS
輸入食料品

Once Japan was a self-sustaining country regarding food. Due to a decrease in agricultural production and a change of lifestyle, it is now the world's largest food importer.

かつては自給自足生活をしていた日本人であるが、農業生産高の減少や人々の生活様式の変化に伴い、今では世界でも最大の食料輸入国となっている。

Major Imported Foodstuffs and Sources • 主な輸入食料品と輸入相手国

(Unit: US$1 million 100万ドル)

(Ministry of International Trade and Industry 通商産業省 1995)

Japanese Dishes with Imported Ingredients • 外国製の日本食

Tempura udon and *nigirizushi* are typical noodle dishes, but most of their ingredients come from foreign countries.

日本の伝統的なてんぷらうどんや握り寿司も、実はそのほとんどが外国から輸入された食品で作られている。

INTERNATIONALIZATION
国際化

Japan is intent on balancing trade with other countries, not just pursuing its own benefits. At the same time, as a member of the "global family," Japan promotes interchange with other countries through culture and sports. It is also engaged in technical cooperation with and economic support to developing countries.

日本は自国の利益だけでなく、他国とのつり合いのとれた貿易に努めている。また、世界の一員として文化、スポーツを通して結びつき、開発途上国への技術協力や経済援助などさまざまな活動を行っている。

ASSISTANCE TO DEVELOPING COUNTRIES
開発途上国への援助

ODA (Official Development Assistance) per Country • 政府開発援助国別内訳

(Unit: US$1 million 100万ドル)

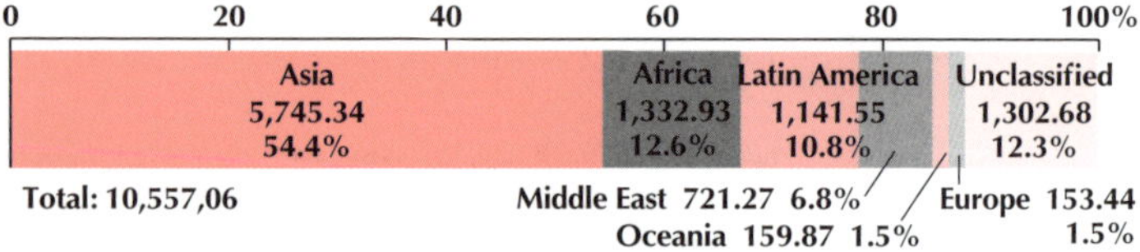

(Ministry of Foreign Affairs 外務省 1995)

Japan Overseas Cooperation Volunteers • 青年海外協力隊の活動内容

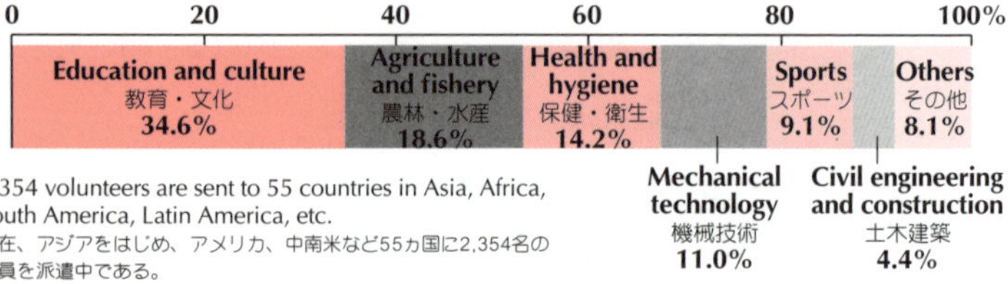

2,354 volunteers are sent to 55 countries in Asia, Africa, South America, Latin America, etc.
現在、アジアをはじめ、アメリカ、中南米など55ヵ国に2,354名の隊員を派遣中である。

(Japan Overseas Cooperation Volunteers 青年海外協力隊 as of June 1996)

JAPANESE TRAVELING ABROAD
日本の海外旅行

The number of Japanese visiting to South-east Asia, Europe, U.S.A. and other areas has tripled in the past ten years, reflecting heightened interest in the world.

東南アジア、欧米をはじめとする各地への海外旅行者は、過去10年間で3倍にも増え、海外への関心の深さがうかがえる。

(Unit: 10,000 persons 万人)

391 (1980)
↓
1,358 (1994)

(Prime Minister's Office 総理府)

Appendix
付録

JAPANESE HISTORY & WORLD HISTORY
日本史／世界史

JAPANESE HISTORY

Before 30,000 B.C. Paleolithic culture.
Ca. 10,000 B.C. Jōmon culture.

Ca. 300 B.C. Yayoi culture. Wet-rice cultivation is introduced.

57 King of the state of Na in Wa is awarded a gold seal by Emperor Kuang-Wu of the Chinese Later Han dynasty.
239 Himiko sends an envoy to the kingdom of Wei in China.

Ca. 300–710 ➤ KOFUN PERIOD

350 The Yamato Court established.
552 Traditional date for introduction of Buddhism to Japan. (One theory dates this 538.)
593 Prince Shōtoku appointed regent by Empress Suiko.
604 Prince Shōtoku promulgates Seventeen Article Constitution.
607 Ono no Imoko appointed leader of the second embassy of Sui dynasty in China.
Construction of Hōryūji completed.
630 First embassy to Tang-dynasty China.
645 Taika Reform initiated.
701 Taihō Code completed.

Prince Shōtoku

710–794 ➤ NARA PERIOD

710 Heijōkyō (Nara) established.
712 Compilation of the *Kojiki* (Record of Ancient Matters) is completed by Ō no Yasumaro.
720 *Nihon shoki* (Chronicle of Japan) completed.
743 Konden Einen Shizai Hō promulgated.
752 The Great Buddha at Tōdaiji is completed.
759 The *Man'yōshū* (Collection of Ten Thousand Leaves) completed.

日本史

旧石器文化
縄文文化

弥生文化、水稲農業始まる

倭の奴国王、後漢光武帝より金印をうける
卑弥呼、魏に遣使

古墳時代

大和朝廷成立
仏教伝来（一説に538年）

聖徳太子、摂政となる
十七条憲法制定
小野妹子を隋に派遣

法隆寺建立
第1回遣唐使
大化の改新
大宝律令

奈良時代

平城京遷都
太安万侶「古事記」

「日本書紀」
墾田永年私財法
東大寺大仏開眼
「万葉集」

WORLD HISTORY
世界史

Ca. 1300 B.C. Chinese characters engraved on animal bones.
中国で漢字が使われる

Ca. 528 B.C. Historical Buddha Gautama gives his first sermon.
釈迦が仏教を説く

334 B.C. Alexander the Great begins his conquest of the East.
アレクサンダー大王の東征始まる

221 B.C. China unified under the Qin dynasty (221 B.C.–206 B.C.).
秦朝、中国統一

27 B.C. The Roman Empire established.
ローマ帝国成立

376 The Visigoths cross the Danube and invade the Roman Empire.
ゲルマン民族大移動

589 Beginning of the Sui dynasty (589–618) in China.
中国に隋朝成立

622 Mohammedan Era begins.
イスラム暦元年

624 China unified under the Bang dynasty (618–907).
中国に唐朝成立

668 Silla unifies Korea with the assistance of Tang China.
新羅、朝鮮統一

794–1185 ➤ HEIAN PERIOD

794 Capital moved to Heiankyō (Kyōto).
805 Saichō introduces the Tendai Buddhism.
806 Kūkai introduces the Shingon Buddhism.
905 The *Kokin wakashū* (Collection from Ancient and Modern Times) completed.

996 Sei Shōnagon writes *Makura no sōshi* (*The Pillow Book*).
1008 Murasaki Shikibu's the *Tale of Genji* is written.
1016 Fujiwara no Michinaga becomes regent.
1053 Construction of the Phoenix Hall completed at the temple of Byōdōin.

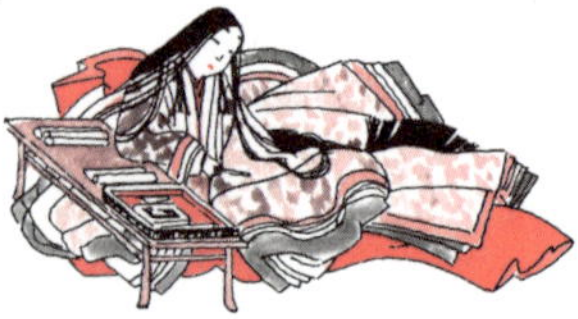
Murasaki Shikibu

1167 Taira no Kiyomori is made grand minister of state.
1180 Taira-Minamoto War begins.

1185–1333 ➤ KAMAKURA PERIOD

1185 Minamoto no Yoshitsune annihilates the Taira family in the Battle of Dannoura.
1192 Minamoto no Yoritomo assumes the title of *seii tai shōgun.*
1203 Hōjō Tokimasa assumes the office of shogunal regent. (*Shikken*)
1205 *Shin kokin wakashū* (New Collection from Ancient and Modern Times) compiled by Fujiwara no Sadaie and others.
1218 Early versions of the *Heike monogatari* (*The Tale of the Heike*) in existence.
1224 Shinran founds Jōdo Shin sect of Buddhism.
1232 Goseibai Shikimoku (The Formulary of Adjudications) promulgated.
1274 First of the Mongol invasions of Japan.

1281 Second of the Mongol invasions of Japan.
1330 Yoshida Kenkō completes the collection of essays *Tsurezuregusa* (*Essays in Idleness*).

1333–1568 ➤ MUROMACHI PERIOD

1333 Kamakura shogunate collapses.
Kemmu Restoration (1333–1336).
1338 Ashikaga Takauji receives the title of *seii tai shōgun,* founds the Muromachi shogunate.
1397 Ashikaga Yoshimitsu begins construction of Kinkakuji (Temple of the Golden Pavilion).

平安時代

平安京に遷都
最澄、天台宗を伝える
空海、真言宗を伝える
「古今和歌集」

清少納言「枕草子」
紫式部「源氏物語」
藤原道長、摂政となる
平等院鳳凰堂完成

平清盛、太政大臣となる

源平の争乱

鎌倉時代

源義経、壇ノ浦の戦いで平氏一門を滅す
頼朝、征夷大将軍となる
北条時政、執権になる
藤原定家「新古今和歌集」

「平家物語」

親鸞、浄土真宗開宗
御成敗式目制定
文永の役（第1回蒙古襲来）

弘安の役（第2回蒙古襲来）
吉田兼行「徒然草」

室町時代

鎌倉幕府滅亡
建武の中興
足利尊氏、征夷大将軍となる
足利義満、金閣寺を造営

800 Charlemagne becomes the emperor of the Holy Roman Empire.
カール大帝のローマ皇帝戴冠

960 Beginning of the Northern Song dynasty (960–1126) in China.
中国に北宋成立

962 The Holy Roman Empire established.
神聖ローマ帝国成立

1066 William, duke of Normandy, is crowned king of England.
ノルマン朝、イギリス征服

1096 The first expedition of the Crusaders.
十字軍始まる

1127 Beginning of the Southern Song dynasty (1127–1279) in China.
中国に南宋成立

1206 Genies Khan conquers Mongolia.
チンギスハンの蒙古統一

1215 Magna Carta issued by King John of England.
マグナ・カルタ発布

1271 Marco Polo sets out on his journey the court of the Mongol emperor Kublai Khan.
マルコ・ポーロ、東方旅行に出発

1279 Kublai Khan establishes the Yuan dynasty (1279–1368) in China.
クビライ・ハン、元朝中国統一

1337 Hundred Years' War begins.
英仏百年戦争始まる

1368 The Ming dynasty (1368–1644) in China.
中国に明朝成立

1404 Tally trade initiated with Ming-dynasty China.
1467 Ōnin War (1467–77) begins.
1483 Ashikaga Yoshimasa begins to construct Ginkakuji (Temple of the Silver Pavilion).

1543 Firearms are introduced to Japan by the Portuguese on Tanegashima.

1549 Francis Xavier propagates Christianity at Kagoshima.

1568–1600 ➤ AZUCHI-MOMOYAMA PERIOD

1568 Oda Nobunaga enters Kyōto.
1573 Oda Nobunaga ousts Ashikaga Yoshiaki; Muromachi shogunate collapses.
1582 Oda Nobunaga is assassinated at the Honnōji by Akechi Mitsuhide.
1588 Toyotomi Hideyoshi issues the order of sword hunt.
1590 Toyotomi Hideyoshi pacifies all of Japan.
1592 First of the invasions of Korea.
1597 Second of the invasions of Korea.

1600–1868 ➤ EDO PERIOD

1600 Battle of Sekigahara.
1603 Tokugawa Ieyasu founds the Tokugawa shogunate.
1612 Shogunate issues directives aimed at restricting Christianity (anti-Christian edicts).
1615 Shogunate promulgates the Buke Shohatto (Laws for the Military Houses).
1636 Dejima at Nagasaki completed.
1637 Shimabara Uprising (1637–38).
1639 Edicts establishing National Seclusion are completed.

Tokugawa Ieyasu

1688 Beginning of the Genroku era (1688–1704); the golden age of *kabuki* and *jōruri*.
1716 Tokugawa Yoshimune becomes *shōgun*; Kyōhō Reforms (1716–45) commence.

1787 Matsudaira Sadanobu becomes senior shogunal councillor; Kansei Reforms (1787–93) commence.

1833 Publication of Andō Hiroshige's *ukiyo-e* (Fifty-Three Stations of the Tōkaidō) begins.

明との勘合貿易始まる

応仁の乱

足利義政、銀閣を造営

ポルトガル人、種子島に鉄砲を伝える

ザビエル、キリスト教を伝える

安土桃山時代

織田信長、入京

室町幕府滅亡

本能寺の変

刀狩令

豊臣秀吉、全国統一

文禄の役

慶長の役

江戸時代

関ケ原の戦い

徳川家康、徳川幕府を開く

禁教令

武家諸法度発布

長崎出島成る

島原の乱

鎖国が完成する

元禄時代始まる；歌舞伎、浄瑠璃が隆盛になる

徳川吉宗将軍になる；享保の改革

松平定信、老中となる；寛政の改革

安藤広重「東海道五十三次」

1455 Johannes Gutenberg completes the Forty-Two Line Bible, printed from movable type.
グーテンベルク、聖書を活字印刷

1492 Christopher Columbus lands in the Bahamas.
コロンブス、バハマ諸島に上陸

1517 Martin Luther's Reformation.
ルターの宗教改革

1588 Invincible Armada of Spain defeated by the English fleet.
スペイン無敵艦隊の敗北

1600 British East India Company incorporated by royal charter.
イギリス東インド会社設立

1618 Thirty Year's War (1618–48) breaks out.
30年戦争始まる

1644 Manchus establish the Qing dynasty (1644–1912) in China.
中国、清朝成立

1688 Glorious Revolution in England.
イギリス名誉革命

1689 English Bill of Rights enacted.
英国権利宣言公布

1776 Continental Congress issues the U.S. Declaration of Independence.
アメリカ独立宣言公布

1789 French Revolution begins.
フランス革命始まる

1804 Napoleon crowns himself emperor of France.
ナポレオン、皇帝となる

1841 Tempō Reforms (1841–43) initiated by Mizuno Tadakuni.

1853 U.S. Commodore Matthew Perry arrives at Uraga.
1854 Kanagawa Treaty (Treaty of Peace and Amity between the United States and the Empire of Japan) signed.
1858 Ansei commercial treaties are concluded.

1867 Formal return of political authority to the emperor by Tokugawa Yoshinobu (Taisei Hōkan).

1868–1912 ➤ MEIJI PERIOD

1868 Restoration of Imperial Rule; Meiji Restoration.
Charter Oath promulgated.
1871 Establishment of prefectural system.
1872 Railroad begins operation between Shimbashi and Yokohama.
The Education Order is promulgated.
1873 Conscription Ordinance enacted. Land Tax Reform Law issued.
1880 Public Assembly Ordinance issued to control the Freedom and People's Rights movement.
1889 Constitution of the Empire of Japan promulgated.
1894 Sino-Japanese War (1894–1895) begins.

Emperor Meiji

1904 Russo-Japanese War (1904–1905) begins.
1905 Natsume Sōseki begins serialization of *Wagahai wa neko de aru* (*I Am a Cat*).
1910 Annexation of Korea.
1911 Treaties signed with the Western powers that restore tariff autonomy to Japan.

1912–1926 ➤ TAISHŌ PERIOD

1914 Japan enters World War I.

1923 Tōkyō Earthquake.
1925 Enactment of the Peace Preservation Law.
Universal Manhood Suffrage Law passed.

日本史

水野忠邦、天保の改革

ペリー、浦賀に来航
日米和親条約締結

安政五箇国条約締結

大政奉還

明治時代

王政復古；明治維新
五ヵ条の御誓文
廃藩置県
新橋―横浜間に鉄道開通

学制発布
徴兵令公布、地租改正条例布告
集会条例制定；自由民権運動弾圧
大日本帝国憲法発布
日清戦争始まる
日露戦争始まる
夏目漱石「吾輩は猫である」

韓国併合
関税自主権回復

大正時代

第1次世界大戦に参戦

関東大震災
治安維持法公布
普通選挙法成立

WORLD HISTORY
世界史

1837 Victoria becomes queen of England (1837–1901).
ヴィクトリア英女王即位

1839 Opium War (1839–42) begins in China.
中国でアヘン戦争始まる

1858 China signs Treaties of Tianjin.
中国、列国と天津条約を締結

1861 Civil War (1861–65) begins in the United States.
アメリカで南北戦争始まる

1870 Franco-Prussian War (1870–71) begins.
普仏戦争始まる

1871 Unification of Germany.
ドイツ帝国成立

1876 The first successful telephone transmission is achieved by Alexander Graham Bell.
ベル、電話を発明

1896 First modern Olympic Games held at Athens.
アテネで第一回オリンピック大会

1900 Boxer Rebellion in China.
中国で義和団の乱

1912 Establishment of Republic of China.
中華民国樹立

1914 World War I (1914–18) begins.
第1次世界大戦始まる

1917 Revolution in Russia.
ロシア革命

1919 May Fourth Movement in China.
中国で五・四運動

1920 League of Nations.
国際連盟発足

1926–1989 ➤ SHŌWA PERIOD

1927 Financial Crisis.
1931 Manchurian Incident.
1937 Sina-Japanese of War (1937–1945) begins.
Kawabata Yasunari publishes *Yukiguni* (*Snow Country*).

1941 The Pacific War (1941–45) begins.

1945 Atomic bomb dropped on Hiroshima and Nagasaki.
Japan accepts the terms of the Potsdam Declaration.

1946 Constitution of Japan promulgated.

1949 Yukawa Hideki awarded the Nobel Prize for physics.

1951 San Francisco Peace Treaty and the first of the United States-Japan Security Treaties signed.
1953 Television broadcasting begins in Japan.
1956 Japan granted membership of the United Nations.

1964 Tōkyō Olympic Games held.

Emperor Shōwa

1972 Okinawa returned to Japanese sovereignty by the United States.
1978 China-Japan Peace and Friendship Treaty signed.

1989– ➤ HEISEI PERIOD

1989 Death of Emperor Shōwa.

1990 Formal enthronement of Emperor Akihito.
1992 Law on Cooperation in United Nations Peacekeeping Operations passes in the Diet.
1993 Non-LDP coalition government is formed.
1994 Political reform bills pass in the Diet.
Ōe Kenzaburō awarded the Nobel Prize for literature.
1995 Great Hanshin-Awaji Earthquake.

日本史

昭和時代

金融恐慌

満州事変

日中戦争始まる

川端康成「雪国」

太平洋戦争始まる

広島、長崎に原子爆弾

ポツダム宣言受諾

日本国憲法公布

湯川秀樹、ノーベル物理学賞受賞

サンフランシスコ平和条約、日米安全保障条約調印

テレビ放送開始

日本、国際連合に加盟

東京オリンピック開催

沖縄祖国復帰

日中平和友好条約調印

平成時代

昭和天皇崩御

天皇明仁、即位の礼

PKO協力法成立

非自民連立内閣成立

政治改革関連法案成立

大江健三郎、ノーベル文学賞受賞

阪神大震災

WORLD HISTORY
世界史

1927 Chiang Kai-shek sets up a Nationalist government.
蒋介石、中国国民政府樹立

1929 U.S. stock market crashes, Great Depression begins.
世界大恐慌始まる

1939 World War II (1939–45) begins in Europe.
ヨーロッパで第二次世界大戦始まる

1945 Potsdam Conference.
ポツダム会談

1945 United Nations established.
国際連合成立

1949 People's Republic of China established.
中華人民共和国成立

1950 Korean War (1950–53) begins.
朝鮮戦争始まる

1957 Soviet Union launches the first space satellite, Sputnik 1.
ソ連、初の人工衛星スプートニク1号の打ち上げ

1966 Cultural Revolution in China.
中国で文化大革命

1969 U.S. Apollo 11 spacecraft puts the first man on the moon.
アメリカのアポロ11号、月面着陸に成功

1975 North Vietnam achieves the unification of Vietnam.
ベトナム全土統一なる

1980 Iran-Iraq War (1980–88) commences.
イラン・イラク戦争始まる

1989 Berlin Wall demolished.
ベルリンの壁崩壊

1990 Persian Gulf War (1990–91) commences.
湾岸戦争始まる

Reunification of Germany.
東西ドイツ統一

1991 Soviet Union dissolved.
ソビエト連邦解体

INDEX • 索引

装幀● 菊地信義
挿画● 野村俊夫

執筆● 乾久美子
イラスト● 高橋満

翻訳● Hisako Nozaki Ifshin
レイアウト● 飯尾緑子

イラスト日本(にっぽん)まるごと事典(じてん)

Japan at a Glance

1997年5月8日 第1刷発行
1998年1月30日 第4刷発行

著 者 インターナショナル・インターンシップ・プログラムス
発行者 野間佐和子
発行所 講談社インターナショナル株式会社
〒112-8652 東京都文京区音羽1-17-14
電話：03-3944-6493（編集）
03-3944-6492（営業）
印刷所 大日本印刷株式会社
製本所 株式会社 堅省堂

ISBN4-7700-2080-5
日本音楽著作権協会（出）許諾第9701593-704号

英語で読む日本史
Japanese History: 11 Experts Reflect on the Past

「英文日本大事典」[編]　224ページ　ISBN 4-7700-2024-4

11人の超一流ジャパノロジストたちが英語で書き下ろした日本全史。外国人の目から見た日本史はどういうものか、また、日本の歴史事項を英語で何と表現するのか。新しい視点が想像力をかき立てます。

英語で話す「日本の謎」Q & A　外国人が聞きたがる100のWHY
100 Tough Questions for Japan

板坂　元［監修］　240ページ　ISBN 4-7700-2091-0

なぜ、結婚式は教会で、葬式はお寺でなんてことができるの？　なぜ、大人までがマンガを読むの？　なぜ、時間とお金をかけてお茶を飲む練習をするの？——こんな外国人の問いをつきつめてゆくと、日本文化の核心が見えてきます。

英語で話す「日本の心」　和英辞典では引けないキーワード197
Keys to the Japanese Heart and Soul

「英文日本大事典」[編]　328ページ　ISBN 4-7700-2082-1

一流のジャパノロジスト53人が解説した「日本の心」を知るためのキーワード集。「わび」「さび」「義理人情」「甘え」「根回し」「談合」「みそぎ」など、日本人特有な「心の動き」を外国人に説明するための強力なツールです。

英語で話す「日本の文化」
Japan as I see It

NHK国際局文化ﾌﾟﾛｼﾞｪｸﾄ［編］　ﾀﾞﾝ・ｹﾆｰ［訳］　196ページ　ISBN 4-7700-2197-6

金田一春彦、遠藤周作、梅原猛、平川祐弘、西堀栄三郎、鯖田豊之、野村万作、井上靖、小松左京、中根千枝の１０人が、日本文化の「謎」を解く。NHKの国際放送で２１の言語で放送され、分かりやすいと世界中で大好評。

ニッポン不思議発見！　日本文化を英語で語る５０の名エッセイ集
Discover Japan: Words, Customs and Concept

日本文化研究所［編］　松本道弘［訳］　260ページ　ISBN 4-7700-2142-9

絶望的な場合ですら、日本人は「そこをなんとか」という言葉を使って、相手に甘えようとする……こんな指摘をうけると、いかに日本人は独特なものの考え方をしているか分かります。あなたも“不思議”を発見してみませんか。

ニッポン見聞録　大好きな日本人に贈る新・開国論
Heisei Highs and Lows

ﾄﾑ・ﾘｰﾄﾞ［著］　216ページ　ISBN 4-7700-2092-9

国際化の進む日本ですが、アメリカのジャーナリストが鋭い目と耳で浮き彫りにしたニッポンの姿は、驚くほど平穏でいとおしく、恥ずかしいくらい強欲で無知なものでした。トムが大好きな日本人へ贈る新・開国論。

「Japan」クリッピング　ワシントンポストが書いた「日本」
Views of Japan from the Washington Post Newsroom

東郷茂彦［著］　256ページ　ISBN 4-7700-2023-6

アメリカの世論をリードするワシントン・ポストに書かれた「Japan」……政治、外交、経済、社会のジャンルで取り上げられた日本の姿を、国際ジャーナリストが解説し、その背後にある問題点を浮き彫りにする一冊。

ベスト・オブ・天声人語
Vox Populi, Vox Dei

朝日新聞論説委員室［著］　朝日イブニングニュース［訳］　280ページ　ISBN4-7700-2166-6

「天声人語」は「朝日新聞」の名コラムというよりも、日本を代表するコラムです。香港返還、アムラー現象、たまごっち、マザー・テレサの死など、現代を読み解く傑作56編を、社会・世相、政治、スポーツなどのジャンル別に収録しました。

誤解される日本人　外国人がとまどう４１の疑問
The Inscrutable Japanese

メリディアン・リソーシス・アソシエイツ［編］　賀川　洋［著］　224ページ　ISBN 4-7700-2129-1

あなたのちょっとした仕草や表情が大きな誤解を招いているかもしれません。「日本人はどんなときに誤解を受けるのか？」そのメカニズムを解説し、「どのように外国人に説明すればよいか」最善の解決策を披露します。

ビジュアル 英語で読む日本国憲法
The Constitution of Japan

「英文日本大百科事典」［編］　208ページ　ISBN 4-7700-2191-7

難しいと思っていた「日本国憲法」も、英語で読むと不思議とよく分かります。日本国憲法を、59点の写真を使って、バイリンガルで分かりやすく解説しました。条文中に出てくる難解な日本語には、ルビや説明が付いています。

イラスト 日本まるごと事典
Japan at a Glance

インターナショナル・インターンシップ・プログラムス［著］　248ページ（2色刷）ISBN 4-7700-2080-5

1000点以上のイラストを使って日本のすべてを紹介――自然、文化、社会はもちろんのこと、折り紙の折り方、着物の着方から、ナベで米を炊く方法や「あっちむいてホイ」の遊び方まで国際交流に必要な知識とノウハウを満載。

英語で折り紙
Origami in English

山口　真［著］　160ページ　ISBN 4-7700-2027-9

たった一枚の紙から無数の造形が生まれ出る…外国の人たちは、その面白さに目を見張ります。折るとき、英語で説明できるようにバイリンガルにしました。ホームステイ、留学、海外駐在に必携の一冊です。

英語で日本料理
100 Recipes from Japanese Cooking

辻調理師専門学校　畑耕一郎, 近藤一樹［著］

268ページ（カラー口絵16ページ）　ISBN 4-7700-2079-1

外国の人と親しくなる最高の手段は、日本料理を作ってあげること、そしてその作り方を教えてあげることです。代表的な日本料理100品の作り方を、外国の計量法も入れながら、バイリンガルで分かりやすく解説しました。

アメリカ日常生活のマナーQ & A
Do As Americans Do

ジェームス・M・バーダマン, 倫子・バーダマン［著］　256ページ　ISBN 4-7700-2128-3

"How do you do?" に "How do you do?" と答えてはいけないということ、ご存知でしたか？　日本では当たり前と思われていたことがマナー違反だったのです。旅行で、駐在で、留学でアメリカに行く人必携のマナー集。

日米比較 冠婚葬祭のマナー
Do It Right: Japanese & American Social Etiquette

ジェームス・M・バーダマン, 倫子・バーダマン［著］　184ページ　ISBN 4-7700-2025-2

アメリカでは結婚式や葬式はどのように行われるのか？　お祝いや香典は？……そしてアメリカの人たちも、日本の事情を知りたがります。これだけあればもう困らない。日米冠婚葬祭マニュアル、バイリンガル版。

英語で話す「仏教」Q & A
Talking About Buddhism Q & A

高田佳人［著］　ジェームス・M・バーダマン［訳］　240ページ　ISBN4-7700-2161-5

四十九日までに7回も法事をするのは、「亡くなった人が7回受ける裁判をこの世から応援するため」だということ、ご存じでしたか？　これだけは知っておきたい「仏教」に関することがらを、やさしい英語で説明できるようにした入門書です。

まんが 日本昔ばなし
Once Upon a Time in Japan

川内彩友美［編］　ラルフ・マッカーシー［訳］　160ページ　ISBN 4-7700-2173-9

人気TVシリーズ「まんが日本昔ばなし」から、「桃太郎」、「金太郎」、「一寸法師」など、より抜きの名作8話をラルフ・マッカーシーの名訳でお届けします。ホームステイなどでも役に立つ一冊です。

ベスト・オブ 宮沢賢治短編集
The Tales of Miyazawa Kenji

宮沢賢治［著］　ジョン・ベスター［訳］　208ページ　ISBN 4-7700-2081-3

「注文の多い料理店」「どんぐりと山猫」「祭の晩」「鹿踊りのはじまり」「土神ときつね」「オツベルと象」「毒もみの好きな署長さん」「セロ弾きのゴーシュ」の代表作8編を精選。ジョン・ベスターの名訳でどうぞ。

ビジネスマン必携！

対訳：英語で話す日本経済Q&A
A Bilingual Guide to the Japanese Economy

NHK国際経済プロジェクト・
大和総研経済調査部［編］

46判 (128 x 188 mm)　仮製　360ページ
ISBN 4-7700-1942-4

NHK国際放送で好評を得た番組が本になりました。クイズと会話形式で楽しく読んでいくうちに、日本経済の仕組が分かり、同時に英語にも強くなっていきます。日本語と英語の対応がひと目で分かる編集上の工夫もいっぱい。

インスタントビジネス日英会話
すぐに役立つコミュニケーションの秘訣
Instant Business Japanese
Real-Life Skills for Real-Life Situations

ジャイルズ・マリー［著］

46判 (128 x 188 mm)　仮製　272ページ
ISBN 4-7700-2105-4

面白く、簡単に読める会話形式で、いざというとき、すぐに役立つビジネスコミュニケーションの例文200を収録しました。キーワードは日本語と英語が対照できるように太字で表示されています。欧米のビジネスマインドと言葉を解説する「物知り英語ノート」付き。

わが家の味を海外に

バイリンガル とってもかんたんマイレシピ
Stone Soup—Easy Japanese Home Cooking

渡辺節子［著］

B5判変型 (189 x 257 mm)　仮製　256ページ

ISBN 4-7700-2061-9

手軽な日本の家庭料理、わが家の味160品目の作り方を英語と日本語で紹介したクッキングブック。作り方や調理器具などのイラスト付き、カロリー計算、調理時間もひと目で分かります。

名作＋名訳＋名画の魅力！

対訳：おくのほそ道
The Narrow Road to Oku

松尾芭蕉［著］　ドナルド・キーン［訳］
宮田雅之［切り絵］

A5判変型 (140 x 226 mm)

仮製　188ページ（カラー口絵41ページ）

ISBN 4-7700-2028-7

古典文学の最高峰のひとつ、「おくのほそ道」をドナルド・キーンが新訳しました。画家、宮田雅之が精魂を込めた41点のカラー切り絵の魅力とあいまって、この名作に新しい生命が吹き込まれた、必読の1冊です。

ビジュアル　日本紹介決定版

英文版　ジャパン：四季と文化
Japan: The Cycle of Life

［序文］高円宮憲仁親王殿下
［イントロダクション］C.W. ニコル

A4判変型 (228 x 297 mm)

上製　296ページ（オールカラー）

ISBN 4-7700-2088-0

日本の文化は「四季」によって育まれてきました。日本人の生活、文化、精神から切り離せないこの「四季」を、美しく新鮮な数々のカラー写真でビジュアルに紹介します。

第1部　自然と風土
第2部　人々の暮らしと伝統行事
第3部　文化と伝統